mondohomo

Your Essential Guide to Queer Pop Culture

edited by
Richard Andreoli

alyson books
los angeles

MANUFACTURED IN THE UNITED STATES OF AMERICA.

THIS TRADE PAPERBACK ORIGINAL IS PUBLISHED BY ALYSON PUBLICATIONS,
P.O. BOX 4371, LOS ANGELES, CALIFORNIA 90078-4371.
DISTRIBUTION IN THE UNITED KINGDOM BY TURNAROUND PUBLISHER SERVICES LTD.,
UNIT 3, OLYMPIA TRADING ESTATE, COBURG ROAD, WOOD GREEN,
LONDON N22 6TZ ENGLAND.

FIRST EDITION: NOVEMBER 2004

04 05 06 07 08 **a** 10 9 8 7 6 5 4 3 2 1

ISBN 1-55583-862-6

CREDITS
COVER PHOTOGRAPHY BY CHRIS MCPHERSON.
COVER DESIGN AND ART DIRECTION BY MATT SAMS.
INTERIOR ART AND INCIDENTAL PHOTOGRAPHY COURTESY OF STEVEN K. THOMPSON

To Carleen Hemric, Glenda Richter, and Carolyn See—
the three women who said, "Yes. It is possible."

Contents

Reel to Real: How Cable TV, VCRs and Video Stores Helped Me Realize
I was a Homo and Bought Me a One-Way Ticket on the Midnight
Express from New Orleans to New York

By Smith Galtney

Hot Chicks Kick Ass! (Or, How Wonder Woman Saved My Life)

By Richard Andreoli

Slave to the Rhythm

By Smith Galtney

Book Learnin' Will Turn a Man Soft and Feminine

By Dave White

one
AUGUST 1958
FIFTY CENTS
THE HOMOSEXUAL VIEWPOINT

I am glad I am homo-sexual

Acknowledgments

This book might never have happened if it weren't for Ron Oliver and Michael Rowe, who introduced me to the fantastic Michael Thomas Ford. Through Michael I met my Alyson family: Angela Brown, the over-worked Whitney Friedlander, my godlike editor Nick Street, and the darling Dan Cullinane, who forced Nick to buy me dinner and listen to my pitch. Thank you all for making dreams come true.

From the book's seven main writers to all of the celebrity contributors—everyone worked very hard for very little—to you I am deeply indebted. Thank you for helping this whimsical idea take shape.

For friendship and helping me "keep it real," as we say in the urban community, I give a shout out to David Glanzer, Anna Marie Villegas, Scott Icenogle, David Heimlich, Brian Dailey, Jerry Cryder, Rodney Alexander Griffis, Alan Stubblefield, Cary Berman, Bernadette Bowman, Brigette Boyle, and my Hollywood power lezzies, Meghan Treese, Molly Snow, Michelle Hagen, and Lynn McCracken.

For assistance, inspiration, and (in some cases) employment, I have to thank Alonso Duralde, Tom Ford, Sean Abley, Brett Freedman, Danny Casillas, Carl Deo, Matt Glaser, Alan Carter, Matt Breen, Darren Frei, Ken Martinez, Dan Allen, Mikel Wadewitz, Jeremy Kinser, Alex Cho, Amy Witry, Allen Fogderude, Troy Williams, Phil Jimenez, and Billy Carroll. My love always goes out to Kurt Heisler, and he knows why. Special thanks go to the kids at *Instinct* magazine, Scott Mosley at Specialty Publications, Gabriel Goldberg (who assisted with this book on levels he'll never know), and Jim J. Bullock for giving us hours of laughs that he never knew about.

To my family, who I'm sure is always curious about what I really do in Los Angeles, and especially to Brianne, Mikayla, Joseph, Maria Pilar, Louise, and Hailee—you kids inspire me every time I see you. To Mom, Kurt, Lauretta (all of whom should skip the dirty parts of this book), and Jeff and John (who will love those dirty parts)—you're the best family I could ask for.

And finally, to Steve, my partner, my fellow dreamer, and my ultimate muse (just like Kira was for Sonny in *Xanadu*): I'm proud to say I love you.

Introduction

Richard Andreoli

In & Out pisses me off. Queer writer Paul Rudnick might be unmatched in his ability to sculpt hilarious characters and infuse spicy dialogue into his movies, but this particular script panders to straight ideas about gay men by leaning on tired jokes about Barbra Streisand and other antiquated stereotypes. While there is some lingering cultural authenticity in Kevin Kline's role, his character is no one I recognize in my 20- and 30-something set. For that matter, I doubt his appetites and sensibilities are representative of many homosexual men under 45 (dare I say under 50?).

This movie would have been perfect in 1985, maybe even 1990. But 1997? By then my head was filled with Madonna's music, *Melrose Place* catfights, and meeting shirtless guys on dance floors. When I still went to see the movie with my friends, I chuckled at many of the lines, but all the while I felt as though the character embodied a joke I'd heard long ago. It was time, I thought, for the next generation of gay men to invent some new stereotypes for themselves.

Mondo Homo was originally conceived to answer that need by recreating, in literary form, those delicious late-night cocktail parties where friends discuss their favorite shows, books, divas, and anything else that excited them while they were growing up gay (closeted or otherwise). I wanted to hear what sources of solace other writers had found, whether they were obvious choices like TV and film, or more specialized areas of popular culture such as fashion, art, and porn. I boldly decided that words like "fag" would be reclaimed and used to add an extra kick to an irreverent attitude so that anyone reading these pages would know, without question, that this was the new face of gay male culture in America. Kevin Kline no more! We are the drag queens from *The Adventures of Priscilla, Queen of the Desert*: complex, filled with desires, dreams, and passions. Most importantly, we're men who don't give a shit about what the rest of the world thinks of us.

Yeah, well, that idea tanked. Sort of...

The problem was that after settling on the first six chapters—Television, Film, Music, Literature, Theater & Art, and Fashion—it became apparent that queer tastes, experiences, and stereotypes varied widely. Some old-school associations such as the Village People or Judy Garland were unavoidable, because 20 years ago—when most of us were just beginning to catch signals on our adolescent or prepubescent gaydar—there just weren't many other icons for us baby queens to latch onto. But the continually evolving gay liberation movement has since contributed many distinctly queer styles, concepts, and behaviors to the mainstream media, which means there's no longer one single gay identity.

Consequently, homosexual men born post-Stonewall have grown up and fallen in love with a new generation of popular culture icons and ideas that are also ever-changing. The thing that's new about this evolution is that while we can often implicitly recognize queer sensibilities in a book or film or TV show, we're hard-pressed to name what specifically creates or defines those sensibilities. So if stereotypes are birthed, murdered, and regenerated faster than you can turn a trick at a gay pride parade, how can we lay down any sort of definitive statement that says, "*This* is gay?"

We can't. The point of *Mondo Homo* is to push past the two-second sitcom jokes and avoid the impossible task of painting a complete picture of queer pop culture, or queer culture, or even what it means for something simply to be queer. That's why we assembled writers who could work as a bridge between generations, men who understood the significance of our queer history but whose work reflected a clear eye and a distinct voice for the future. Together, we could create a composite portrait of queer popular culture by assembling snapshots of the changes each of us has observed and experienced over the course of his life. The idea is that each of these small slivers of queer history reflects the Big Picture, which becomes easier to see when you use all the slivers to make a larger mirror. This was not only possible, but to me, far more interesting.

To expand that idea, we realized the second section of the book needed to dish about familiar aspects of contemporary queer life such as body obsession, clubbing, traveling, and drinking more cocktails on a Friday night than most straight people consume in a year. We also needed to know where these patterns of connecting, hooking up, and relating came from. So we created chapters on the rise of queer media—which makes it possible for you to hold this book in your hands today—the rise of gay ghettos, and the development of gay gatherings across the country.

Those classic queens who reveled in Judy and Barbra also came of age at a time when one could be arrested if he was suspected of being a homosexual. There's simply no way to see our culture clearly without reflecting on how the experience of queers in the past continues to influence the lives of queers today.

From there we decided two final areas needed some attention: porn and sex. The importance of porn is fairly obvious—queens obsess over their favorite porn stars with the same enthusiasm they have for their favorite Disney characters. Sex, however, is different. Unlike music or literature, sex isn't something you collect or become freakishly knowledgeable about (I say that in the sweetest possible way).

Because we live in a world where the major identifiable difference between me and some random guy walking down the street is that I enjoy butt love, sex necessarily becomes an aspect of how we gay boys view the world. I know there are activists and educators who don't like hearing that—who want us to blend in with everyone else and prove that being gay isn't any different than being straight. But it just ain't so. All of these chapters take a distinctively, queerly sexual point of view that distinguishes us from heterosexuals. As humorist Dave White proves in his sex chapter, that's what makes us fan-fucking-tastic.

Each chapter is punctuated with lists of important things for readers to remember, reminisce about, or laugh at—after all, this is meant to be fun. And, yes, you will read about Judy Garland and *The Boys in the Band* because, again, those are our roots.

In no way are these lists meant to be the be-all and end-all for a fulfilling queer life, but they do work as starting points for larger discussions. There are also shadow boxes that elaborate specific topics, and to this end we've enlisted queer professionals—from Dead or Alive's Pete Burns in Music to John Cameron Mitchell in Theater—to offer some celebrity insight and perspective.

Ultimately, the point of *Mondo Homo* isn't to slam new stereotypes or to try to pinpoint a gay sensibility in any given piece of pop culture. If queer life has taught us anything, it's that we actually lessen the beauty of something when we capture and label it instead of just seeing the thing or experience, enjoying the way it makes us feel, and accepting that it's inherently "part of us." Rather, these personal essays are like gay mosaic (homosaic?) pieces, which when taken together offer a larger picture of the gay experience of men who grew up post-Stonewall and in the time of AIDS. It's funny, touching, insightful, and truthful, as told by the men who actually lived it.

In closing, for those homos who still feel guilt about their love of pop culture, I'd like to quote the brilliant Cristal Connors from *Showgirls*: "But you *are* a whore darlin'..."

Because, really—aren't we all?

Chapter 1: Film

Reel to Real: How Cable TV, VCRs, and Video Stores Helped Me Realize I Was a Homo and Bought Me a One-Way Ticket on the Midnight Express from New Orleans to New York

By Smith Galtney

I could start with the time I went to see *Star Wars,* when I waited in the longest line I'd ever seen to watch some movie I'd never even heard of. Or the time I sat next to my mother and had no idea why she was crying through the end credits of *Close Encounters of the Third Kind.* Better yet, I could tell you how I was a different human being after experiencing *Saturday Night Fever* and *Grease*—how they made me want to do strange, fey things like put on boogie shoes and belt out show tunes. But really, if I'm going to tell you movies instilled me with enough courage to embrace the love that dare not speak its name, I'd have to (1) begin with a film called *Midnight Express,* and (2) confess that I didn't even see the movie in a movie theater. I was watching it at home instead, on a VCR.

The setting was like some clichéd coming-of-age flick: In the early '80s my newly divorced mother took two of her five children—my teenage sister and soon-to-be teenage me—and moved us into a funky duplex across town, a new home with a spiral staircase in the middle of the living room. We got cable for the first time, with all the trimmings: HBO,

Cinemax, Showtime, the Movie Channel. Meanwhile, video stores were spreading like kudzu, and soon the converter box was perched atop a brand-new, silver JVC videocassette recorder. With so many movies to watch, rent, record, and archive, I became something of a junior scholar in cinema studies. Not only had I watched *National Lampoon's Vacation* 50 times, but I could tell you it was directed by Harold Ramis, who, in turn, costarred with Bill Murray in *Ghostbusters* and *Stripes*, after cowriting the screenplay for *National Lampoon's Animal House*.

The first video I ever rented was *Fame*, which—given its tossed-salad jumble of hot-lunch jams, *Rocky Horror* and homosexuality—I related to from head to toe and loved every second of it. I watched it twice, each time noticing the credit "Directed by Alan Parker." So I did a little research on this Parker guy—all through reference books at the school library, or from the display copy on the back of VHS boxes, since we didn't have Google or IMDB.com back then. I was happy to learn that, like, wow! Parker had directed all these movies I loved, like *Bugsy Malone* and *Shoot the Moon*. And like, cool! He also directed *Midnight Express*, which I'd never seen before and which I knew was coming on Showtime that month. And like, awesome! I knew the score was going to be great, too, because Giorgio Moroder did it, and I knew he was the guy who worked with Donna Summer and also did Blondie's "Call Me" from *American Gigolo*, and like, I totally remembered when the "Chase" song from the *Midnight Express* soundtrack was on the radio in the '70s. So like a good little film geek, I set the timer on our VCR and prepared to absorb another opus in the Alan Parker oeuvre—although I wouldn't have used that word, since I had no idea what it meant at the time.

But nothing—and I mean nothing—could have prepared me for *Midnight Express*.

For those of you who don't know the story, it's a highly fictionalized account of the experience of Billy Hayes, a young American man who was thrown in a Turkish prison for drug smuggling. The film offers a harrowing depiction of the brutality and inhuman conditions Hayes suffered during his incarceration—although his travails may seem tame to some jaded *Oz* habitués. Today, it's probably most famous for the scene where Billy's girlfriend visits, and he begs her to press her bare breasts against the glass partition so he can jerk off. (Jim Carrey later parodied this scene in *The Cable Guy*.) But it was the breakout film for a then-unknown screenwriter named Oliver Stone, as well as for a young actor named Brad Davis, who would go on to become a gay icon, thanks to his role in Rainer Werner Fassbinder's *Querelle*, before dying of AIDS in 1991. (And no, he was straight. Unfortunately, he was also a one-time drug addict.)

To say Davis was "handsome" or "gorgeous" is to undermine his dynamic sex appeal. Both boyish and entirely masculine, he looked like he could have been the captain of the football team—only the sweetness in his eyes convinced you he never teased anyone in the locker room. So when Davis, as Hayes in the movie, struck up a close friendship with a blond,

GUILTY PLEASURES

Beastmaster • Spice World • Straight Talk •
Tarzan the Ape man (the Bo Derek version) •
Two of a Kind • Troop Beverly Hills

ESSENTIAL QUEER MUSICALS

The Best Little Whorehouse in Texas •
Cabaret • Chicago • Grease•
The Sound of Music• Victor/Victoria

CHICK FLICKS FOR DICKS

Beaches • Moonstruck •
My Best Friend's Wedding • Pretty in Pink •
Pretty Woman • Steel Magnolias •
Thelma & Louise • Working Girl

LITTLE GIRLS DOING BIG THINGS

13 Going On 30 • Desperately Seeking Susan •
Flashdance • Freaky Friday • Legally Blonde •
Mean Girls • Nine to Five • Party Girl •
The Princess Diaries • Tootsie

bearded, ruggedly beautiful prison inmate, my teenage brain didn't think it was *going* anywhere. I certainly wasn't thinking they were fags.

Still, they grew closer and closer, doing yoga, staring deeply into each other's eyes and repeating the mantra, "Prison. Monastery. Cloister. Cave." Next thing I know Hayes is in a steam-filled shower, cleansing his taut upper-thigh in slow, soapy circles. His friend's hand appears onscreen, and it softly runs up Hayes's arm, over his shoulder, around his neck. The two share a couple of long, closed-mouth kisses before Hayes pulls back. He kisses his friend on the hand. He politely shakes his head, and he walks offscreen.

End scene.

I was worked up, horny as hell, and hard as a rock. But when I tried to jerk off, I couldn't. This wasn't like the hard-core porn I'd seen once at a friend's house, or like the softer stuff I'd seen on the Playboy Channel. This was just so real, so pure—more sensual than sexual—and I didn't want to just have sex with myself. I wanted to make a connection with another human being, another man. For the first time I was beginning to feel what romance was like.

Of course, well before I saw *Midnight Express,* my body had begun dropping more than a few hints that I might possibly be gay. I was around 14 then, already well practiced in the art of self-abuse, and thus well aware how images of naked men were more "climactic" for me than naked women. But mentally entertaining such taboo prospects while having a wank was one thing; wanting to make them a tangible reality another. And this whole attraction to the same sex was starting to feel less like postpubescent curiosity and more like an unshakable destiny—one I promised not to embrace until later in life. *Much* later in life—

like when I had my own money and my own place to live, in case my mother decided to kick me out of the house.

In the meantime, I figured it would be best to do some research on the life that potentially awaited me down the line, and movies seemed to be the most accessible way to go about it. Cable TV and video stores became like libraries to me—these amazingly bountiful resources that showed me so many people, places, and things beyond the world I knew (which, back then, didn't extend much farther than uptown New Orleans).

What I found wasn't always encouraging. In fact, it rarely was. Gay people were either getting murdered—like the queen in *Eyes of Laura Mars*—or they were doing the murdering, like the serial killer in *Cruising*. Mostly, they seemed pretty fucking miserable, as was Harry Hamlin in *Making Love* or Hugh Grant in *Maurice*. If not, they were laughingstocks or so unbelievably fey that I didn't want to have *anything* to do with them (i.e., Lamar from *Revenge of the Nerds* or the requisite sissy from all those '80s teen-sex comedies).

But no matter how unappealing I thought gay people looked in movies, my destiny proved unavoidable. Besides, my research was giving birth to a new obsession: New York City. Not only were many of my favorite movies set there—*Fame, Tootsie, Arthur, Ghostbusters,* to name a few—but movies set in New York always seemed to have at least one gay person in them. Like *Only When I Laugh,* in which James Coco plays the original queer friend and neighbor. I rented a cult film called *Liquid Sky,* which was jam-packed with homos. Yes, they were all junkies and necrophiliacs, but they lived in these really cool apartments with really cool views of the Empire State Building.

One night my oldest sister took me to see Martin Scorsese's *After Hours.* She'd just returned from her first visit to Manhattan, and throughout the whole movie she offered a running commentary. When a cab hightailed it downtown: "That's how it *is.*" A cashier did a pirouette before opening the register: "That's what it's *like.*" A yuppie unwillingly got half a Mohawk in a nightclub: "You gotta *watch it* in New York, I'm tellin' you." But I was only half-listening, since I was completely enthralled by the movie, particularly a scene where two leather queens were making out in a bar. They were in the corner of the screen, sort of in the background, going at it like crazy. Everyone in the theater—everyone in New Orleans, that is—was pointing and laughing at them. No one onscreen, though, even notices them. No one in Manhattan bats an eyelash.

Then at the start of my junior year in high school, just as our guidance counselors started hounding us to consider where we wanted to go to college, I taped a small independent film on cable called *Parting Glances.* One of the first—if not *the* first—films to deal with AIDS, it showed me something I'd never seen before: a family-tight group of friends—some gay, some straight—living on the Upper West Side, knowing a strange deadly virus will soon claim one of them. Some of the queers were butch and preppy, others were fey and flaming. Some were total assholes, others were kind and sweet. There was no dramatic death scene, and at the end you're left with this snapshot in your head of a circle of people who just feel lucky to be part of each other's lives. For a "gay" movie, that seemed pretty damn normal to me.

One particular scene sealed my fate as a college student, and it's best to let it speak for itself. Nick is a jaded rock star with AIDS, played by Steve Buscemi in his first major film role. Then there's Peter, an overly confident college student, played by Adam Nathan—who, according to IMDB.com, went on to have a bit part in Michael Jackson's "Bad" video before he dropped off the radar completely.

The two bump into each other in a stairwell and talk about Nick's ex-boyfriend, Michael, who Peter has a crush on.

PETER
You want to know why I'm crazy about Michael?

NICK
(*sarcastically*)
Well, I'm, like, trembling with curiosity.

PETER
First, you have to admit that I'm imminently irresistible.

NICK
Bullshit. You're a ditz-ball twinkie.

PETER
Who are you calling a twinkie?

NICK
You're beyond twinkie. You're in the realm of the super-twinkie.

PETER
But you were a twinkie once.

NICK
Never.

PETER
You were.

NICK
Alright. Maybe I was a quasi-twinkie.

PETER
I'm crazy about Michael 'cause he don't give a shit about my irresistibility. Everyone else is after me all the time. But Michael? He's, like, so cool.

TEEN ANGST MOVIES WE LOVE

Footloose • Heathers • The Outsiders • St. Elmo's Fire • Welcome to the Dollhouse

JUST BECAUSE YOU SHOULD

The Color Purple • Delicatessen • Happiness • The Hours • The Lion in Winter • The Princess Bride • Safe • Who's Afraid of Virginia Woolf? • Y Tu Mamá También

DIRECTORS WHOSE FILMS YOU SHOULD KNOW

Pedro Almodóvar • John Hughes • Every John Waters film up to and including Hairspray • Every Tim Burton film excluding Planet of the Apes • Christopher Guest

AUSSIE FILMS YOU ABSOLUTELY MUST SEE

The Adventures of Priscilla, Queen of the Desert • Muriel's Wedding • Strictly Ballroom • Moulin Rouge!

CHILDREN'S FILMS QUEER BOYS SHOULD KNOW

Beauty and the Beast • The Dark Crystal • The Iron Giant • Labyrinth • The Last Unicorn • The Little Mermaid • The Muppet Movie and The Great Muppet Caper • The Neverending Story • The Secret of NIMH • Spirited Away

(*beat*)
Makes me crazy. I like the chase. I'm a wolf in twinkie clothing.
(*another beat*)
So, I got a chance?

NICK
(*resigned*)
Let me sit down.

They plop down on a flight of stairs; PETER seated two steps higher than NICK. Both light up cigarettes.

NICK
When I first met Michael, he was a freshman at NYU. I'm hanging out in the Village—

PETER
(*interrupting, exhaling smoke*)
I'm a *Columbia* freshman—

NICK
(*overlapping*)
Will you shut up a minute?
(*beat*)
I'm hanging in the Village—and I'm a couple of years older than Michael—and I see this Midwest, nerdy-type kid walking down the street.

PETER
(*interrupting*)
Michael?

NICK
(*as if saying, "duh"*)
Yeah.
(*beat*)
So I chat him up a little bit. He don't know anything. I mean, the whole scene is happening four blocks from where he's going to school. And he doesn't even know it.

PETER
(*blowing more smoke*)
No shit.

NICK
I show him around. We go bar-hopping that night. Terry had this place on Barrow. So we go there. There's a party going on. Michael went wild. He almost flunked out his first year.

NICK scoots up a step, until he's almost eye-to-eye with PETER.

NICK
We tore this town apart, man. That's what you need. Find somebody your own age. Get your hair messed up a bit.

For me, that was it. That's when the fantasies started. Not only was there this college in New York—*way* far away from New Orleans, where none of my high-school classmates were going—but it was located in the heart of Greenwich Village, where the whole scene was happening!

I applied to NYU soon after. The only college I applied to, in fact. I was going to New York City, or I wasn't going to college at all. And I was going to have an apartment just like Sigourney Weaver's in *Ghostbusters*. Only I would decorate it like Molly Ringwald's bedroom in *Sixteen Candles*.

Relocating from New Orleans to New York at the age of 18 might have been a dream come true, but sometimes it felt like a nightmare—one where everyone is 10 feet taller than you, and even your best friends are speaking in a language you can't understand, much less recognize. But the longer I lived there, the city's sheer magnitude came into clearer focus and I was able to draw my own conclusions. For instance, there was the New York one sees in the movies, and the New York that New Yorkers move through on a day-to-day basis, and the two had little more than a backdrop in common. Basically, it didn't take me long to realize that few people have apartments like Sigourney Weaver's in *Ghostbusters*. And the ones who do wouldn't decorate them in homage to a teenager's bedroom.

By this point the only time I went to the video store was when I simply wanted to watch a movie. Not that my research was complete—it was just that now it was taking place in the real world. One could say I was living out my own cinematic history and had moved beyond what I'd seen in any movie. I was cruising guys on the street and in the subways, making new friends in bars and during class, and dating my first boyfriend (who would soon by my first *ex*-boyfriend). And all the while no one knew about this new part of my life. Not my family, not even my new friends in this new school in this new city. And it was feeling weirder every day: to be turning over so many new leaves and keeping it all inside, to taste urban independence yet remain terrified of getting kicked out of the house. Movies might have showed me a new world and given me new direction, but they weren't making me a stronger person.

Modern Camp Movies You Must Know (and Why)

Can't Stop the Music (the Village People)
Glitter (the silver stripe)
The Lonely Lady (the nozzle of a garden hose...and that's all we're sayin')
Mommie Dearest ("Barbara, please!")
Showgirls ("She looks better than a ten-inch dick and you know it.")
Valley of the Dolls ("They drummed you out of Hollywood, so you come crawling back to Broadway. But Broadway doesn't go for booze and dope...Now get out of my way, I've got a man waiting for me!")
Xanadu (the story of a muse who inspires a young man and Gene Kelly to achieve their dreams of opening a roller disco-nightclub)

Classic Queen Movies to Learn From

All About Eve (Clawing your way to the top was never so much fun!)
Auntie Mame ("Life is a banquet, and most poor suckers are starving to death!")
Pillow Talk (Rock Hudson and Doris Day—what's not gay about that?)
The Women (The classiest bitch-slapping you'll ever see. "So who cares, Edith?")

Then in 1990, at the end of freshman year, a movie called *Longtime Companion* came out. It was hyped as the first mainstream movie to deal with the AIDS crisis and its effect on the gay community. Alas, I couldn't see it, since it was released in New York a few days after I headed back to New Orleans for summer break. And by the time it came to New Orleans, I'd already started my second year at NYU.

However, when I was back home during Christmas break, I found myself in a video store—the same one I'd been hovering in all those years before—renting *Longtime Companion* on the sly. Unlike *Parting Glances,* it makes you experience the death of not one but *three* close friends. Even more devastating is how the film's first 10 minutes—when the characters have never even heard of AIDS—are such a joy to watch: men gallivanting on Fire Island, skipping in the sand, huffing poppers, cracking each other up, dancing their butts off, falling in love. Watching it late at night in my mother's living room with the sound down low, I wondered, *Jesus, if I died tomorrow, what kind of life could I look back on?*

This time it wasn't about sex, or romance, or boyfriends. Like destiny calling, "later in life" suddenly became "right now." For the first time I was tired of living a lie.

The next night I did something unthinkable: I showed the movie to my mother, claiming we needed to watch it because Bruce Davison's performance was generating Oscar buzz. She said okay and grimaced during the love scenes, and didn't ask any questions as to why *exactly* we were watching this.

The following March I was home for spring break, and since Bruce Davison had indeed gotten an Oscar nomination, *Longtime Companion* came up again.

"That was a *good* movie," she said.

"Really?" I asked.

"Yeah!" she continued. "I'm so glad that guy is up for an Oscar. That scene was just devastating."

Encouraged, I found myself uncorking.

"I *really* like it, too. It's sort of interesting because it does this really good job of depicting the gay world, how it's really like a bunch of nice people who really care about each other, who aren't just a bunch of freaks and rejects. You know, I've made a lot of gay friends up at school, and they say the movies often get it wrong..."

And I kept going, saying too much and not saying enough—just like Michael Stipe sang in R.E.M.'s "Losing My Religion," which was a huge hit at the time.

DOCUMENTARIES THAT CHANGE LIVES

Bowling for Columbine • The Celluloid Closet • Common Threads: Stories From the Quilt • Crumb • Farhenheit 911 • Grey Gardens • Paris Is Burning • Roger & Me

GAY FILMS ACTUALLY WORTH WATCHING

Another Country • Beautiful Thing • My Beautiful Laundrette • Bound • The Broken Hearts Club • The Crying Game • Death Trap • Edward II • Head On • Latter Days • Making Love • Midnight Cowboy • Midnight Express • No Skin off My Ass • Parting Glances • Trick

In any case, Mom wasn't stupid. When I came home later that night she was perched in the living room—the same place where she and I watched *Companion* together—ready to talk.

"I get the feeling you're trying to tell me something, Smith."

"Well..." I muttered, before sucking in a deep breath and telling my mother everything. I was 19 years old.

Maybe it's presumptuous to say that I never would have come out to her if it weren't for movies. Maybe inspiration would have come after reading the Sunday *Times* or *Giovanni's Room.* I know people older than me who had similar epiphanies in the '70s after reading magazines like *Interview* or *After Dark,* and people older than that who had them via trashy

pulp novels. Still, those magazines and paperbacks were hardly as accessible as cable TV and VHS tapes. In a way those media were like the Internet before it even existed: They brought so much information right into my home, right to my fingertips. Some of that information was scary. But thankfully I could fast-forward through the tough parts and slow-advance through the good stuff—I got a "sneak preview" of a life I thought I could handle, and was eventually ready to live.

So, to hell with it: The movies changed my life. They made my friggin' dreams come true. If that sounds like a clichéd crock, get this: The other day I came home from having dinner with my boyfriend. I put my keys on the table in the hall. I hung up my coat. Sitting down to watch TV I noticed the Empire State Building glowing in my window—almost like I'd never seen it there before. And you know what? I felt just like Sigourney Weaver in *Ghostbusters*. That and, um, my apartment was just as messy as Molly Ringwald's bedroom in *Sixteen Candles*.

MOVIES THAT WEREN'T INTENDED TO BE GAY BUT ARE SO INCREDIBLY GAY

Bachelor Party • Clash of the Titans • Flash Gordon • A Night In Heaven • Porky's • Tap Dogs • Top Gun • Tron • Weird Science • X-Men

BEST COCK SHOTS

All the Right Moves • American Gigolo • Breathless • Looking for Mr. Goodbar • Maurice • The Pillow Book • A Room With a View • The Talented Mr. Ripley • Testosterone • Trainspotting • Velvet Goldmine

PUNK CINEMA YOU MUST KNOW

A Clockwork Orange • Breaking Glass • The Decline of Western Civilization • The Great Rock 'n' Roll Swindle • Ladies and Gentlemen...The Fabulous Stains • Sid and Nancy • SubUrbia • Times Square

Science Fiction Double-Feature

By Richard Andreoli

Let's do the time warp again!
Let's do the time warp again!
It's just a jump to the left...

This is "The Time Warp!"—the group-dance song that was played at school proms and roller rinks across the country was one of the anthems in *The Rocky Horror Picture Show*. Released in 1975 and based on the stage musical, this B-movie parody follows the adventures of Brad Majors and Janet Weiss, a young, ordinary, healthy couple played by Barry Bostwick and Susan Sarandon. One night they leave their hometown of Denton, Ohio, and run into some trouble.

EXT.—DARK ROAD, RAINING—NIGHT
AN EXPLOSION as the tire of Brad and Janet's car blows out.

JANET
(*panicked*)
What was that bang?!

BRAD
We must have a blow out!... Didn't we pass a castle back down the road a few miles? Maybe they have a telephone I could use.

JANET
I'm coming with you. Besides, darling, the owner of that phone may be a beautiful woman and you might never come back again.

Well, the owner of that phone isn't a beautiful woman, but rather a sweet transvestite from Transsexual Transylvania, played by Tim Curry. All it took was a campy plot and a score of rocking songs, and suddenly midnight movie screenings started popping up across the country. Die-hard fans dressed in character, sang along, and danced in the aisles.

But *Rocky Horror* was more than just some performance art piece because the audience was as important to the evening's entertainment as the film itself. And yes, I'd been a part of that magic. I'd held up my lighter during the song "There's a Light" and shot my water pistol when it was raining on-screen. I even performed the Barry Bostwick role during screenings—and I say "performed" because none of the live cast ever actually acted during the film. We simply mimicked the characters' on-screen actions. And I did all this at the Ken Cinema's weekly screenings of *Rocky Horror* in San Diego, where some motivated individual in our group had decided to reunite us after 10 years.

I explained all this to my current circle of friends—all of whom have seen the movie— and they acknowledged that, yes, it would be a hoot to watch a group of 30- to 40-somethings jiggling around in their underwear and mimicking the motions of...

Janet?
Dr. Scott!
Janet!
Brad!
Rocky!
Ugh!

...and this would spawn hours of small talk for future dinner parties. But they couldn't fathom why on God's green earth I was so excited about spending a weekend with the lost, disenfranchised youth of San Diego that I grew up with. Well, these friends might have seen *Rocky Horror,* but I soon realized that they definitely didn't get it.

I'm not exactly sure why this is, but those of us at *Rocky* struggled with more than just the usual coming-of-age dilemmas that plagued everyone else.

It was the early '80s, and some of us were exploring sexual freedoms we never thought possible in our highly academic lives—admittedly, many of us were nerds. Others in my group were discovering personal philosophies for the first time, entertaining feminist theories, or investigating alternative religions like Wicca, and discovering how that impacted their spirituality. These radical journeys made many of us feel exactly like the class freaks that everyone else had condemned us to be, and nothing in our lives seemed to offer any stability. Nothing, that is, except for *Rocky Horror.*

Because when you were "in" at *Rocky,* whether as a "cast member" or simply as a bemused observer in the audience, you were suddenly more important than you could ever hope to be in the normal world. You knew what to yell and when to yell it at the screen. You knew the songs, the dances, the choreography, and you *belonged* in a world that the "normal" kids thought was different, alternative, even cutting edge in some cases. Suddenly you were on the inside looking out rather than the outside looking in. And it was this sense of belonging, of importance, of a ritualized normalcy amid the everyday insanity that gave each of us the strength to face those internal struggles. That's such a valuable gift—something that people who never "got" *Rocky* never got to experience.

You know, now that I'm older I can freely admit that in many ways I was lost during those years, but at least I always knew how to find my way home: Fridays and Saturdays, midnight, *Rocky Horror* at the Ken theater.

Dan Jink's Top 10 Movies Every Queer (or Straight Person) Should See

1. *All About Eve*—This is my favorite movie. Some people, like my ex-boyfriend, find it a bit slow for the first 20 minutes, but I think the whole film is brilliant. Bette Davis has never been better.

2. *A Star Is Born*—The Judy Garland-James Mason version, of course. This is a wonderful musical love story starring one of the great gay icons in a smashing performance. I first saw this at a revival house in Greenwich Village, and the audience cheered like it was a Broadway opening. Strange, but there were very few women in the theater.

3. *Auntie Mame*—Try watching just a few minutes of this hilarious comedy and you'll be hooked for the whole thing. The best dialogue of any comedy I've ever seen, and Rosalind Russell is sublime.

4. *Cabaret*—Along with *Singin' in the Rain,* this could be the best movie musical ever made. Based on the stage show and directed by Bob Fosse. People who only know Liza Minnelli as a punch line on late-night talk shows should see why she became famous in the first place. She's perfect.

5. *Casablanca*—One of the great love stories of all time. Beautifully shot and wonderfully performed.

6. *Citizen Kane*—There is nothing remotely gay about this film, but many people feel it's one of the two or three best movies ever made. They're right. Orson Welles was only 25 when he wrote, directed, and starred in this classic about a man with strong similarities to William Randolph Hearst.

7. *The Godfather* I and II—Way before *The Sopranos* came the Corleone family. Marlon Brando, Al Pacino, and Robert De Niro in perhaps their most memorable roles. Just writing this makes me want to see it again.

8. *Gone With the Wind*—Does this need an explanation? If you haven't seen it, put down this book and run out and get the DVD. (*Editor's note: Then immediately return to the book and continue reading.*) It's four hours long, but it's four of the best hours you'll ever spend.

9. *Schindler's List*—Again, not a very gay movie, but I think the best movie of the last 20 years. I couldn't get it out of my mind for weeks. Incredibly moving and powerful.

10. *Some Like It Hot*—Tony Curtis and Jack Lemmon have to hide from the mob, so they dress up as women and join an all-girl band led by Marilyn Monroe in this phenomenal comedy directed by Billy Wilder. Many have tried to imitate it, none have come close.

I hate having to leave off *One Flew Over the Cuckoo's Nest, The Graduate, Grease, Dog Day Afternoon, The Philadelphia Story, His Girl Friday, The Unforgiven, Jaws, Alien, E.T., Lawrence of Arabia, Annie Hall, Chinatown, What's Up, Doc?, Close Encounters of the Third Kind, Psycho, It Happened One Night, Bonnie and Clyde, Raiders of the Los Ark, The Sting, The Lady Eve, Sunset Boulevard, The Apartment, The Deer Hunter*, and *Airplane!* But I can only list my Top 10.

Dan Jinks won the Academy Award in 2000 for producing *American Beauty.* He also produced *Big Fish, Down With Love, The Forgotten* and *Nothing to Lose.*

Chapter 2: Television

Hot Chicks Kick Ass! (Or How Wonder Woman Saved My Life)
By Richard Andreoli

Sydney Bristow is in big trouble and I'm about to have a heart attack!

For those of you just tuning in to *Alias*, the hottest chick show on ABC television, Sydney (portrayed by Jennifer Garner) has just returned from a major CIA operation. She's taking some much-needed downtime with her best friend and roommate, Francie, which drives my boyfriend and me absolutely insane because we know that good Francie was murdered by an evil doppelgänger Francie during Sweeps Week just a few months earlier. Still in the dark, Syd—her friends call her "Syd"—checks her cell phone messages, one of which is from her buddy Will, who warns her that this Francie is really Evil Francie!

My heart races like I've just done two lines of coke with a Red Bull and vodka chaser. But—pro that she is—Syd remains calm, casually hangs up, and offers Evil Francie some coffee ice cream. When she accepts, Syd makes a nonchalant excuse so she can retreat to her bedroom. I simply marvel at how cool she is. Even after battling terrorists, jetting across the globe, and discovering that her best friend has been replaced by an evil freak and most likely murdered in the process, Sydney's hair, makeup, and smart little black pantsuit are still absolutely flawless! God, I wish we were friends!

"I forgot," Evil Francie says, her voice startling me as much as the gun she's got pointed at my favorite heroine, "Francie doesn't like coffee ice cream." And suddenly the show goes *off the hook* as these two fierce ladies engage in the greatest bitch fight since Lynda Carter's Wonder Woman fought against Lorene Yarnell's Formicida. Or was it Jaime Summers versus

the Fembots on *The Bionic Woman*? Or Alexis and Krystle in the pool on *Dynasty*?

Sigh. I love powerful women—I always have. And like many homos my age, that obsession started with Wonder Woman—as portrayed in the aforementioned Lynda Carter series, not to be confused with the abysmal Kathy Lee Crosby TV movie, which all true Wonder Woman fans block out of their minds. That was simply a bad dream created by some hetero TV exec on acid. *Wonder Woman* was distinctly campy and homoerotic and, for many of us 30-something gay boys, it's the first queer TV program we remember.

Take the competition to determine who will represent the Amazons in Man's World. All of the tall, beautiful babes wore their contestant numbers on upside down pink triangles sewn between the breasts of their costumes. Or consider later episodes where the high-fashion, hair, and makeup of Wonder Woman's alter ego, Diana Prince, was so stunning and timeless that these styles can still be spotted on fashion runways or episodes of *America's Next Top Model*. There were also the numerous girl-on-girl scenes—Stella Stevens straddling Wonder Woman's hips as they wrestled in the War Department offices, Wonder Woman grunting and rolling down a grassy hill on top of the Baroness Von Gunther—that spawned secret cheers of delight from the fags in the audience who embraced the program's over-the-top sensibility. And, looking a little deeper, consider the Amazing Amazon's early comic book escapades, which teemed with S/M and bondage imagery. A simple coincidence or a distinct Jungian connection to the existing gay male obsession? I'll let you decide.

On the surface power-chick programs like *Wonder Woman, Buffy the Vampire Slayer, Xena: Warrior Princess,* or *Alias* seem written specifically for straight male viewers, which means gay youths can easily disguise their budding homosexuality behind their heartfelt and enthusiastic obsession with these shows. Indeed, my own heterosexual masquerade began when I was 5 years old. I was sitting inches from the television when my father walked into the room and asked what I was watching. After I told him, he said, "*Wonder Woman*'s pretty good, huh?"

I turned, wide-eyed, in awe, and said, "Yeah! And boy, what a body!" To my father—who recounted that story whenever someone asked about his youngest son—this was proof positive that my watching a crime-fighting hottie in a bathing suit was a good thing. But what neither Dad nor anyone else in the family knew was that I had a secret—a secret so important that it felt as though the safety of the free world depended on my leading a double life. And it wasn't that I was gay.

You see, sometimes I would run into the backyard and to the side of the shed. After looking left and right to make sure no one was watching, I'd gracefully stretch out my arms to shoulder level, crank back my upper body, hum that snappy '70s tune, and spin into Wonder Richard. My secret persona included tinfoil bracelets and a slip-knot lasso hooked to my belt loop by a wire tie I'd taken from the produce department of the local Big Bear supermarket. Once my spin-transformation was complete, I'd mimic Princess

Diana's first season check—belt-tiara-lasso—and I was ready to take on anyone!

In case you were wondering, back in 1977 Richard met Diana Prince and discovered her secret identity as Wonder Woman when she was captured by modern-day Nazis; don't ask me how Richard managed to get into the Nazi's lair. Anyway, Diana displayed a whole new power never before seen on any season of the TV show or the *Superfriends* cartoon, and with a solemn nod she granted young Richard permission to spin. He did and became Wonder Richard, deflecting the Nazi's bullets and freeing Diana so she could spin into

Why the World of Sid and Marty Krofft Matters

Rumors abound that their shows contained multiple drug references, but there are other reasons why they were important to queer kids everywhere.

Bigfoot and Wildboy—You figure it out.

The Bugaloos—Benita Bizarre (Martha Raye) was a big drag queen who lived in a giant jukebox.

Dr. Shrinker—"Dr. Shrinker, Dr. Shrinker, he's a madman with an evil mind. / Dr. Shrinker, Dr. Shrinker, he's as crazy as you'll ever find." Sounds like your first boyfriend, huh?

Electra Woman and Dyna Girl—These sexy superheroes drove around in the coolest buggy, and their Electra-Comps could do anything.

Far Out Space Nuts—Bob Denver (Gilligan) and Chuck McCann hung out with an alien named Honk who had a horn coming out of its head. Don't know if that's gay or not, but it's pretty damn queer.

H.R. Pufnstuff—Witchiepoo was freakin' cool, and who wouldn't want to live on Living Island and meet Mama Cass at the annual Witch's Convention?

Land of the Lost—The Sleestaks were prototypes for queens in a K-hole, and Will was dreamy. And when Uncle Jack came searchin', we hoped he'd find us.

Lidsville—There was Weenie the Genie and Charles Nelson Reily in a flying top hat. What's not to love?

The Lost Saucer—Jim Nabors and Ruth Buzzi: Again, what's not to love?

Sigmund and the Sea Monsters—"Johnny and Scott are friends..."

Wonderbug—A junked-out car that turns into a superbuggy when you squeeze the horn. Hmm...

Wonder Woman, and together they kept the world safe for democracy.

Deep down I knew it was wrong to liken myself to Wonder Woman, skip around in my backyard, and pretend to be the only boy allowed on Paradise Island, home of the Amazons. Which is why I'd assume the identities of characters like Aquaman or the Hulk when I played super-heroes with the neighborhood kids. But when left to my own devices

HOW AARON SPELLING TURNED OUR COUNTRY GAY

Beverly Hills, 90210 • *Charlie's Angels* • *Dynasty* • *The Love Boat* • *Melrose Place* • *Models Inc.* • *Velvet*—The two-hour pilot about aerobics instructors who are actually spies!

OBVIOUS GAY TV CHOICES

American Chopper (At least we think it's an obvious choice.) • *Ellen* • *Queer as Folk* • *Six Feet Under* • *Sex and the City* • *Will & Grace*

REALITY TV THAT TURNS US ON

American Idol • *America's Next Top Model* • *Boy Meets Boy* • *Jackass* • *The Jeff Corwin Experience* • *Newlyweds: Nick & Jessica* • *The Real World* (up to the San Francisco season) • *The Simple Life* • *Solid Gold* • *Star Search* (the original) • *Survivor* (because Richard Hatch is an evil motherfucker)

I'd quietly open my toy chest and push aside my Matchbox cars to reveal those magical items that I used in the only game I was ever any good at. There—next to the *Isis* amulet I'd made two years earlier and the *Electra Woman* Electra-Comp I'd assembled just six months before—lay the magic bracelets and lasso that made me feel adventurous, happy, and special.

Obviously these fantasies can't last forever if one wants to function in the world, but gradual maturity only meant my obsession transformed itself into a fanatical desire to learn every obscure fact about these shows. I could eventually recite the dates of specific broadcasts and guest stars—even details about different edits. In this way I was *publicly* interesting, happy, and special. I could now share this aspect of myself with other people, which still made me odd (but not gay), funny, and entertaining (but not nelly or "too strange"). I could safely relish my favorite television ladies without all the secrecy—and by extension, without all the shame.

I look at this as my trial coming-out period: "Hey, you know how I'm all *quirky* and *eccentric*? Well, keep looking just a little more to the left and there you'll find me—on the Paradise Island of Gay."

Anyone who *did* look was too polite or clueless to confront me about my potential gayness. Thus I blissfully went on to discuss *Charlie's Angels* with delight and to refer to Jill Munroe as an LA T-bird, Sabrina Duncan as the lesbian Angel, or Jaclyn Smith as my personal favorite. I scored laughs when I proclaimed that TV's only salvation was Lynda Carter's and Loni Anderson's stunning detective show *Partners in Crime* (and when I mourned its horribly premature cancellation). My personal style was inspired by *Scarecrow and Mrs. King*: I sported Bruce Boxleitner's square-cut knit tie, and I begged the Supercuts stylist to give me his parted-down-the-middle penis haircut. Hell, somewhere in there I even scored points with the straight guys by knowing everything about Erin Gray and her one-piece spandex uniform in *Buck Rogers*.

Only later in life did I realize that one of the best things about television obsession is how it helps gay men find one another. Consider the numerous parties, bars, or outings you've attended where you've overheard someone say, "Melrose Place." You immediately drop whatever boring conversation you're having and find Mr. *Melrose Place* so you can discuss favorite episodes, laugh at hilarious moments, and be mutually saddened by the mediocre finale that capped a series that so touched your life.

For those of us who really savor television (or music or fashion or any other form of pop culture), that common experience helps us spot "our people." These are the guys who will become lifelong friends because they have a perspective on the world that we can truly, even deeply, relate to. They "get it" the same way we do, and rather than being on the outside (like most of us were when we were growing up), we're suddenly "in."

Certainly some of that attraction to classic TV is simply nostalgia—a fond recollection of who we were when a show first touched our lives. At the same time we also tend to relate to specific TV characters that offer us glimpses of qualities in ourselves that we don't see mirrored in the "real" (read: straight) world around us. In terms of actual relatability, it wasn't until I closely examined the shows I gravitated toward while I was growing up gay that I understood how much the entire cast of characters in my TV world collectively reflected my life.

When I grew into queer adolescence and teendom the characters I most closely identified with were from sitcoms. I adored *Alice*. I dreamed of having Flo's brashness, but I often felt scared like Vera. I cheered when Vera stood up to Mel, her bully of a boss (and I got teary-eyed when, later, I realized that Mel actually cared about her). The show taught me that the surest means of survival was to belt out a song like Alice herself and to assume the best qualities of all three ladies.

Action Shows Worth Remembering

Battlestar Galactica (the new show)—Because it's so smart and well done!

Buffy the Vampire Slayer—Willow and Tara had some emotional gay shit. And Buffy kicked ass!

Buck Rogers in the 25th Century—One-piece white spandex body suits, and Erin Gray!

Smallville—No other show has had a hotter ad campaign.

V and **V: The Final Battle**—Only the miniseries, *never* the TV series.

Voyagers!—Jon-Erik Hexum in a pirate shirt. Yum!

Xena and **Hercules**—It's the *Shazam/Isis Power Hour* without the Winnebago.

Children's Shows That Will Never Go Out of Style

The Electric Company—For Rita Moreno singing.

He-Man and **She-Ra**—He's such a fag and his sexy sister had killer boots and bodice.

Jem—Not only are Jem and the Holograms' songs truly outrageous, but the Misfits kick ass! This was the height of lezzie girl gangs that made The Bangles, The Go-Go's, and Fuzzbox envious.

Johnny Quest—Johnny + Hadji + Race Bannon = the latest Falcon video release.

Josie and the Pussycats—Valerie and Alexandra were doing it on that phallic spaceship in outer space while Alan watched.

Kids Incorporated—"K-I-D-S. Kids Incorporated! We're gonna have fun!"

The Peanuts specials—Marcie and Peppermint Patty were into lezzie love.

Popeye—Olive Oyl never did much for him, but Bluto always got him excited.

Sesame Street—If you need an explanation for Bert and Ernie, then you need to come out.

Scooby-Doo—Shaggy was a druggy, Velma a lesbo, and Daphne had killer boots!

The Smurfs—One Smurffette to all those guys in hot pants: You figure it out.

Spiderman and His Amazing Friends—Iceman was a dreamy nude stud, and Firestar had such pretty hair (and killer boots).

Superfriends—Meanwhile, at the Hall of Justice...

In the same fashion, I watched *The Facts of Life,* I wanted to be pretty like Blair, butch like Jo, fun like Tootie, everyone's best friend like Natalie, and protected by someone like Mrs. Garrett. But it was *The Golden Girls* that really taught me how to be a well-rounded homo.

You had Blanche, the whore we all wished we could be (or secretly were) and who made us feel empowered because of her unabashed appreciation for her libido. By contrast, Rose portrayed the innocence and vulnerability I sometimes felt as the odd but optimistic outsider in this terribly straight world. Then there was Dorothy, the smart-talking, confident dame I hoped to become. Like Linda Lavin's Alice, she was the one I most hoped to emulate in order to survive outside the cocoon of my family. And finally there was Sophia, the mother I really wanted (and the mother I discovered I actually had once I stopped thinking of her as a parent and instead related to as a friend).

Now this is all well and good, but it raises two major problems: (1) Maybe we can see aspects of ourselves in wacky sitcom characters, but women like Wonder Woman, Buffy, and *Alias*'s Sydney are still pretty different from us. So what's the real source of the attraction? And (2) with the recent explosion of gay visibility and culture what I'm discussing in these pages might seem a little anachronistic; maybe young people today no longer need to escape into Wonder Richard's world. Well, let me tackle the second point, because it's easier.

Some people might argue that with *Queer as Folk, Will & Grace,* and *Queer Eye for the Straight Guy,* gay kids don't need to search for straight female idols to identify with because they're readily available in gay male form. That might seem to be true on the surface, if you think these programs depict gays in a way that could be considered heroic. But they most emphatically don't. Will and Jack, the asexual gay and the wacky queen, are sanitized for

Why *Mary Tyler Moore* Matters

- Cloris Leachman was the Queen in the *Wonder Woman* pilot movie and Mrs. Garrett's sister on *The Facts of Life.*
- The Dan-O-Rama *Mary Tyler Moore* music video kicked ass and helped him get work with Madonna and Cher.
- Lou Grant is a daddy bear.
- Hazel Frederick, the woman who scowls at Mary when she tosses her hat during the opening credits, is forever burned into our consciousness.
- Sue Ann Nivens makes Martha Stewart look like an amateur.
- Veal Prince Orloff.
- Because Mary showed us that we really could make it, after all!

heterosexual consumption. Meanwhile, the characters on *Queer as Folk* are so preoccupied with their gayness that, on one hand, you feel this intense pressure to be out and, on the other, you can't help worrying that the shit will inevitably crash down on you if you are. And, yes, the Fab Five are very entertaining, but are men who tell us how to use hair dryers and style window treatments really people we should look up to? Well, for some guys, yes. But so much more is possible in the lives of gay men than the options these five men offer. Claiming the Fab Five as your role models profoundly limits your exploration of your total personality.

Which leaves us with my first question: How is it that these kick-ass chicks reflect real aspects of ourselves?

We identify with characters like Diana Prince and Sydney Bristow because they're forced to keep secrets about who they are and what they know—and, like it or not, most gay kids still have to keep secrets. Call me cynical, but when a young person wakes up to his homosexuality—no matter how many queer characters he sees on television— it's still going to be difficult to reveal that truth to his family and friends. Most straight people who are steeped in mainstream American culture still consider gay men strange at best and candidates for a good stoning at worst. That sort of mentality forces gay kids into survival mode: They often construct a public persona that masks their true experiences and emotions, and they only reveal their "true selves" when they're absolutely certain they're safe.

Until us gay kids have real gay heroes to emulate, these ladies will serve as metaphors for ourselves; within each of us is a powerful champion for good like Wonder Woman or a survivor like Sydney Bristow. We're still outsiders in our own world, and at the same time our experience as outsiders equips us with powers and skills that allow us to handle some pretty difficult situations. Coming out—*really* coming out—is simply a matter of awakening to that understanding.

I'm not saying that the current crop of gay programs is bad. In fact, I rejoice every time a new queen or lezzie pops up on TV precisely because their visibility is important, and that *does* make life better than it was for many of us when we were kids.

But, whatever their value as entertainment or information, the fact of the matter is that those programs aren't made for young people who are growing up gay. They're created solely to make money for networks, production companies, actors, and everyone else who has a hand in the business. The *business* of making money is what the entertainment industry is all about.

I still relish television and I even entertain fantasies of seeing Jem and the Holograms in concert from time to time. To tell the truth, I *need* that mental outlet—I *need* to geek out over obscure facts that other people miss. But now I cultivate these obsessions in a saner, more balanced, and happy place in my life.

Ultimately, what gives me peace of mind is knowing that for all the other young gay boys in the world who feel alone, in need of a friend, and burdened by their secrets, there will always be a Wonder Woman or Sydney Bristow on television to protect them. Maybe they'll even be inspired to unleash their own personal superpowers.

Wilson Cruz's Top 11 TV Shows Every Gay Man Should Watch

(As told to Richard Andreoli one night at Here Lounge in West Hollywood.)

1. Dynasty
2. Soap
3. My So-Called Life
4. thirtysomething
5. Designing Women
6. The Golden Girls
7. Life Goes On
8. Ellen
9. Six Feet Under
10. Sex and the City
11. Alias

Wilson Cruz played Rickie on the 1990s TV drama *My So-Called Life*.

Who Made the Writers Hard?

TV crushes from the cast of *Mondo Homo.*

Richard Andreoli: I fell in love with John Wesley Shipp when he played Kelly on *Guiding Light.* After I'd become a comic book geek I wanted him to save me as The Flash. However what I *really* wanted was to call him Daddy just like Dawson did on *Dawson's Creek.* Of course, none of those fantasies compares to when I met Antony Hamilton from *Cover Up* (he replaced Jon-Erik Hexum, who accidentally shot himself in the head while playing Russian roulette with a gun loaded with blanks) while I was kicking everyone out of the steam room at the Athletic Club in West Hollywood. Good times.

David Ciminelli: Captain James T. Kirk's tight polyester shirt and black pants coupled with his fearless leadership, perfect skin, and knack for maintaining an unshakeable coif even while fending off alien creatures was pure ecstasy. My libido was set to stun during one particular episode of *Star Trek* in which, after a fierce battle, Kirk's shirt was slashed in just the right spot to expose his left nipple. That scene alone had me fantasizing about transporting into Kirk's pants. Then there was Jon from *ChiPs*: a tight cop uniform, leather boots, and reflective shades on a bearish, ex-frat boy-looking straight guy with shoulders and an ass like a linebacker? It just didn't get any better than that for a horny grade-schooler in heat in the early '80s. Yep, watching *ChiPs* was usually an interactive experience for me whenever Ponch's pal was onscreen.

Smith Galtney: (1) Robert Hays: First I saw him in *Angie,* then in the *Airplane* movies. Cute, cute, cute. Not your Marlboro Man, Steve Austin type. More your boy-next-door all grown up into a successful, suit-wearing doctor. Preppy, wholesome. (2) David Naughton: He was adorable in *Makin' It* and as the "Be a Pepper" guy, but it wasn't until *An American Werewolf in London* that I really lost my shit. (3) Patrick Duffy: Bobby Ewing was a doll. Too bad I wasn't around for any *Man From Atlantis* reruns. (4) Gregory Harrison: In the title sequence of *Trapper John, M.D.,* opening the shower door, all bare and hairy-chested, dripping wet, and smiling.

Aaron Krach: Okay. So you watched *CHiPs*. That meant you either liked sugar (Larry Wilcox) or spice (Erik Estrada). It's not like I would have kicked either of them out of my twin bed, but I wanted their boss, Sgt. Joseph Getraer, played by the grinning salt-and-pepper-haired Robert Pine. He was the proverbial daddy, and Ponch and Jon were the very bad boys. But Mr. Pine never came down too hard on them. At least not as hard as I fantasized (fondly) that he might come down on me.

Drew Limsky: Steve Austin, *The Six Million Dollar Man*. Clean-cut, big hairy chest, and just vacant enough to project any kind of fantasy onto. The zipper of his tracksuit was always lower than it needed to be, and I especially liked the way the show's writers kept inventing situations in order to get him undressed, like the time he and the Bionic Woman ran through a hurricane and he stripped down to his boxers, explaining, "I can move faster this way." So can I. But try explaining that to the cops in the Ramble in Central Park.

Christopher Lisotta: I was always a *St. Elsewhere* fan, but when Mark Harmon started playing the dreamy Dr. Bobby Caldwell, I hoped against hope I could move to Boston and ask Bobby for a nose job. And of course, in the irony of ironies, he got cut up by a psycho redhead while they were having sex during a vacation in Cape Cod. She also gave him AIDS. See what sleeping with women gets you?

Parker Ray: I could easily have said Tom Selleck from *Magnum P.I.* (he can solve my case anytime), or George Clooney from those first few seasons of *E.R.* ("Um, doctor, I need you to check out my boo-boo"). But if I'm going to be honest, give me Sherilyn Fenn from *Twin Peaks* any day. This buxom babe was reintroduced to me when my straight husband and I used to watch his *Twin Peaks* DVD collection, downing Jack and Cokes in our underwear in college. We would look at each other in our drunken stupor every time she slinked onscreen and nod in agreement. Later on those nights, in my bed, I imagined her as the seducer during our little rendezvous in my head. Funny thing, she was more of a "top" than the guys I was seeing back then.

Dave White: In the '70s when I was a kid it was bear-template Dan Haggerty from *Grizzly Adams*. Of course, Dan Haggerty's most important qualities were best displayed when he appeared on *Battle of the Network Stars* in crotch-hugging track shorts and nothing else. In the '80s I loved MTV VJ Kevin Seal because he was dorkishly cute, had a sexy perpetual 5 o'clock shadow, and was the first host to actually make fun of MTV on the air. Currently I'm in love with Kevin James from *The King of Queens*. It's the uniform.

The Cable Guy

By Smith Galtney

Is it a coincidence that a friend informed me about masturbation months after my family got cable? Or was it kismet?

My parents divorced and moved into separate residences, thus rearranging the world as I'd known it. With three of my siblings off studying at Ole Miss in Oxford, Miss., my mother moved my sister Eleanor and me into an apartment in uptown New Orleans, just off the river. Compared to our old stucco house, where my Dad was still living by himself, this place looked like a set from a wacky sitcom about a dysfunctional family. (*"Find out what happens when a newly divorced mom moves into a new neighborhood with her belligerent teenage daughter and effeminate son..."*)

Our apartment was in a triplex with two terraces, the upper one of which allowed me to spy on our hippie-looking neighbors while they had sex. The whole setting was like a teen-sex comedy.

TOP SHOWS OF ALL TIME

Absolutely Fabulous—Without Patsy and Edina you wouldn't have *Will & Grace*'s Karen Walker or all those other messes on TV.
Battle of the Network Stars—Because you'll never see it again.
The Simpsons—Always intelligent and fresh.
So Graham Norton in the U.K. or *The Graham Norton Effect* in the U.S.—Because it's fan-fagging-tastic!.

Perhaps in some bid to one-up my father, who only had HBO, my mother requested HBO *and* Showtime. However, when the cable guy came to our house he brought the wrong converter box, one equipped with ALL PREMIUM CHANNELS.

"My apologies," he said. He promised to return with the correct box soon. "In the meantime, I'll just hook up this one." Thankfully, the guy never came back. I enjoyed free movie channels from ages 11 to 15...including the Playboy Channel!

Soon after that, my father took a friend and me to the Super Bowl to watch the Saints play. We were hardly paying attention to the game, so I suggested to my friend—whose name just happened to be Willie—that we go get nachos and Cokes. While we munched on our nachos we started talking about sex, and I told him about the stuff I'd seen on the Playboy Channel. Then he said there was something you could do to yourself, something that feels *almost* exactly like sex. All you had to do was curl your hand around your penis, rub up and down, and picture a naked woman doing naughty things in your mind. "It'll feel really, *really,* REALLY good," he promised.

"It's called masturbation," Willie said, only I misheard it as "mascavation." Anyway, it wasn't long before I was at school informing my friend David about this really cool thing called "mascavating."

"Man," he said, grossed out. "That's jackin' off. You *do* that?"

"Of *course* not," I insisted.

Nevertheless, I watched as much of the Playboy Channel as I could, late at night with the sound down low so it wouldn't wake my mother or my sister, but not *too* low, since I wanted to hear the moans and groans. I quickly realized that amid the tangle of painted lips, bare breasts, and shaved vaginas, what *really* got me going was seeing a guy's ass, or his pubic region, perhaps a testicle or two, sometimes a whole penis. In some movies a woman would go down on a guy, and the scene was shot showing the back of her head so as to obscure an erection or actual penetration (this was soft-core, after all).

Sometimes the guy would put one hand on the back of her head or slowly lie back and contort his manly face into any number of pleased expressions. When these things happened it felt as if my entire biology was shifting into overdrive.

I filed these images, sounds, scenes, motions, and expressions into my head and used them over and over again. I became steadily more skilled at pleasing myself; in fact, it got to the point where I could make myself have an actual orgasm! What's more, I learned that the right word for my new favorite activity was "masturbation." Meanwhile, those sights and sounds from the Playboy Channel began to morph and splice themselves together. The women slowly dissolved from each scene, to be replaced by men from other scenes—and, eventually, by my freshman-year homeroom teacher. (He was a coach, you see.)

By the time I was 14, I was no longer watching other men do these things to each other in the corners my mind. I was actually joining them. Yes, it was all still happening in my imagination, but now I was conjuring real people in real places with real emotions. That's when the act of pleasing oneself became an incredibly dirty, unbearably shameful, quite intoxicating, thoroughly addicting, and ultimately inescapable art.

To this day, I'm still trying to paint my masterpiece.

QUEER TV ESSENTIALS

You must get E!, Lifetime, HGTV, and the Food Network. Everything else is secondary.

COMEDIES

Absolutely Fabulous • Designing Women • The Golden Girls
Frasier • Friends • In Living Color • Kids in the Hall
South Park • Strangers With Candy • Three's Company

CLASSIC QUEEN SHOWS

Batman
You figure it out...
The Beverly Hillbillies
Jane Hathaway was a huge dyke.
Bewitched
Samantha was the only nonqueer on the show, but she made
up for it by being a huge fag hag.
The Brady Bunch
Jan was another huge dyke.
Gilligan's Island
The Skipper + Gilligan = daddy + boy. Ginger = drag queen.
Maryanne = fag hag. The Professor = closet case.
Mr. and Mrs. Howell = your clueless parents.
The Odd Couple
Fags
Whelan and Madam
She was his drag persona come to life.

Chapter 3: Music

Slave to the Rhythm
By Smith Galtney

I was born in 1971, two years after Judy Garland died, and thus I had the pleasure of growing up in one of the gayest decades the 20th century had to offer. Who's to say exactly *why* the '70s were so fabulous, but Garland certainly had a lot to do with it. On Friday, June 27th, 1969, the night of her funeral, a couple of Manhattan drag queens kicked off the Stonewall riots—an event that convinced urban gays it was their human right to have a good time. So they hit the clubs with a vengeance, danced as hard and fast as they could, and ended up building an entirely new culture from the underground up. It was called disco, and by the mid '70s it was no longer just a gay thing. This gay thing was *everywhere*.

What does this all mean to a young 5-year-old living in uptown New Orleans? Well, I was plopped in front of our home entertainment center, taking it all in with my eyes and ears. One could honestly separate my childhood into two parts: "before *Saturday Night Fever*" and "after *Saturday Night Fever*." The "before" section can be summed up in one moment: when my oldest sister played me her copy of Elton John's *Goodbye Yellow Brick Road,* and I simply had to know why that man on the album cover wore heels bigger than my Mom's.

The "after" part is somewhat similar: My other sister came home with the *Fever* soundtrack, and I listened to it endlessly. This time, though, I was no longer just an observer. I wanted to *be* John Travolta. I wanted to wear a tacky white suit, and point my finger in the air while I posed on a dance floor underlit by blue, yellow, and red lights. There was something about the music—it had a beat that made me want to dance and melodies that made me want to sing. And when I did both at the same time, I felt like a completely new person.

That *Fever* would have such a profound impact on me is a no-brainer. After all, the movie's central character was disco. And really, what was Tony Manero if not a big old queen rewritten as a macho Brooklyn badass. He had big dreams and secret desires that only came alive when he was in a dark room, moving his body to throbbing, pulsating rhythms. To Tony, that act alone was just as good, if not better, than having sex. Tony utters one of *Fever*'s most memorable lines after Joey asks Tony if he's going to fuck their friend Annette. "Y'know, Joey," Tony says, in his iconic Brooklynese, "you make it with some of these chicks, they think you gotta dance wit 'em."

Watching the movie today, it's undeniable how sensitive and ultimately *gay* Tony Manero seems. Unlike his cronies he's careful not to bash a gay couple that walks past the gang on a Saturday afternoon. What's more, his life changes when he strikes up a platonic relationship with a woman, who, by the movie's end, has helped him realize his true potential. No surprise, then, that the next time we saw Tony Manero on the big screen, he was a Broadway dancer, wearing leg warmers and flashing jazz hands in 1983's *Staying Alive*.

If disco gave a blue-collar punk enough courage to head for the Great White Way, you could say it had a similar effect on me. As a very shy 8-year-old who never tried out for plays or sang loud in music class, I found myself starring in and producing a talent show with my sister—just so I could dance to the Bee Gee's "You Should Be Dancing" in full view of all our friends and neighbors. We picked out an olive green leisure suit for my big moment. We also got my brother, Ford, and his friend Hayden to do the lights, which basically involved standing on a Ping-Pong table behind a few rows of patio furniture and using high-beam flashlights as spotlights.

Ford and Hayden were teenagers. They smoked pot and played basketball, and when their spotlights hit me, I was terrified—not only because I was having my first bout with stage fright, but I was also having my first bout with gay-boy paranoia. Even after the applause, I couldn't stop wondering, *Do they think I'm a sissy?*

Both disco and the '70s had to die before I got my answer. As it does with all gay boys, puberty brought the strange realization that I might be turning into something other than normal. Yeah, it's fine if a boy wants to dance when he's a child. But if he gets a little older and he *still* wants to dance, folks are likely to get suspicious. And by the time I was 12, Ford was extremely suspicious.

I distinctly remember the first time I ever heard Lionel Richie's "All Night Long" on the radio. I was in carpool with about seven other kids as somebody's mom drove us home from school. There were, like, three conversations going on at once, so I couldn't completely hear the song. What I did hear, though, blew me away—especially that "Jumbo! Jumbo!" part near the end—and I couldn't wait to hear the song again.

A few days later the video came on MTV when I was alone at my father's house. (Or at least I *thought* I was alone.) I got up and started dancing, and when I say dancing, I mean *dancing*: twirling around, doing flying leaps off the sofa with my hands in the air, legs split and toes pointed. During one enthusiastically executed twirl, I happened to see my brother leaning against the kitchen doorway. He just shook his head and walked away, as if he'd caught me doing something unspeakable.

Later that night he and I were having dinner with my father when Ford said to Dad, "You know what I caught Smitty doing this afternoon?"

Dad said, "What?"

Ford said, "Dancing in the living room. I'm telling you, he's gonna be a fag."

My father, bless him, defended me. "Ford, don't say that. The boy likes to dance. So what? It's okay."

GRACE JONES / SLAVE TO THE RHYTHM

But for some reason, I didn't feel comforted or reassured. My father's defense—*"The boy likes to dance!"*—often replayed itself in my mind. And the more I heard it, the more I felt like a fag.

Things began to feel worse when I was 14. In fact, one moment remains so sharp and crisp in my memory I should switch to the present tense to truly do it justice:

The year is 1985, and I'm a freshman in high school. My best friend, Lee, and I have decided we're going to exchange presents for Easter. Both of us are avid watchers of MTV. We both own Walkmans and boom boxes, and we both wish our cassette collections were bigger than they actually are. So, with our proposed Easter exchange come two requirements: (1) The gifts must be cassettes, and (2) we'll trade them in social studies, the first class of the day we had together.

Lee doesn't hesitate to tell me what he wants: a Lone Justice tape. (FYI: Lone Justice was a new wave-country group. They made two so-so albums, broke up in 1986, and aren't important to this story. Or to anything, really.) I have to think a while before I tell Lee what I want. Not because I don't know what I want. I know exactly what I want—an album by one of the most gay-identified artists of the 20th century: *Slave to the Rhythm* by Grace Jones.

Not that I even know Grace Jones is a humongous gay icon. I don't know she's a former model who kicked off her singing career by performing for throngs of homosexuals in discos across the world. All I know is what I've seen on MTV: this towering, hulking, mannish woman with skin so black it looks blue, with lips so heavily painted they look plastic, and a flattop Afro so sleek and stylized it looks like a pillbox hat.

MTV has been running this video of her performing "Demolition Man," a hit by the

Police that Grace's monotone growl of a voice has rendered unrecognizable. In the video, which I only see late at night on weekends, she stands on a gray staircase, wearing black stiletto heels, charcoal slacks, and a matching blazer, without a shirt. The whites of her eyes pop out at the camera like characters in old cartoons after the lights are turned out.

I have lived in uptown New Orleans all my life. I have never seen anything like this. Not even during Mardi Gras.

A few weeks after I first see Grace on MTV, my obsession intensifies when I spot the cover of *Slave to the Rhythm* in a record store. It's just a picture of Grace's face, with her mouth wide open as if she's yelling. But the photo has been enhanced and rearranged with an X-Acto knife, with four slashes across her mouth and three through her hair. As a result, her wide-open mouth has been extended a good few inches—making it look *really* wide open, like an anaconda's—and her Afro has been stretched above her head like a nappy, leaning Tower of Pisa.

My jaw drops; my own mouth feels as wide as Grace's. I'm transfixed, and feel kind of funny and peculiar inside.

The thing is, I don't know any other 15-year-old boys—who live in uptown New Orleans and go to an all-male Christian Brothers high school—who know who Grace Jones is. Okay, they've probably seen her in *A View to a Kill*. And they'd probably recognize her as "that Amazonian black chick," the one who had Arnold Schwarzenegger complaining that she was

GUILTY PLEASURES
Boy bands • Britney Spears • Debbie Gibson • Hanson • Spice Girls • Tiffany

DIVAS WE LOVE
Celine Dion • Cher • Christina Aguilera • Kylie Minogue • Madonna • Mariah Carey

FOR QUEER EARS ONLY
Anastacia • CeCe Peniston • Crystal Waters • Deborah Cox • Jody Watley • Kristine W. • Pepper Mashay • Taylor Dayne

GAY, GAY, GAY—OH, MY GOD—THEY'RE SO GAY!
Elton John • Erasure • George Michael • Indigo Girls • k.d. lang • Melissa Etheridge • Pet Shop Boys • Queen • Rufus Wainwright • Scissor Sisters

being too rough on the set of *Conan the Destroyer*. Maybe some even know she's a singer too, but I seriously doubt they're walking around with Grace Jones cassettes in their backpacks.

Which is why I feel a rush of relief when I mention *Slave to the Rhythm* to Lee. "Dude, I saw that album in the record store." he says. "The cover is *totally* cool!"

It was all the courage I needed. "That's what I want for Easter," I say, before I start to feel nervous again. "Just, um, do me a favor."

"What?"

"When we make the exchange in social studies, try and pass me the tape without anybody seeing it. I kind of don't want anybody to know I've got a Grace Jones tape."

"Sure," Lee says, smirking. "Whatever."

You know what happens next.

Lee walks into class, hoisting the cassette high above his head and shouting, "I have your Grace Jones tape, Smitty!" All of my classmates raise their heads. I keep mine as low as possible. But there's nowhere to hide. Lee stands right in front of me—laughing his ass off—shoves the tape in my face and wags it in his fist. One by one, the students around me start to chuckle too, following the lead of my best friend. Oh god, even gape-mouthed *Grace* looks like she's laughing at me.

SINGERS LESBIANS LOVE
(And Whose Work Every Gay Man Should Own)

Cris Williamson • The Gossip • Jane Siberry • Team Dresch •
Patty Griffin • Phranc • Rickie Lee Jones • Shawn Colvin •
Tori Amos • Tracy Chapman • Two Nice Girls • P.J. Harvey

Humiliating as that felt, my love affair with music was far from over. Some teenagers want cars for their 16th birthday. I wanted a stereo—one of those *really* nice ones that doesn't come in one piece and that has a tape deck, so I could make mix tapes. Once I got one a desire was born that remains unquenched to this day: to amass not just a record collection, but a comprehensive music library. I aspired to build a music archive filled with not only the hot new releases (I was the first kid in school to know about Edie Brickell & New Bohemians) but also the must-have classics (a good deal of my allowance was spent on David Bowie and Roxy Music albums). Basically, I was doing my best to become an educated musicologist; if record-shopping could be considered an extracurricular activity, I was an overachiever.

For Christmas my sister got me a subscription to *Rolling Stone* and a copy of *The Rolling*

Stone Record Guide, which grades every album ever released on a five-star rating system, and which I read like the Bible. I also read anything about rock history that I could get my hands on, and in my research, I quickly learned this: Rock à la the Beatles was deemed "meaningful art," whereas most disco was considered to be a weightless indulgence, nothing more than a fleeting good time. So in my mission to familiarize myself with Great Music, I bought as many albums as I could by "important" artists like the Stones, Neil Young, and the Velvet Underground. Plus, it was easier to buy a Bob Dylan album without worrying whether the cashier thought I was a fag.

This was the '80s, though, and the lines between "macho" and "homo" were beginning to blur a tad. By mid-decade, disco had morphed into new wave, allowing androgynous idols like Boy George and Annie Lennox to create hits even jocks could sing along to. Hair-metal bands sported more makeup and bigger coifs than most girls at the local mall. By contrast, dance music itself was taking on a more rock-like feel, thanks to groups like New Order and Depeche Mode. So it was easier to test out other genres without feeling like I was subscribing to a new lifestyle. So easy, in fact, that I found I could turn my friends on to a song by Book of Love called "Boy," a bouncy synth-pop ditty in which a woman pines to "be where the boys are / but I'm not allowed."

It helped that none of us had the faintest clue what she was talking about. Had I known, I probably would've only listened to the song when I was absolutely sure the house was empty—like I did when I listened to my copy of Bronski Beat's "Smalltown Boy" 12-inch single. When I bought that one I couldn't even look the cashier in the eye; I felt like I was buying a nudie magazine. I bought a lot of singles, in fact—some by the Pet Shop Boys and the Smiths. I never bought their albums because I never considered Morrissey or Neil Tennant to be serious artists. I thought Morrissey was whiny and the Pet Shop Boys were cheesy. Besides, I knew kids in school who dug the Smiths and the Pet Shop Boys. They looked gay, and I knew I didn't want to be associated with that.

Not yet, anyway.

When it came time to think about college, New York University was the only school I applied to; it was the one I *had* to go to. It was another no-brainer: I was gay, it was far away from home and located in the heart of Greenwich Village. There was simply no other choice.

What happened next isn't so unique: I got to NYU, started smoking pot with the stoners, listened to lots of Dylan and Pink Floyd on bright days with the shades pulled down. Around sophomore year the gayness inevitably burst out of me, and soon I was coming out to my family and friends. My sister hooked me up with a friend who lived in New York too, and one afternoon I went to his place for a chat.

The first thing I noticed was that his roommate had decorated the place like it was a monument to Cher. There were Cher posters on the wall, programs from her concerts on the coffee table, and not one, not two, but *all* of her albums on the CD shelves—next to the complete works of Billie Holiday, Diana Ross, Patti LaBelle, and Madonna. That's when I noticed a fascinating connection: This guy—this *homo*— seemed more serious about his music than all the *Rolling Stone* scribes I was reading and all the Dylan-smitten stoners I was hanging out with *combined*.

Suddenly I was filled with an undeniable sense of liberation—I could freely and openly and shamelessly embrace the music I'd loved since I was a kid. Talk about being let loose in a candy store: Now there was all this fantastic new music to discover (Chaka Khan, Jennifer Holiday, Sylvester, Donna Summer *albums,* not just the hits). All of it was a direct link to this new community I was exploring and eagerly becoming a member of.

It wasn't long before I started to hear other music in a new way. Like that Book of Love song? I could tell it was obviously about a fag hag, and that the "boy bar" the woman was singing of was a reference to Boy Bar, a gay bar in the East Village I'd been to once or twice. Plus, my perspective on the Smiths and the Pet Shop Boys did a complete 180. If I couldn't understand Morrissey when I was in the closet, lyrics like "There's a club if you'd like to go / you could meet somebody who really loves you / so you go and you stand on your own/and you leave on your own / and you go home / and you cry and you want to die" were making a shit-load of sense. My newfound pride quickly careened into arrogance, and I found myself standing cross-armed in front of my stoner friends, arguing that "Rent" by Pet Shop Boys was *every bit* as powerful as anything Dylan wrote. They also dissed Madonna's *Erotica.*But for me, it was more than just a cheesy dance album. It was the soundtrack for my new life: music written with a gay man, using sounds from gay clubs, wrapped in a package that was just gay, Gay, GAY! Then again, Madonna's entire songbook was coming through in a whole new key.

The most liberating moments by far, though, were hearing all this music out in gay clubs as I participated in the nocturnal rites of gay passage—an epiphany not unlike Tony Manero's in *Saturday Night Fever*. It just made all the sense in the world that my finally dancing in a gay club didn't just mark a new chapter in my life, but also *justified* the parts of my life that had always seemed suspect.

Whenever a DJ broke out disco classics like "Bad Girls" or "Funky Town," it was such a sweet slap in the face to realize where this music came from. I was now dancing to it in a roomful of people who'd made the exact same discovery at some point in their lives. Once the DJ even broke out "Slave to the Rhythm," and when I realized the woman dancing next to me who looked like Grace Jones actually *was* Grace Jones, I didn't feel as if I'd come out. I felt like I'd come full circle.

Pete Burns's Top 11 Albums Every Queer Kid Should Own

1. Sonny & Cher—*The Beat Goes On*
In 1964 there was a TV show called *Ready, Steady, Go!* and I remember hearing these amazing voices and seeing this vision on the TV of these two beautiful guys who looked like they'd escaped from a Cherokee reservation. And I thought, *I'm not alone in the world! I want to grow up to be a man just like him.* And of course that was Cher I was talking about. I didn't even grasp that she was a woman, I just thought she was the most beautiful man I'd ever seen.

2. The Ronettes—*Greatest Hits*
When the Rolling Stones were causing yawns, the Ronettes were causing riots, and when I first saw them on the TV I thought, *Those three guys look fabulous!* Gender didn't register in my head then, but they also didn't look like any of the women I was being exposed to at the time. Everyone who was coming out then in Britain was blond, but everyone from America was multicultural and dark. They seemed so exciting, and I perceived that their music was really the soundtrack to their personalities.

3. David Bowie—*The Rise and Fall of Ziggy Stardust and the Spiders From Mars*
One particular day on the TV—on this children's show, of all places—I saw Bowie singing "Starman." Naturally, I flipped! So when I returned to school I had neon hair, no eyebrows, an earring, and yellow trousers. This amazing silence fell over the entire school. Days later this bastard skinhead dragged me into the leisure room where we could play records, and he put on "Lady Stardust." I was supposed to die of embarrassment, but to me it sounded fabulous. And if you listen to Lady Stardust you would probably say this guy was psychic, because it predicted what I would become. So I became known as Lady Stardust, and I didn't think that was such a bad nickname at all.

4. Patti Smith—*Horses*

In the summer of '76 when the punk movement began and before it became mainstream and ruined, Patti Smith's music filtered over here. When I got *Horses* and heard "Gloria," I was smitten. Here was this fantastic poetry by this absolutely beautiful androgynous woman. Her albums take me right back to that wonderful summer of '76. Her vocals, music, and poetry absolutely flip me. That was the start of my journey, really.

5. Judy Garland—*Live In London, 1969*

God, where do I start? I mean, it's Judy! She's at The Talk of the Town in London, and technically her voice was dreadful and she was hallucinating and out of her head. When she sang "Over the Rainbow" she sounded two-thirds of the way over, herself. Her voice would break down and then when you didn't expect it, it would suddenly soar. It's car-crash listening. By the end of that album you know she's going to never be able to sing again. It's the essential album to all singers who are suffering. [Note: This album was never officially released on CD, so you'll have to search the Internet to find copies.]

6. Carly Simon—*No Secrets*

The first song that struck me was "His Friends Are More Than Fond of Robin" because my first sexual experience was with a Robin. But then I branched out and heard "Carter Family." When you're young you think you know everything, and so you don't want to listen to what people have to say, and then suddenly when they're gone you think, *I could've just listened to them.* That's a rule I live by now. Listen to people, even old people who you think are just crazy, because their opinions matter. At a certain age that song should be a part of the educational curriculum.

7. Sylvester—*Greatest Hits*

Oh! What can I say? Some time after Bowie I came home and there was this vision on the TV, so I turned the sound on and it was a voice from heaven! "You Are My Friend" is a live recording with Martha Wash that gets standing ovations. "Don't Stop" is another favorite. There's not much I can say other than if there's one album to get, it should be a law to own this one. His voice reflects joy to me. Real, pure joy.

8. Hole—*Celebrity Skin*

I think it's an unquestionable fact that Courtney Love has a lot to say in her lyrics. She's just amazing. The girl's got her problems and she loves fame, but I think she looks fabulous and she writes fabulous music. She's got incredible amounts of rage and frustration in her. I don't think anything she's doing is any stranger than Judy

Garland, but now it's held up and laughed at and derided like an item of mockery. I love her and have great respect for her as an artist. I admire her.

9. Mary J. Blige—*Share My World*
God she's fantastic. The track "Seven Days"—not only do I love the song but I've lived it. There's pain in her music that she's singing to everyone. And on TV she looks like she's some kind of queen. Her hair and nails and clothes are so beautiful— emblems of success. She throws it all on. She looks regal and tribal and in my mind and heart she really has made it. She's a goddess.

10. Victoria Beckham—*Victoria Beckham*
I think she's fabulous and I don't have a crush on her husband. "Mind of Its Own" is a classic '60s style love song. Her voice is so plaintive and she's not trying to do Christina Aguilera operatics. I play "Mind Of Its Own" and "Not Such an Innocent Girl" once a day. They remind me of being a kid and listening to Sonny and Cher and the Ronettes. Don't listen to the media who say she's mediocre. She makes you happy and that's enough.

11. Dead or Alive—*Evolution: The Hits*
When I did this album I was afraid of digging through the archives and listening to them in their entirety, because I thought I'd hate them. But when I heard the songs compiled I thought, *This really is a good body of work.* "What I Want" is a favorite. It's where my heart was. You know, there are many things in life that I can't do, and I get this 6-year-old's frustration. But then I think about how I wrote all those songs, and on that I can sleep well at night. What can I say? I'm proud of the collection.

Pete Burns is the lead singer for Dead or Alive.

DISAPPEARED DIVAS By Dave White

Everyone's not Madonna. These women had a hit or two and then—*poof*—they were gone without a trace. Having one name was no guarantee of longevity. We miss them.

1. Martika
2. Stacey Q
3. Cherelle
4. Sinitta
5. Regina
6. Alicia
7. Stacy Lattisaw
8. Nia Peeples
9. Karyn White
10. Pebbles

This Is a True Story...

In September 2001, Steve Thompson and a group of friends participated in the Canada-U.S. AIDS Vaccine Ride. Their trip began in Montreal and ended in Maine, and the quickest route to their homes in Los Angeles was to take a puddle-jumper flight from Maine to Boston, then a transcontinental flight from Boston to LA. Meanwhile in Los Angeles, Madonna was on her "Drowned World Tour." At the last minute she added an additional performance in Los Angeles that coincided with the completion of the AIDS Ride. In a desperate bid to see their favorite diva in concert, Steve and his then-boyfriend scrambled to purchase tickets for the new show, even though it meant flying back a day early. The two of them boarded an American Airlines flight from Boston to Los Angeles on September 10th, instead of their original plan to fly back on American Airlines Flight 11, on September 11th.

Never forget: Madonna saves lives.

Queer Punk

"Jock-o-Rama on the brain / Redneck-a-thon driving me insane..."

By Parker Ray

When I first heard the song "Jock-o-Rama" by the Dead Kennedys I was 7 years old. I remember thinking Jello Biafra, the lead singer and one-time San Francisco mayoral candidate, was scary, what with his ripped shirt, phallic microphone in hand, and arm waving around at the scary-looking crowd that had gathered to see him scream. I was at a D.K. concert in San Francisco, on the shoulders of my sister's jock boyfriend, listening to something that was far different from the harmless *Sesame Street* songs I had just abandoned.

Looking back, I can honestly say Jello turned me on. So did my sister's boyfriend. Actually, both of my older sisters—one 9, the other 8 years older than me—dated hot, popular jocks throughout high school. I remember their bribing me to stay in my room when my parents were out so their boyfriends could come over to "watch movies." I always managed to say hi to the guys and let them know that I was there to play with if they got bored with my sisters—not exactly aware that this impulse was a product of my budding queerness.

But I quickly discovered I was a little too queer to ever fit in with the jocks. I enjoyed playing sports, but, to be quite honest, I was a little too intellectual to even pretend that I enjoyed talking in one-syllable words all the time. Why should I waste precious hours memorizing baseball facts to impress the guys I thought were hot, but whose lifestyle bored the hell out of me?

However, I still felt this overpowering urge not to be the stereotypical "sissy" queer in high school. I started listening to music that flew in the face of the Rush and Guns N' Roses-listening dumb-asses who taunted me by calling me "faggot" 20 times a day. Funny thing is, this taunting depressed me, but at the same time it spurred me to be as individualistic as possible. That's where punk rock came in.

Sonic Youth, the Dead Kennedys, the Sex Pistols, this tiny band called Nirvana, the local Gilman-Berkeley scene with Operation Ivy, and another tiny band called Green Day: They were all angry and smart. And, though I wasn't exactly clear on this point at the time, they were even more masculine in my mind than the jocks could ever be. Masculine in that "Fuck you, I'm gonna wear a dress and kick your athletic ass because your hours in the gym are no match for my fury" kind of way.

But, looking deeper, it was masculine in that "I don't need to prove to *you* that I'm a man" way, and I started to embrace the fact that I didn't want to be either a sissy *or* a man who showed my affections by punching another guy in the shoulder. Punk rock allowed me to just be myself in contrasting extremes, what with my steel-toed Army boots and plastic little-girl bracelets, with my electric blue hair and my affinity for the water polo players' bodies. I wanted to kiss guys in that romantic way, but also slam into them at concerts.

Then punk went mainstream in the 1990s and you had football players trading Axl Rose for Kurt Cobain, even though he sang about wanting to be attracted to guys and came out and told all of the homophobes to stop buying Nirvana's records. The jocks still tormented me because, well, that was how they filled their time when they weren't busy barely passing their remedial classes. Of course, I still secretly lusted after them like one might twistedly lust after his enemy. And even though I heard "faggot" thrown at me, the volume was lower, and more often than not it made me smile.

In fact, I secretly got together with jocks during my last two years of high school; my first boyfriend was an all-American water polo player. I felt vindicated when, in 1995, Green Day came back to Oakland for two sold-out shows at the 10,000-seat Henry J. Kaiser Auditorium and had Pansy Division—the biggest queer punk band at the time—open for them.

You had all these screaming jocks and their witless girlfriends (who, probably later in life, became fag hags) yelling, "Get off the stage, faggots!" and "Fuck you, cocksuckers!" as P.D. played songs like "Bill & Ted's Homosexual Adventure" and "Ring of Joy."

Chris Freeman, the bassist, pointed out into the crowd and said, "Hmm, well I'd fuck you, and you, but not you—you're ugly and I feel sorry for your girlfriend."

The middle fingers went down and the jocks just started anonymously screaming "faggot." *What pussies*, I thought, *hiding behind anonymity like that.* Then my girlfriend, Shannon, pushed another girl because she was yelling some derogatory comment. The girl didn't know what to do, and before her boyfriend could step in, Shannon had these punk rockers (me included) get between her and Mr. Big Johnson T-shirt. He scowled but didn't say a word. The vibe I gave off was: Unlike you, I don't need to conform to some bullshit jock programming to be masculine. So if you want to come here to listen to our music (whether "our" means punk or queer or both) it's *your* turn to be the faggot.

In the background P.D. played "Smells Like Queer Spirit," which Kurt happily gave them permission to parody. But, as Mr. B.J. backed down, I couldn't help but think, *He's hot, and after I kick his ass I'd sure like to fuck it.*

Once Gay Club Hits/Now Jock Jams

Bizarre Inc.—"I'm Gonna Get Ya"
Black Box (ewww!)—"Strike It Up" and "Everybody Everybody"
C+C Music Factory—"Gonna Make You Sweat (Everybody Dance Now)," "Here We Go Let's Rock & Roll," and "Things That Make You Go Hmmmm"
Corona—"The Rhythm of the Night"
Culture Beat featuring Tania Evans—"Mr. Vain"
Haddaway—"What is Love?"
La Bouche—"Be My Lover" and "Where Do You Go"
The Real McCoy—"Another Night" and "Run Away"
Robin S.—"Show Me Love"
Snap—"Rhythm Is A Dancer"
Technotronic—"Pump Up the Jam"

Best Songs for Being Dramatic and Contemplating Suicide

"Asleep"
—The Smiths
"Boys Don't Cry"
—The Cure
"Creep"
—Radiohead
"Delicate Cutters"
—Throwing Muses
"Forever Young"
—Alphaville
"Here's Where The Story Ends"
—The Sundays
"Hideous Towns"
—The Sundays
"I'm Stretched on Your Grave"
—Sinéad O'Connor
"Loser"
—Beck
"Love Will Tear Us Apart"
—Joy Division
"Nothing Compares To You"
—Sinéad O'Connor
"Song To The Siren"
—This Mortal Coil
"Small Town Boy"
—Bronski Beat
"Somebody"
—Depeche Mode
"Sour Times"
—Portishead
"There Is a Light That Never Goes Out"
—The Smiths

Chapter 4: Literature

Book Learnin' Will Turn a Man Soft and Feminine

By Dave White

If you're holding this book in your hand, you're not part of the problem. You're just an endangered species—one of the last remaining faggots who actually reads books. In fact, you're kind of a freak. You know what I mean. Go to your friends' houses. Where are their books? Probably nowhere. Or worse, they're used decoratively, because, you know, books make you look all smart and shit. *Will & Grace* star Sean Hayes (who I'm not saying is a homo or anything, because I don't know if he is or not, and I don't actually care) recently was on Ellen DeGeneres's talk show prattling on about how he bought big, important looking law books to put on the shelves in his fancy new house so it would look like he was into books, or something like that. Motherfucker actually *confessed* this on national TV like it wouldn't sound stupid. Gay or not, this is a man who needs his ass kicked.

If you don't read books, then don't front like you do by going out and buying them. It doesn't matter. Just *be* the nonreading type. Who cares? And if you're gay and don't read, then you should *especially* stay away from bookstores. Buy trinkets and scented candles for your shelves. Little glass animals or whatever. That will leave more books for *me* to have, and we won't accidentally meet in a bookstore where I might cruise you thinking you're all hot and bookish and find out you're just a big faker. Personally, I own 1,761 nonlaw books, and they live in my too-small apartment, where I've organized them according to what I like to call the Davey Decimal System. Fiction lives next to autobiographies, biographies, and memoirs, then comes anthologies, essays, and interviews, criticism, zines, comics and graphic novels, children's books, art, architecture and design, cook books, books about tel-

evision, books about film, books about books, history/sociology and gay stuff, religion and reference. It makes sense to me, anyway. And I'm not being braggy about the number. Some people own more. Some own less. It's just a number I know. I know because I counted. I counted because I'm obsessive. I'm obsessive because I'm a fag. I'm a fag because my parents gave me books instead of baseball gloves.

Okay, I can't prove that. But it's true that they did give me more books than anything else. (Here comes all that *David Copperfield* crap.) I simply didn't want to go out and roll around in the mud with the other little boys and my parents didn't know what else to do with me. It wasn't because they were serious readers themselves. The only other books I even remember in my childhood home were my mother's paperbacks. Her drug of choice, after Tareytons and iced coffee, was the Harlequin romance novel. While she was sunning herself on a plastic lawn chaise in our backyard, she'd read them the way drunks knock back can after can of Pabst Blue Ribbon. Then my father would sneak up on her and douse her with water. He thought this was very funny. They divorced when I was 9.

Anyway, I had books. I had more Dr. Seuss books than I knew what to do with, and the ones I didn't own I'd check out of the library over and over. For some draconian reason, 6-year-old children weren't allowed to have their own library cards in Rye, N.H., the tiny town where I lived for the first 12 years of my life. I was a prisoner of my mother's library-going whims, and she didn't want to go as often as I felt necessary. When I finished the eight or so picture books she'd allow me to check out (like *Corduroy, Harry the Dirty Dog,* and, because no one told me that boys didn't like her, *Madeline*), I'd say, "My books are due," whether they were or not, just so we could go back.

When you're a budding little faggot—the sort who shoots off his stupid little smart-ass mouth at bullies who are just *dying* to fuck him up, the sort who doesn't want to be outside with other filthy boys whose idea of fun is to lacerate each other with pieces of orange plastic Hot Wheels track as warm-up for the Smear the Queer marathon—you end up spending a lot of time inside. And if there was no decent kids' movie playing downtown for me to beg my mother to drive me to, and if there was no good TV show on, and if I'd already played with all my toys too many times, I'd read. And if I'd already read all the books I owned and all the books I'd taken from the library and all the back covers of the Harlequin romances (giving the clinching cover couple a quick once-over to see if the guy had a hairy chest—for some reason, even at 6, I was really into that part of the male physique) and the underwear pages of the Sears catalog, I'd memorize that day's listings in *TV Guide*. ("The Partridge Family's tour bus is invaded by a skunk.")

This little gay read *Charlotte's Web* (six times), *Stuart Little* (once), *The Trumpet of the Swan* (almost didn't finish), most of the *Pippi Longstocking* and the *Little House* books (got bogged down and bored when Mary went blind), *Charlie and the Chocolate Factory* (four times because kids being juiced to death was too awesome only to read once), *Charlie and the Great Glass Elevator*(once), *Harriet the Spy* (four times), *From the Mixed-Up Files of Mrs. Basil E. Frankweiler*(three times), *Mad* magazine, those horrible *Partridge Family* and *Brady Bunch* tie-in books where they all went off and solved lame-o mysteries, dozens of paperback compilations of *Peanuts* daily strips, and a dieting-for-kids book called *The Hundred Hamburgers* (because when you're inside a lot you come to learn that nobody doesn't like Sara Lee).

At age 10 I picked up *Are You There God? It's Me Margaret*. All the girls were reading it. In fact, all the girls were reading all the Judy Blume books and none of the boys were, which seemed grossly unfair to me. They had a secret they weren't sharing—those little bitches—and I was going to find out what it was. Turns out, it was about their periods, which even after reading *Are You There God? It's Me, Margaret,* I still didn't really understand. After that, I started-ed stealth-peeking at a copy of *The Exorcist,* which my Dad's then-girlfriend was reading and laughing her way through while chain-smoking Virginia Slims and telling me there was no God. My stealthiness sucked, however, and I was apprehended in the middle of chapter 1 and forbidden to touch it again. Not that I cared so much. By then I had discovered the super-liberated girlfriend's not-so-secret stash of *Playgirl* magazines. And when I say not-so-secret I mean she kept them on her coffee table. She had a son my age who'd pick them up and dance around and shout, "Hey, wanna see a guy's thingie? If you like it then that means you're a fag who loves men." This kid also said stuff like, "Don't read that *Reader's Digest* version of *Jaws,* gaywad! The real one has all the sex stuff!"

I'd checked out the condensed version from my 5th grade teacher Mrs. Zerbinopolous's book wall. I stopped reading that once I had the full-length version in my hands—the dog-eared pages guided me to the sex fantasy scene between the characters who, in the film, were played by Richard Dreyfuss and Lorraine Gary. I thought she looked weird. He got a pass for the sexy beard and Jew-fro. Anyway, I substituted hotter people in my mind when I read it. That's the power of reading, after all. You're not bound to envision the actors who play them in the movie if you don't find them fuckable.

I waded through Judy Blume's *Forever* for the same reason I took on *Margaret*: The girls were having all the fun. The boys didn't seem to be reading *anything*, much less the cool books about sex. I also somehow managed to steal copies of Gay Talese's *Thy Neighbor's Wife*, a non-fiction book about swinging orgies in the suburbs, and *North Dallas Forty*, thinly-veiled fiction about swinging orgies in the NFL. I really liked to read about orgies. I don't think a "classic" book entered my life until my junior year in high school, when the youth minister at my Southern Baptist church in the small New Mexico town to which I'd been relocated (Okay it was Roswell. And shut up.) told me that *The Catcher in the Rye* was "ungodly." So I went out, bought a copy, read it, and told him that it was my new favorite book. In the South they call that "bein' ugly," and I'd like to thank the books in my life for helping me become that way. Thanks, books!

As a young adult closet-case figuring out what it meant to be queer, I turned to books for assistance. I have no idea why I did this. It wasn't like other fags I was encountering wanted to spend our stolen moments talking about Gogol's *Lost Souls*. But somehow, along the way, I had gotten it into my head that this particular form of sexual perversion required one to be fairly well-read, and I didn't want to be left behind. I was in college, show-offy and annoying, so I went out of my way to read books other people were calling "transgressive." None of it was bad writing. In fact, it's stuff I still love today. But it took me a second reading of each title to realize that the first pass I took was just a skim-job to make me look cooler.

My comparative literature classes may have required me to slog through Joseph Conrad and Stendahl, but I carried around Kathy Acker because it was more punk rock. And *Naked Lunch* and Mary Gaitskill and *The Broom of the System*, zines like *Chemical Imbalance*, and uglified black-and-white "comix" from Gary Panter and Mark Beyer. That was my shit. Matt Groening's *Life in Hell* and Lynda Barry's *Ernie Pook's Comeek* and the RE/Search titles were just as important to me as anything prescribed in my undergraduate syllabi.

And I learned after college that none of it mattered to anyone, anywhere. I actually ate dinner one night with a college friend two years after graduation, a woman I knew and liked a lot. She asked me how my second year of teaching high school English in what's euphemistically referred to as a "low-performing" school was going.

"I'm exhausted, that's how it's going," I said, "This shit is like Kafka's *The Trial*."

"Who?"

"Kafka. Franz Kafka."

"Never heard of him."

A BUNCH OF GAY BOOKS WORTH CHECKING OUT

Bastard out of Carolina and *Trash* by Dorothy Allison
Lost Illusions by Honore de Balzac
Rubyfruit Jungle by Rita Mae Brown
Other Voices, Other Rooms by Truman Capote
Frisk and *Closer* by Dennis Cooper
The Hours (or any book) by Michael Cunningham
My Big Fat Queer Life: The Best of Michael Thomas Ford by Michael Thomas Ford
Maurice by E.M. Forster
Invisible Life by E. Lynn Harris
The Swimming-Pool Library by Alan Hollinghurst
A Single Man and *The Berlin Stories* by Christopher Isherwood
Blue Heaven by Joe Keenan
Faggots by Larry Kramer
Sarah by J.T. Leroy
Rolling The R's by R. Zamora Linmark
Stranger Among Friends by David Mixner
Borrowed Time by Paul Monette
Flesh and the Word anthologies by John Preston
City of Night by John Rechy
Barrel Fever (or any book) by David Sedaris
And the Band Played On by Randy Shilts
The Man Who Fell in Love With the Moon by Tom Spanbauer
The City and the Pillar and *Myra Breckinridge* by Gore Vidal
A Boy's Own Story and *The Beautiful Room is Empty* by Edmund White
The Picture of Dorian Gray by Oscar Wilde
Oranges Are Not the Only Fruit by Jeanette Winterson
Mrs. Dalloway by Virginia Woolf

"You know, that guy who wrote *The Metamorphosis*."
"Don't know it."
"Yeah, you do. It's the one about the dude who gets turned into a bug."
"Nope. Never read it."

Later that same night, I went out to my local gay bar (by this time I had moved to Fort Worth, Tex.) and picked up a guy. When we got to my place and finished the business at hand, he looked around and said, "You read all these?"

"Most of 'em, yeah."

"What are the rest for?"

"For when I'm ready to read them."

"How do you know what you want to read before you read it?"

"I just do. There're the ones I know I like and the ones I think I'll like and then the ones friends tell me I'll like."

"Oh... have you read *The Bridges of Madison County*? That's my favorite book."

So. About being gay and literary? Forget it. You're an irrelevant minority within a minority. There may be a long tradition of great queer contributors to the world of decent books, but no one out there gives a flying heck. And I could tell you that reading Jacqueline Susann and André Malraux and Lisa Carver and Walker Percy and Travis Jeppesen and Gustave Flaubert and Dorothy Allison will make your life round, warm, and full (and if you check this chapter's sidebars, you'll see us make good on that promise). But I've made that case for years to anyone who would listen—even to my literate friends who don't seem to care that much. Check it: All the bookstores are *closing* except for those soul-slurping chain stores. And the gay ones are disappearing quicker than the rest. The survivors have turned half their floor space into coffee shops (which is actually a nice touch: You can read, cruise, drink tea, and eat powdered sugar-dusted lemon squares while you do it). If you're carrying around that Jean Genet or Dennis Cooper book to impress people or as some sort of code for "Hey hot stuff, I'm *that way* too," it won't work. Faggots will look at you and go, "Who's that?" Then when you tell them, they'll crinkle up their nose and go "Ewww." You're fucked either way. You're that guy who goes to dinner or the movies alone and brings a book. You might as well be a serial killer. Or a stinky hippie. Or Oprah.

And there is no solution. If you're a reader and queer, you've sentenced yourself to a marginal, neobohemian (speaking of stinky hippies) existence. You're on your own. Outnumbered. You'll always be single and you'll have to dust a lot. So get used to it and learn to be happy. And if being happy alone isn't your bag, you could scour the earth for a boyfriend who likes to read too, trap him, train him, and then seclude yourselves. That's what I did. Half of those 1,761 books are his. (See? I don't sound so braggy now, do I.) Our collections merged, and duplicates were mostly given away to third parties to prevent the threat of gay divorce. In fact, I recently found a love note he wrote to me that I'd stuck in a duplicate copy of Anne Fadiman's *Ex Libris,* a book I'd put down and always meant to pick up again to finish. I treasure that note like the book it lives in. It reads: "Do shut up."

Christopher Rice's Top 10 Books That Every Gay Man Should Read

© Brian Orter

1. *Becoming a Man* by Paul Monette. A rich and riveting memoir about coming to terms with oneself by way of coming out of the closet. This book should be considered mandatory reading for anyone who has just taken their first awkward steps out of the closet.

2. *The Gay Metropolis* by Charles Kaiser. This brilliantly documented historical record has the narrative force of a great novel. A fascinating and enlightening journey for anyone who thinks gay life in America began with "Queer Eye for the Straight Guy," or the Stonewall riots for that matter.

3. *Love Undetectable* by Andrew Sullivan. Sullivan is a master essayist and a courageous intellectual. This collection contains some of his best writing on the changing nature of the AIDS epidemic and the myriad of spiritual and political responses available to gay men.

4. *A Queer Geography* by Frank Browning. A fascinating glimpse into what same-sex desire can look like beyond American borders. It's a provocative piece of journalism that calls into question some of our most basic assumptions about male homosexuality.

5. *Vamps & Tramps* by Camille Paglia. The essay "No Law in the Arena" offers provocative answers to some of the most pressing social and psychological questions facing the gay community. The best collection of writing from this invaluable independent intellectual.

6. *Vulgar Favors* by Maureen Orth. A searing exploration of one of the most notorious villains to come out of contemporary gay culture: spree-killer Andrew Cunanan. The unbiased Orth shines a sometimes harsh light on the darker side of gay life today.

7. *Like People in History* by Felice Picano. This wildly entertaining novel has been rightfully dubbed "the gay *Gone With the Wind*." It's a colorful, sexy, and tear-jerking journey through the last few decades of gay America.

8. *The Married Man* by Edmund White. One of the more recent works from this undisputed master of gay lit, *The Married Man* is also one of his most haunting.

It brings gentle answers to the brutal question of how to be a proper lover to a dying man.

9. *The Catch Trap* by Marion Zimmer Bradley. A sprawling romance about a love affair between two male gymnasts during the World War II era. One of my favorite accidental discoveries in the used books section.

10. *Sex Toys of the Gods* by Christian McLaughlin. Hysterically funny and deliciously sexy, this campy expose of gay Hollywood is the most fun I have ever had between two covers. I couldn't read it late at night because my laughter kept my roommate awake.

Christopher Rice is the author of *A Destiny of Souls* and *The Snow Garden*.

CHILDREN'S BOOKS WE KNOW AND LOVE

Miss Nelson is Missing! by Harry G. Allard (author),
James Marshall (illustrator)
The Wonderful Flight to the Mushroom Planet by Eleanor Cameron
The Little Prince by Antoine de Saint-Exupéry (Richard Howard's translation)
Harold and the Purple Crayon by Crockett Johnson
Where The Wild Things Are by Maurice Sendak
The Lorax (or any book) by Dr. Seuss
Sylvester and the Magic Pebble by William Steig

BOOK SERIES TO COLLECT

The Chronicles of Narnia
Dune
The Great Brain series
Harry Potter
The Hitchhiker's Guide to the Galaxy
Weetzie Bat

Comic Books Every Queer Should Read

Special thanks to New York members of the Gay League (www.gayleague.com) for their assistance with this list.

Age of Bronze—Eric Shanower's retelling of *The Iliad* is gorgeous to look at and contains that ancient Greek gayness we know and love.

Alpha Flight—During the comic's first two years, before Northstar broke down the closet door, John Byrne wasn't allowed to say the character was gay, so instead he introduced an entirely visual queer subtext and gay life for the character. From a historical standpoint it's amazing.

The Authority—For Apollo and Midnighter.

The Cavalcade of Boys—Gay soap opera in comic form.

Codename: Knockout—Gayer than gay, and written by a gay guy.

Enigma—Groundbreaking at the time, from Vertigo (DC).

Gay Comix—Edited by Andy Mangels. For the invaluable historical content.

Gotham Central #7—Renee Montoya's lesbian story line.

The Invisibles—Lord Fanny was a drag-queen shaman from Brazil.

The Legion of Super-Heroes—Utopian themes, cute costumes, a huge gay following, and let's just talk about Invisible Kid and Chemical King, shall we?

The Mirror of Love—Alan Moore and José Villarrubia's epic poem about the history of same-sex love.

Pedro and Me—Judd Winick's chronicles about his time with Pedro Zamora.

Rawhide Kid—For better or worse, it got tons of media attention and was a milestone for Marvel Comics, who normally shy away from the love that hath no name.

Sandman—Neil Gaiman's series was full of queer themes, imagery, and supporting characters.

Strangers in Paradise—Check it out and you'll immediately know why.

Any *X-men* book—They're the ultimate metaphor for queer life.

Wonder Woman—Just because.

Beat Generation Books Every Homo Should Know

Naked Lunch by William S. Burroughs
The Happy Birthday of Death by Gregory Corso
A Coney Island of the Mind by Lawrence Ferlinghetti
Collected Poems 1947-1980 by Allen Ginsberg
The Herbert Huncke Reader by Herbert Huncke and Benjamin G. Schafer (editor)
On The Road by Jack Kerouac

Chapter 5: Theater and Art

Strange Love: Or, How I Learned to Love Theater From the Middle of Nowhere

By Aaron Krach

Thank God for the *Los Angeles Times* Calendar section. It was in its dusty but hallowed pages that I first read about Reza Abdoh, an off-the-charts intense and inventive theater artist. Abdoh is little known today, but during the '80s and early '90s, he shot to the top of the avant-garde theater world and produced a dozen mind-blowing plays before dying of AIDS in 1995.

I should also thank my high school journalism teacher for introducing me to Reza Abdoh, and to "theater" in general. Ms. Grace Huerta, tough-as-nails and as queer as could be, told me that "anyone who mattered" read the newspaper *every* day ("Even the sports section," she said, "because you need to know at least something about everything.") So Ms. Huerta was the reason my 16-year-old ass was reading about an Iranian-born, British-bred, LA-via-New York avant-garde theater maven instead of skipping over the unfamiliar drama pages to get to the movie reviews. It was while I was deep inside a feature on Reza Abdoh and his newest play, *The Hip-Hop Waltz of Eurydice* (1990), that my gaydar went off like a metal detector in an old man's sunburned hand as he walks along the beach. When I finished the article, I did what any overly curious gay-in-training would have done: I went to see *The Hip-Hop Waltz* for myself...on my own.

The show was downtown, which in LA is a place that is only rumored to exist. I went anyway, and found a small theater filled with people who didn't look like anyone from my suburban neighborhood. I was scared and excited.

The Hip-Hop Waltz scared me. The show was so different, so sexual, and so weird—I didn't know how to react. Abdoh's rejiggered, rethought, and remixed version of Orpheus losing Eurydice and going down to hell to get her back was a tale of two lost souls played by actors of the opposite sex (Eurydice was played by an enormous man and Orpheus by a petite but strong Juliana Francis). Both of them had shaved heads and amplified but angelic voices.

The play seemed to have fallen out of a Norman Rockwell-meets-Edward Hopper America into a blood-and-lust world of sex and heartbreak. Think David Lynch without the hetero-erotic violence. Abdoh's Orpheus and Eurydice find a kind of sad redemption by the end of the play: Both of them fall back through Abdoh's rabbit hole and, like Dorothy in *The Wizard of Oz*, they watch all their previous experiences fly out their kitchen window.

I left the experience—my first real trip to the theater—in a daze of excited confusion. The show was almost *too* exciting—which ended up being disheartening, because I had no one to talk to about it. I remember telling my mother something, but her reaction (if there was one) doesn't exist in my memory bank. I tried desperately to find a place in my mind to file away such a crazy experience. Gays were supposed to love the theater, I knew, so maybe it was my destiny to be so moved. But gays were supposed to love Stephen Sondheim and musicals and their larger-than-life female stars. The song-and-dance aspects of *The Hip Hop Waltz* were skewered like the roasted pig in *Lord of the Flies*.

A year passed, and I didn't think about Reza Abdoh much. I filed him away in the back of my head near the section called "Real Life is Out There...Somewhere." Then I heard

THEATER THAT'S JUST FUN

Beautiful Thing
Debbie Does Dallas
The Full Monty
Hairspray! The Musical
I Should Be So Lucky (the Kylie Minogue musical that most of us have never seen)
Mamma Mia!
Thoroughly Modern Millie
The Wiz
Xanadon't

PLAYWRIGHTS TO KNOW

Edward Albee
Charles Busch
Lillian Hellman
Larry Kramer
Terrence McNally
Joe Orton
William Shakespeare
Neil Simon
Tennessee Williams
August Wilson

about his next show, which would also be staged at the LA Theatre Center. The advance word was that *Bogeyman* (1991) was even fiercer. With HIV burning through Abdoh's 30-year-old body, he was pushing his work to new heights of aggressive, psychosexual, and political theater-making. Again, I bought a ticket—just one—for opening week.

The curtain never came up on *Bogeyman* because it had been removed. Instead, the audience sat down to face the scrubby facade of an apartment building filled with hookers and junkies, families, outcasts, and homeless freaks as they yelled from stoops, propositioned, taunted, raped, seduced, robbed, and stole from each other. Then the facade lifted to reveal a *Hollywood Squares*-style grid of nine rooms—and hell literally broke loose.

The bottom area featured a gang shower where men stripped down, got wet, and pleasured each other. Above, there was a square half-filled with water where a man was strung up—also naked—and dunked, tortured ferociously. Another square was styled as an enormous vagina (or was it an asshole?) through which ranting, angry people emerged and retreated. Altogether, it was an insane collage of chaos and order, rhythm and madness. The sacred and the very profane merged into performance, ritual and—yes—Theater with a capital *T*. I cried and left with my stomach in my throat. I was in awe of how live performance could make me feel. This strange, realer-than-real feeling was, or is, why gays love the theater. I may not have understood that at the time, but I know it now.

Consider These Gay Favorites...

The Wizard of Oz—The story of a young woman who escapes her black-and-white world, only to find herself hunted by the wicked establishment for being independent. In the end she realizes she just should have stayed in her safe black-and-white world and left well enough alone. (Okay, not a stage musical, but it might as well be!)

Grease—The story of a sweet young girl who falls in love with a "bad boy" and realizes the only way she can ever get what she wants is to dress and act like a slut.

Chicago—The story of two women who commit murder and spend the entire musical attempting to cover their tracks, and subsequently hurt many innocents in the process.

Rent—The story of a group of artistic friends who don't work, don't want to pay their rent, and either use drugs or practice unsafe sex so they've contracted AIDS. And that means we're supposed to feel bad for them.

No wonder gay men are so fucked up!

Bogeyman was the end-all be-all, crazy-as-hell theatrical experience of my life. I have never been as excited, scared, turned on (I had such a raging 17-year-old boner sitting in that theater), and thrilled by theater since then. Okay, Tony Kushner's *Angels in America* pretty much rocked my world a few years later, but that was such a different beast. Things happened on Abdoh's stage that I had only dreamed of, fantasized about, wished for, and feared.

When I saw *Bogeyman,* I was a senior in high school. I actually had a boyfriend (although no one who wasn't paying close attention knew about him). I was gaining confidence and had a few good friends who knew I was a big ol' art fag (the kid who went to the museum while the other kids went to see *Forrest Gump*). This small group knew I only watched foreign-language films and read *Artforum* in the library, so I invited them to come back with me the next week to see *Bogeyman* again. I was so blinded by my excitement that I didn't even consider that they might not "get it"—that they might be seriously confused and even offended by the queer exuberance on stage. Lucky for me, they were shocked, but only momentarily. My friends were more worried about me. It was as if I'd taken them to my secret drug den and shown them I was an addict. I thank my lucky stars that their intervention didn't last beyond a painful meal of cheeseburgers after the show.

Theater Queens Miles Away From Queens (or Broadway)

How in the hell did I, a young man in the suburbs of Los Angeles, not only discover the thrill of theater (albeit my own twisted kind) far from the land of *West Side Story* and *Cats*? Far from Broadway and off-Broadway—in short, far from New York City, the drama capital of the world? If I'd grown up in New Jersey and had parents who took me into Manhattan at a very young age to see *Dreamgirls* or *A Chorus Line,* I might understand. But it didn't happen that way for me, and I am sure it doesn't happen that way for millions of gay men who grow up outside New York City. Yet there is something mysteriously magical about how "the theater" insinuates itself into our very gay lives.

Robert, a 29-year-old who works in publishing, says, "I feel like gays are supposed to say they like theater because it's the right thing to say. But then again, I do. There is something thrilling about theater that is better than anything else."

If only. What about all the bad gay theater that clogs stages everywhere, travels the gay circuit during the summer, and—like *Naked Boys Singing*—filled the same Greenwich Village theater for five and a half years? How does one even begin to explain the success of these shows, which everyone agrees are lame and not even very titillating?

Is it as simple as the experience of losing oneself in entertainment? It can't be, since television and the movies are equally—if not more—escapist forms of entertainment. Is it something about live performance? Maybe. There was something radical and mind-warping (at least to me) about seeing men simulating sex with each other in *Bogeyman*. Is it the audience, and the plea for acceptance and adoration from it by the actors? Love, attention, and adoration are all available to the needy souls on stage if they do their jobs correctly. This relationship is a microcosm of all relationships. Maybe that's what we see and relate to. But we can't forget exactly what the performer's job is. Actors must make believe and pretend—they must *act*.

"I don't think a love of theater is universal among gay men," says Don Shewey, author and journalist for *The Advocate* and *The New York Times*. "Virtually nothing is universally true of gay men, not even sexual practices. You'd think every guy loves sucking cock, but it's not true. Ditto getting a blow job. Certainly not true of fucking or getting fucked. That being said, most gay men learn at a very early age something about pretending to be somebody

ESSENTIAL ART BOOKS

Beefcake by F. Valentine Hooven (Taschen)
David Hockney: Paintings by Paul Melia, Ulrich Luckhardt, and David Hockney (Prestel USA). (If you can find any out-of-print books about his work, snatch them up right away.)
Devil's Playground by Nan Goldin (Phaidon)
A Hidden Love: Art and Homosexuality by Dominique Fernandez (Prestel USA)
Homo Art by Gilles Néret (Taschen)
Pierre et Gilles: The Complete Works by Pierre et Gilles, Bernard Marcade, and Ian Cameron (Taschen)
Tom of Finland: The Art of Pleasure by Micha Ramakers (Taschen)

they're not. So you grow up from an early age with an understanding of a central principle of theater, which is that it's make-believe by choice."

There's a lame joke about gays and Jews being the only two groups of people who like theater. Of course this is not entirely true. Look at Anytown, U.S.A. When the traveling version of *Hairspray! The Musical* comes to town for its few weeks' run, there simply aren't enough gays or Jews in Atlanta to fill the seats. But like all jokes, there is an element of truth behind this one. The relationship between gay men and the theater—onstage and behind the scenes—is significantly more important than the numbers imply. There are more than 280 million people in America. In New York City there are fewer than 50 Broadway productions each year, a couple hundred more off-Broadway shows (whose audiences average a couple hundred per night), and several hundred off-off-Broadway shows (in theaters with fewer than 100 seats and which usually don't run for more than a week or even a weekend).

So when we talk about a "community" of theatergoers, we aren't talking about large numbers of people. Yet theater is considered an art form. It may not be supported by the government (as it is by almost every other Western government) but it's written about, covered by the press, and taught in universities as a major like anything else. The Tony awards are broadcast nationwide to minimal ratings each year, and yet CBS continues to show it during prime time as if it was a duty.

Let's take Tony Kushner's *Angels in America,* for example. It is the most critically acclaimed and popular gay-gay-gay play (actually two plays) of the last 20 years. Tony Kushner's "gay fantasia on national themes" (his subtitle) won the Pulitzer Prize for Drama and two Tony awards for Best Play, two years in a row. Part 1 ran for 20 months; part 2 ran for 15 months, both at the Walter Kerr Theatre, which seats 947 people. That is an average of 8,000 people a week for 68 weeks, meaning that only 544,000 people saw the plays in their award-winning Broadway run.

Angels in America was seen by less than .2% of the American population. And yet it has a permanent place in our culture. Even before the high-power HBO version on cable, the play had run in cities around the country and around the world. It caused widespread protest by religious groups who didn't want any public money spent on even the smallest production by some little group in Podunk, Nowhere. And it has been studied in school. Classes read it and write about it—and not just in queer theory classes but in English classes too. So the queerness of Kushner's six-hour opus has infiltrated mainstream culture in ways that are immeasurable.

Theater as Church, Country Club, and Secret Hideout

Where am I going here? So we've got theater, which literally no one goes to (quantitatively speaking), and we've got gays, who go to the theater in relatively large numbers and wield massive influence over theatrical institutions as actors, directors, writers, publicists, etc. Why? And how does a subculture drive an art form so peculiarly "small"?

Obviously, gay men go to the theater because they love it, like it, and find it important to their lives. I know gay men in New York who see just about everything on Broadway and off-Broadway—and they take an annual pilgrimage to London to see even more. Why do they love it? Because they see something there that reflects their lives in a way that feels more powerful than books, television, or even the movies. Whether it's Blanche DuBois in Tennessee Williams's *A Streetcar Named Desire* or the gaggle of gays in Terrence McNally's *Love! Valour! Compassion!* gay audiences see emotions, yearnings, disappointments, and pathways to redemption that they covet, fear, and recognize.

Why is theater such a distinct pleasure—both intellectual and aesthetic—for gay men? Conceptually speaking, Shewey is right when he says gays love theater because it's "about playing, about taking on roles, clinging lightly to identities, putting them on and taking them off, taking on energy, seeing all that stuff as fluid and highly entertaining. It takes a certain amount of courage to get up and perform, and the gay kids who have the courage to embrace (however consciously) their homosexuality often make for very, very entertaining performers—in the family, at school, and perhaps professionally."

Economically, the reasons for gay men's affinity for theater are numerous, yet most have to do with the word *small*. Budgets for most mainstream New York shows are expensive. A flop on Broadway or even off-Broadway can leave investors millions of dollars in debt. But the hundreds of other shows off-off Broadway and in towns across America cost considerably less. And because less money is at stake—because budgets are smaller—a greater degree of creative freedom is possible.

Another secret to theatrical success is small audiences. With so few people in the seats, it's less likely someone's going to take offense at something artistically risky or edgy (you never hear about fundamentalists taking to the street and actually scaring theater queens back into the closet). Theater queens often bemoan the size of audiences, but perhaps they should look at the glass as half-full. Five years ago there was a small revival of Mart Crowley's *The Boys in the Band* in Chelsea. The theater probably sat less than 75 people. The show was a "hit" and ran for a few months. It was imperfect; it lacked the verve of the movie (and, I assume, of the original theatrical production). But the show was packed most nights—and almost exclusively with gay men of all ages. These men wanted, apparently, and needed to see the theatrical version of such a controversial and yet essential story in the gay canon.

The Boys in the Band is, or at least was, loathed by generations of gay men who were horrified by what they saw as stereotypical behavior by the characters. Younger generations (X, Y, and whatever) don't have the same problem with it. My friends and I love it for its camp value, for the characters' sense of vicious individuality, for their quick wit, and for their struggle for love, all of which feel universal and unchanged over the 30 plus years. Unintimidated by the queeniness of the cast, my generation has added the most original lines ("Turning, turning...") to our personal lexicon. Theater has a way of becoming a part of our daily lives whether we are conscious of it or not, and in that way it feels even more special. Maybe *that's* why gays love theater.

From high to low, gay theater artists have been able to create wildly idiosyncratic imaginings: Write them, perform them, and send them out into the world. Think of Charles Ludlam and his "Theater of the Ridiculous." He and his collaborators basically invented off-Broadway theater in the '70s and '80s as a place of fantastic low-budget invention. In the '90s, performance artists Tim Miller and John Fleck were only the two best known of many radical queer artists who used the stage to tell stories of gay life, AIDS, political subordination, and sexual exuberance. And they were the best known because of the National Endowment for the Arts crackdown on controversial work, which led all the way to a Supreme Court loss that left artists at the whim of political conservatives if they took money from the NEA. Well, fuck them. All four of the NEA plaintiffs (in addition to Miller and Fleck, Karen Finley and Holly Hughes were targeted for attack), have gone on to careers in performance art, theater, writing, and teaching—and even TV. (Fleck was on *NYPD Blue* for years.)

All of these artists wouldn't have had careers if we didn't fill the seats, pay them money, want to hear what they had to say, and want to watch them do their thing.

Into the current decade, Alan Cumming and his exuberantly gay friends have pushed theater again. Cumming's troupe, The Art Party, staged an outlandish and shocking version of Jean Genet's play *Elle*. Cumming's boyfriend Nick Philippou directed, *Angels in America* veteran Stephen Spinella costarred, and the show was shove-your-ass-in-the-Pope's-face fabulous—which is exactly what Cumming did with his cute little British tush.

Cumming—the star of *X-Men 2* and Broadway's *Cabaret*—took his own money and funded the company. Then he rewrote the script and cast himself in the lead. As the Pope, he roller-skated onstage like a hovering deity. He wore a big white dress and landed on stage with flashing smoke like a hatch opening on a spaceship landing on an unexplored planet. In all honesty, Genet's sexy, angry prose is hard to follow at times, but when Cumming flaunted his papal ass in our collective faces—there seemed, if only for a moment—to be another gay man taking the theatrical bull by the horns. Like Abdoh before him, Cumming took his love of theater in all its fabulous permutations and danced around in it until we were all smiling wickedly.

I have long since moved to New York City—I've left behind the theatrical desert of Los Angeles for a place where one couldn't see everything if he tried. When I went to see Alan Cumming's *Elle*, I went with Chris, a supersmart friend and total theater queen. In the audience were all the art fags with the connections needed to get tickets (which doesn't mean money—mostly it means access to the little gay assistants at PR companies). Everyone liked the show—well, almost everyone. People clapped and cheered, and I bet no one left there to go have cheeseburgers with friends who felt he needed to be "talked to" about his wicked taste for live theater.

John Cameron Mitchell's Top 10 Theater Pieces Every Queer Kid Should See, Read, and (if Possible) Work On:

1. *Angels in America* and anything else by Tony Kushner. Just 'cause it's all brilliant.

2. *The Normal Heart* and *The Destiny of Me* by Larry Kramer, who led the way during the early AIDS crisis.

3. *Entertaining Mr. Sloane* and *What the Butler Saw* by Joe Orton. Two of the funniest plays of all time—even the Beatles thought so.

4. *Sister Mary Ignatius Explains It All For You* by Christopher Durang. More hilarity, Catholic-style.

5. *The Black Rider,* an Expressionist musical written by Tom Waits and William Burroughs, directed by Robert Wilson. It totally inspired Hedwig, along with...

6. *Without You I'm Nothing* by Sandra Bernhard and John Boskovich. Check out the movie!

7. Plato's *Symposium,* which reads like a play.

8. Anything by Oscar Wilde, Tennessee Williams (check out *Kingdom of Earth,* his most insane play), Edward Albee, Craig Lucas, Terrence McNally, John Osborne, Michael John LaChiusa, and John Guare.

9. Any solo piece by Lily Tomlin, Lisa Kron, Marga Gomez, Dael Orlandersmith, Anna Deavere Smith, Margaret Cho, Sarah Jones, David Cale, David Greenspan, or John Leguizamo. 'Cause they rock queerly (including John).

10. And maybe my favorite play: *Happy Days* by Samuel Beckett, about a woman buried up to her waist in a mound of dirt. A part I'd like to play some day.

John Cameron Mitchell is the creator and star of the hit off-Broadway musical and film *Hedwig and the Angry Inch*.

QUEER ARTIST Q AND A

james huctwith

Painter James Huctwith was born in Scarborough, Canada, where he was adopted and immediately whisked away to Cayuga, a small farming town two hours outside of Toronto. He eventually escaped, attended university, and has been living off his art since 1995. He primarily shows at The O'Connor Gallery in Toronto (www.oconnorgallery.com).

R.A.: Did you discover your homosexuality through your art?
No, that came through horniness.

When did you discover you were a poof? That's such a horrid word.
Not when you're dainty like I am... All through high school I didn't feel particular gay, per se, I just felt different. And because I was an artist people would say, "He's not gay. He's artistic!" You know—the 1980s excuse. Or, "He's sensitive," or, "He's musical." I don't know what they use today. "He bakes mincemeat pies?" I don't know.

When did you start becoming a fan of art?
When I was about 7. We had this series of books called the *Bookshelf for Boys and Girls,* and it was generally pretty cool stories and fairy tales and illustrations. But there was one book, *The Bookshelf Parents Guide,* which I adored because it would talk about contagious diseases and terrible things that can happen to children. It's for parents and how to deal with their unruly children in the 1950s. It was pretty fabulous. Another book, called *Art and Music,* had black-and-white reproductions of paintings and sculptures. Now the sculptures came off pretty well, but the paintings looked really scary and very strange. There was a reproduction of a painting called *The Tempest* by an Italian artist named Giorgione. The

painting just riveted me from a young age and has probably been a lifelong influence on my artwork. There's another painting by Diego Velásquez that had a huge influence as well, the painting of Prince Prosper. So that's where I really started to realize the magnetic and psychic power of these images. That never left me.

What do you like to paint?

Weirdly, men seem to be very natural to paint, and that's probably for a number of reasons—desire, and I would say I have an easy visual relationship or identification with my own moods and my own self. But also painting men ties into my sense of architecture. Men to me are architectonically built and constructed. They have a direct identification with the mind that's easy for me to transmit meaning onto a canvas. The female body to me, although special, is somewhat "other" and it's not as direct. I sort of reserve it for special occasions in my artwork, whereas the male body for me is a very direct and useful and a complicated instrument of transmission of meaning.

At this point James became very spritely about the whole interview process and our discussion turned to movies starring Divine. That evening he sent this note:

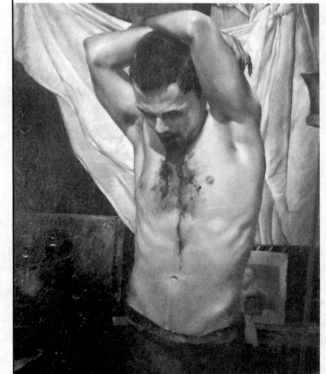

Pitch

Here are some names and ideas that I prattled off to you...

Symbolist art is very important to me. Some artists I like in this movement:
Pierre Puvis de Chavannes
Odilon Redon
Gustave Moreau
Fernand Khnopff
Aubrey Beardsley
Gustav Klimt
James Ensor

Classic artists who've influenced my work:
Giorgione (especially The Tempest)
Velásquez
Titian

Caravaggio
Rembrandt
Goya

Modern Art Influences

Painting:
Odd Nerdrum
Walter Sickert
The Group of Seven
Max Beckmann
Tony Scherman, Margaret Priest
Alex Colville
William Kurelek
Ivan Leonidov (drawings)
Attila Richard Lukacs (first show)

Video:
Floria Sigismondi
Michael Cunningham

Photography:
Joel-Peter Witkin
Allan Stone
George Platt Lynes
Minor White
Diane Arbus
Matthew Barney
Helmut Newton

Methamphetamine Sweat

James met his birth mother a few years ago. She's been a children's book illustrator most of her life, published a number of craft and decorating books, and has recently returned to oil paintings. His half brothers work in graphic design, and his grandmother is also a painter.

tom atwood

Tom Atwood's photography has been exhibited at numerous venues, including Louis Stern Fine Arts in Los Angeles, the Museum of Modern Art in New York, the George Eastman House, and the International Museum of Photography and Film. At ClampArt on West 25th Street in New York, he was part of the "Boys of Summer" exhibit alongside Bruce Cratsley, John Dugdale, Robert Giard, Nan Goldin, Horst P. Horst, Bill Jacobson, George Platt Lynes, Robert Mapplethorpe, Paul Meleschnig, Duane Michaels, Jack Pierson, and Arthur Tress. His photography has won awards from Kodak, the Applied Arts Photography Annual, and the Advertising Photographers of America, which showcased Tom as one of three featured photographers in an international competition sponsored by the Getty Museum and the Armand Hammer Museum. He currently resides in Los Angeles and can be contacted at www.tomatwood.com.

R.A.: What is Urban Fruit?
It's a documentary of the gay community—portraits of gay men at home engaged in everyday life. I explore what people's personal spaces—their lifestyles, their living arrangements, their decor—say about their personalities and gay culture. I bring to life multidimensional personalities with interesting stories—beatniks, bohemians, artists, investment bankers—as well as celebrities from the gay community such as John Waters, Joel Schumacher, John Bartlett, Todd Oldham, Edmund White, Michael Cunningham, Ross Bleckner, Edward Albee, John Ashbury, Ned Rorem, Carson Kressley from *Queer Eye for the Straight Guy,* Junior Vasquez, and Tommy Tune. There's a profound need for such a photo documentary—a body of work to strengthen the identity of the community.

Describe your photos.
I strive for every piece to be a work of art and chock-full of information and color. Some people keep portraits simple, with no distractions and just a face, but I like to challenge people's eyes by throwing as much in as possible. That's one of the ways that I convey people's lives and personalities. I try to keep every object in focus, background and foreground, person and surroundings, because I like to show that one's living space is a metaphysical extension of one's self.

What makes your work distinctive?

Most "gay" photography is about skin and flesh. I'd say 95 percent of it. My photography is different because it's not sexual. I don't care whether people are cute or beautiful. In fact, I've purposely sought out people of all age groups and persuasions. Also, I offer a candid window into the lives and private spaces of some of the most intriguing personalities in urban America. My intent is to produce fine art prints rich in beauty, grace, and clarity—so much so that you can hear these sub-

Mother Flawless Sabina, Urban Fruit Series

jects speak. And I strive for extemporaneous images with subjects unaware of the camera's gaze. The way I bring out somebody's personality is sort of a subconscious process. I'm a social person, and I see photography as a social endeavor.

What other artists have influenced you?

I admire David LaChapelle, Ferdinando Mondino, Simen Johan, and Gregory Crewdson tremendously—those are my favorites. But other photographers haven't substantially affected my work. I am entirely self-taught, especially in terms of creative direction, and what's influenced me most has been my life experiences. I've been to the major art museums around the world, and I had access to classes in art history—I studied at Harvard and then Cambridge University in England for graduate school. But I take pride in my art being personal and unique. I consciously want my photography to be something organic that comes from within and reflects how I see and interact with the world. So while I appreciate formal conversations that take place in the art world, taking my individual path ultimately makes me more likely to produce work that stays fresh.

John Waters, Urban Fruit Series

jorge palomo

In 1979 Jorge Palomo's family fled El Salvador's civil conflict for Miami, returning to their native country after five years. He attended the University of Pennsylvania and became heavily involved in gay and lesbian activism, and eventually he worked at the embassy of El Salvador in Washington, D.C., as both the trade and cultural attaché because he was the only person who knew anything about art. Jorge soon realized he wasn't suited for political life and followed his first passion—art—traveling to Los Angeles where he earned bachelor's and master's degrees in fine art from Otis College of Art and Design. He has since returned to El Salvador and can be contacted at LAGeorge2001@yahoo.com.

R.A.: How would you describe your art? "Dirty little pictures"?
[*Laughs*] Sometimes... They are appropriated images from Internet [webcam sites], and I turn them into small little squares that are 1 inch by 1 inch. From far away these pieces look like oriental rugs, wall mosaics or tile mosaics, and the closer you get you go from an abstraction to a figuration where you see these really graphic images. My main interest has become one of questioning authorial originality.

Why use this method?
Whenever you're dealing with nudes, whether male or female, if this person turns [you] on and [you] paint them, that painting is really about the X number of hours you took to paint. What's left is a performance about your libido, but the viewer standing before [the painting] doesn't always connect to that desire the same way you do. In other words, the spectator isn't going to have the same experience you are, because what it was for me as an artist was those five hours in front of the model wanting to touch him, but painting him instead. So [this art is] still about my desire for that image, but they work differently because anybody can access a photograph.

How did you come up with this idea?
I didn't consciously see webcams as something to make art out of. They were just entertainment. [*Laughs*] But eventually I downloaded hundreds of images. I had to organize them somehow, so I started categorizing by webcam—I have 17 images of so-and-so, or guys [who] are only wearing their watches—then grouping by really mundane things they

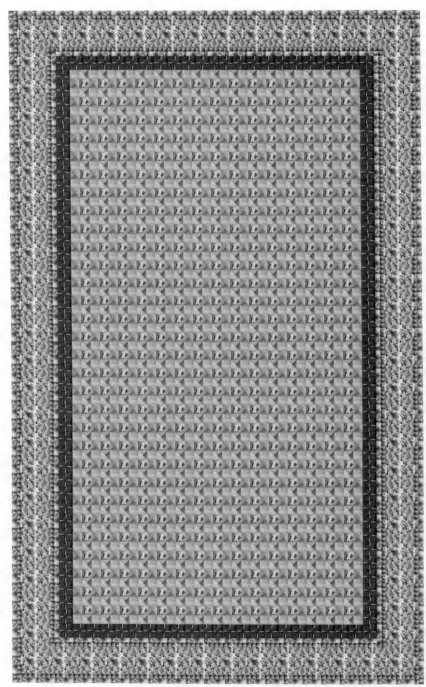

Mandala, 2002, 47 1/2" x 47 1/2", C Print on Sintra

had in common: These are all people in bathrooms, these are all body parts. So I started patterning them, doing checkerboards. I'd have a picture of a close-up asshole next to a shot of somebody's feet at the toilet with their pants around their ankles. I think there are certain narratives you can build when you have two images together like that and you make associations. As I got better on the computer the designs and the patterns got more and more complex. I don't alter the colors. The only thing I do is to crop them to a square. Eventually they became these rugs that you see now.

You're one sick puppy!

I've always had some sense of humor in the work. I want to pick images that are interesting to look at once you get up close because I absolutely love that specific moment where people [*gasp*], "Oh, my God!" And that comes from the whole activism thing, the whole shock tactic.

Jorge's Early Influences
Michelangelo
Caravaggio
Bernini

Museums Art Fags Should Visit
The Vatican Museums (Rome)
The Louvre (Paris)
The Museum of Modern Art
  (New York)
The Metropolitan Museum
  of Art (New York)
The Whitney Museum of
  American Art (New York)

Figurative Painters
Lucien Freud—grandson of
  Sigmund

Mandala, detail

John Sonsini—one of my figure-painting teachers in LA
Monica Majoli—Her work is all based on fantasies that other people have told her about.
Hugh Steers—haunting paintings of bathroom/drag/medical themes
Wayne Thiebaud

Artists Who Look Closely at Gay Subject Matter
Paul Cadmus—magico-realist
Tom Knechtel—He tries to show you the universe as he sees it. He's out of this world.

Artists With a Great Pop Sensibility
Andy Warhol
Jasper Johns
Robert Rauschenberg
David Hockney
Larry Pitman

Must-Visit Sites for Art Fans

Berlin:
Gay Museum, Erotic Museum
Chicago:
Leather Archives and Museum
Greece:
Everything ever produced by the ancient Greeks is cool.
London:
The Tate Museum
Los Angeles:
Los Angeles County Museum of Art, Erotic Museum, Tom of Finland Foundation, One Institute, J. Paul Getty Museum
New York:
Metropolitan Museum of Art, Whitney Museum of Art, Museum of Sex
Spain:
Guggenheim Museum Bilbao, Museum of El Prado
St. Petersburg, Fla.:
Salvador Dalí Museum

joe phillips

From cards and magnets to *Xodus* magazine and Bud Light beer ads, Joe Phillips's artwork is everywhere. His well-sculpted males have become a staple image in the gay community, and his art book from Bruno Gmünder became an immediate top seller. He currently resides in San Diego and can be reached at www.joephillips.com.

R.A.: I've heard you don't drink or have any vices.
I have vices: boys and Sara Lee [*laughs*]. Makes me sound like I'm one of these people with an entourage of beautiful boys lounging all around me.

Technically you do, in your artwork. How would you describe it?
I come from an American illustrator background, like Rockwell and Leyendecker, where you take the idea of fine art and put it to a commercial end. There was a point in American history where there [were] a lot of pinup girls and they had this sexy yet innocent, playful attitude. I always wanted to see some guys with that attitude, but Tom of Finland was very sexually charged. It was fine but nothing you could leave on the table, because it not only spoke of your desire for men but it was very specific [with] what you wanted to do with them. That was a turnoff for me, so [when I became] tired of doing comic books I started [drawing] male pinup art.

Who were your influences?
George Petty, Gil Elvgren. When you think of pinup girls from the '30s and '40s it's invariably one of their pieces. Rockwell, of course. Joseph Christian (JC) Leyendecker was a big influence. He predated Rockwell, is the only person besides Rockwell who's done 360 different *Saturday Evening Post* covers, and he invented the New Year's baby and the American Santa Claus character. [Charles] Dana Gibson, who did the Gibson Girls back in the '20s. James Montgomery Flagg who did the "I Want You" poster with Uncle Sam. Of fine painters my influences have been Gustav Klimt and Alphonse Mucha. A lot of artists like shape and color, but since I'm color-blind, I...

Wait, I'm sorry. What? You only see blacks, whites, and grays?
No, I'm not a dog. I'm red-green color-blind. There are certain colors in the red-green

spectrum that assimilate with the other colors. So if you have a red that has the same amount value of black and white as a green or a brown, I couldn't tell them apart. I'd have no idea which one was which.

Then how do you ink?
It's sort of like [how] Beethoven was deaf but music is mathematical, so he could still write because he knew what it would sound like. I learned color theory really early on to combat my color-blindness, so I know what a color is. And working with a computer is great, because all the colors have a number value and I can just look at the numbers—sort of like in *The Matrix*—and tell you what color it is. When I paint I usually have an assistant [double-check me].

What were your first public pieces?
I started doing comic strips for *XY* magazine, and then I saw these [refrigerator] magnets of David and Venus where you could put clothes on them and I thought, *What if I drew cute guys and did that?* So I created the "Dress Me Magnets" and now there are like 12 different characters.

And suddenly you went from zero to hero. Joe Phillips's artwork was everywhere.
There was an audience built in. You've got this disenfranchised group that is desperately seeking validation—visual public validation—so any time you give them a product that identifies them as being valid they're going to flock to it. Doing pinup boys was basically saying, "Hey you can be gay and you don't have to hide this away, because it's not porn." Some is, but 90% is not, so they can put it on the coffee table. Or they can stick it on a magnet or a bumper sticker or a T-shirt and be proud of who they are without having to squirrel it away and only show this to gay friends. And there's always going to be a few pieces that push the boundaries. But that's the nature of art.

I'm sort of like a surfer. I've got my board out, and I'm riding this wave of acceptance, [while] at the same time I'm not just trying to placate anybody. I'm [creating art] that means something to me, because you can't sell something that you don't believe in. And I'm "selling it," like when you're on stage singing and you've got to *sell it*! You've got to make them believe it, sing to the cheap seats in the back. So that's what I'm doing. I'm trying to belt it out!

What's been your best compliment?
People say, "I want to live in Joe's world." I'm like, "Me too!"

MIXED MEDIA ARTISTS FOR BENT BOYS
Nayland Blake • Vaginal Davis • Gilbert & George • Felix Gonzalez-Torres • Bruce LaBruce • Robert Mapplethorpe • Andre Miripolsky • Jack Pierson • Ed Templeton

PAINTERS ART FAGS ADORE
Don Bachardy • Francis Bacon • Ross Bleckner • Paul Cadmus • Jerome Caja • Janet Cooling • Keith Herring • Ellsworth Kelly

PHOTOGRAPHERS WITH A QUEER EYE
Rick Castro • Anthony Goicolea • Greg Gorman• Chris Komater • David LaChapelle • Bruce of Los Angeles • Ryan McGinley • Bob Mizer • Cathie Opie • Herb Ritts • Cindy Sherman • Wolfgang Tillmans • Arthur Tress • Bruce Weber

NEW YORK 1980'S EAST VILLIAGE SCENE
David Wojnarowicz • Peter Hujar • Nan Goldin • Mark Morrisroe • Frank Moore

DEAD GUYS YOU SHOULD KNOW
Jean-Michel Basquiat—painter from the 1980s • **Andy Warhol**—If you don't know why, put the book down now and do some research • **Baron Wilhelm von Gloeden**—German photographer from the 1800s • **George Platt Lynes**-American photographer from the 1930s and '40s

Chapter 6: Fashion

Why the World Needs Another Pair of Goddamn Cargo Shorts, Although This Time, Maybe in Cashmere

By Aaron Krach

What they were made of or how they actually felt—I can't tell you; I don't remember. What I can tell you is how I felt wearing them: a pair of shorts, a sort of one-piece thing with overall straps in baby blue.

I was about 5 years old when I wore them, if the pictures don't lie, and usually with a white shirt. Wearing that outfit made me feel like the most handsome child in the whole wide world. Take me to the Sears Portrait Studio, pronto! Because in this outfit, I not only looked my best—I *was* my best. I felt so good, so *myself*. Of course, it helped that I could easily reach my hands in the open sides and sort of play with myself, just hold my little 5-year-old penis and scrotum, which was still the size of a walnut. Holding my little package felt good.

Needless to say this led to a "conversation" with Mom, in which she carefully explained that "touching myself was fine, but it was only to be done in private." So I tried that. I hung out in my bedroom with my hands inside my pants, but I got bored. It was only me in there, no one else. Playing with myself was fun, but...

Fast-forward 30 years to today. When I look at a picture of myself in what was my first favorite outfit, I still feel good. I can see my little gay face and I know I was the happiest 5-year-old in the world. Since then, I've had numerous favorite outfits, ensembles I felt comfortable in—felt so much like myself in, that I eventually wore out the clothes. My mother literally started throwing things away that she thought I'd outgrown. She'd rip my favorite shirts in two or throw my favorite shoes in the garbage... on the curb.

Does this happen to straight guys? Not that I know of. Women, girls—that's a whole 'nother story. Gay guys, well, there's a remarkably strong bond between us and our clothes, and with fashion in general, as an idea, a career, a hobby, even something to supposedly hate. I can't begin to unravel the mystical mapping of queer fashion consciousness, but I think, basically, it has to do with feeling good, comfortable, and developing a clear sense of ourselves—like I did in my first favorite shorts. Maybe because we're born into a world that makes us feel different we're more attuned to finding ways to feel comfortable in our skin, even if it's our second skin.

Sixth grade: A pair of black and white checkered slip-on Vans that I wore might as well have been booster rockets. I believed I could run faster in them than in any other shoes I had ever owned. Junior high: Levi's 505s came into my life through a horribly hokey mall store called Miller's Outpost, and for once I had pants that I felt good about, that made me feel like I looked better than the awkward dork I really was. But, unfortunately, I only felt they looked their best on me right after they'd been washed, when they were crisp and clean. Thus, it was Clash of the Titans every few days when my mother found them in the hamper ready to be washed again after only one wearing.

"Everyone else in this family wears their jeans two or three times before washing them," she'd say. "Why are you so different?"

At 13, I wasn't quite ready to explain all the differences, so I started washing my jeans myself after she went to bed.

Today—20 plus years after my midnight rinse cycles—no one would call me a fashion plate, fashionista, or a fashion victim. Yet I have favorite shirts and carefully consider everything I wear in order to represent myself as I imagine (or hope) I am (or want to be).

Currently, my favorite shirt is a short-sleeve blue button-down that I feel is the perfect balance between professional and sporty. It's dressed-up enough for my office but tight enough in the arms to show I have man-made biceps. If I'm going on a date, or to meet a trick, or even just to do a little prowling around, there's a black Gap T-shirt that couldn't be more ordinary. But wearing it, I feel like Sharon Stone must have felt at the Oscars—a million bucks wrapped inside a $15 price tag.

Why? How? I mean, really...who died and made clothes so important for gay men? Okay, so maybe they aren't that important to you—you singularly unfashionable cowboy in Idaho—but you are in the minority, buster (and you're probably not reading this book).

Let's Talk About Sex, Baby

Matthew Bank, publisher of *HX* magazine in New York, once suggested that while for some gay men, the equivalent of sports in their life is porn, he thought the real sport for gay men is fashion.

"Of course, we may watch those athletic games just like other men, but aren't we also looking for something extra-special from those sports stars? Something sexy, something creative, something exciting?" Bank once wrote. "Gay men get all that excitement and more from the runway. Clothing designers can be our team owners and our coaches. And the models—who could overlook the gorgeous models?—can be our superstars. Even better, after gazing at them in magazines, we can buy the clothes they're wearing for ourselves. Fashion can be a spectator or a participant sport."

But do gay men really love fashion in this unholy way? I've never seen a gay man cry over a piece of clothing or a pair of shoes, at least not like Carrie does on *Sex and the City*. Or like my fashion-illiterate sister, who wept openly when she first put on her wedding dress, as if wearing the accoutrements alone were enough to signify the upcoming change in her life. I don't think gay men actually love clothes as much as we enjoy them, use them, and try our best to overcome them. I say *enjoy* because if we weren't having fun with all the trends we've run through over the decades, we would have become as boring as straight men.

Number 1 Reason Gay Men Care About Fashion: Sex

"Fashion helps guys get laid," says David, a 40-year-old advertising executive in New York. "Fashion helps men feel like they are looking their best. It helps them express their personality, which might even be reinforcing their rejection of the status quo. For others it may have to do more with bolstering their self perception or trying to impress others with external cues reflecting good taste, being a trendsetter or having money.

"Gay men are also very visual; aesthetics please them, and therefore looking good pleases them. And they are very visual in regard to sexual attraction: Think of peacocks strutting in front of each other in search for sex or love."

From time immemorial—or at least in the 150-odd years since gays started being gay—clothes have been key. Dress a certain way and you can find each other, hook up, do the nasty, fall in love, live happily ever after. Think of dandies and Oscar Wilde. Think of Weimar-era Germans. Think of the fancy ball scene in Manhattan during the early 20th century. Think plumage, a top hat, a suit, maybe a poofy pocket square. "Dressing up" was gay fashion. "Dressing up" set you apart.

Gays added "dressing down" to their fashion lexicon during and after World War II. The war was a turning point for gay men in many ways. So many guys thrilled to be among so many men away from home (and tradition) for so many months—even years—at a time. Well, we can only imagine.

After the war these men who discovered their love of other men didn't have to go home to Topeka or Tustin. They could move to big cities where they might find others just like them. Thus the birth of San Francisco as a gay Mecca (which is a ridiculous metaphor, I admit, since the idea of a Muslim city welcoming gays is as yet unimaginable).

It is impossible to say what factors were most important in introducing casual blue-collar styles into gay culture. First and foremost there were more gays actually in blue-collar jobs, so jeans and boots were practical.

By the '50s, the great teenage revolution was in full swing, and clothes became more casual in response to the increasing influence of youth culture on fashion. Leather jackets and pants for women were radical introductions. Elvis Presley threw his two cents into the fashion kitty. The movies did their fair share of fashionable expansion (*Rebel Without a Cause*) and Broadway as well (*West Side Story*).

During the '60s, the emergence of a counterculture pushed fashion for fashion's sake over a new line. Hippies developed their own sense of fashion (boot cut jeans, low-slung cords, thick leather belts with holes all the way around, loose gauzy shirts, beaded necklaces) to match their novel lifestyle (recreational drugs, communal living, untraditional relationships, political dissent). For them style was an essential part of the agenda. Members of the counterculture (including everyone from lesbian feminists to black power militants to gay radicals living in communes from the Village to the Castro) chose what they wore just as deliberately as what drugs to take and whom to sleep with. Their fashion decisions were a way of defining themselves in contrast with mainstream America.

True, there were a lot of gay hippies, but there were many more straight ones, quantitatively speaking. And yet hippie central was San Francisco, whose status as the center of gay life was well established by this point. The not-so-separate movements pushed each other further down their respective paths of stylistic self-determination. An example of queer hippie synergy is the theater troupe-communal performance group, the Cockettes, who are memorably chronicled in the documentary *The Cockettes*. The film shines an illuminating spotlight on the queer side of San Francisco's radical underground. The Cockettes mixed glitter and glamour with dried flowers and burlap to create an overwhelming vision of life as a continuous piece of performance art. Want to become a twisted fairy godmother? Go right ahead. The main tenet of fashion belief for the Cockettes, the hippies, and the gays: Wear whatever you damn well please.

Wally, a member of the Cockettes (ca. 1969)

Robert Richards, a New York artist, was in attendance on opening night of the Cockettes' infamously doomed New York theatrical run. "I remember exactly what I wore: a pair of jeans with holes ripped all over them. And remember, this was way before ripped jeans were at all cool."

What did Richards think of the Cockettes and their San Francisco thrift-shop couture? "It was awful," he says. "We'd seen it and done it all before."

His comments betray the traditional East Coast-West Coast rivalry, but more importantly they point to pluralism in gay fashion. By the early '80s gay men could wear just about anything they wanted to—and they did. The Cockettes could dress however they wanted, Robert could wear whatever he wanted, Yoko Ono could wear whatever she wanted. As long as you were outside the mainstream, fashion could be anything you wanted it to be.

Pluralism meant an entire gay bar subculture emerged to celebrate "leather and Levi's." Gay nightclubs dedicated evenings to drag. Some bars played new wave or country and western. Others courted preppies and catered to a white-collar crowd. Uniform nights were common at some establishments. Most important was the fact that any and every gay man could, if he wanted to, go to any club he fancied as long as he changed his clothes. Call it postmodern, for lack of a better word, but gay men could trade their exteriors (and identities) with ease. And they enjoyed it.

Such a state of fashionable flux intensified through the '80s and continues today. Look at Wigstock, the drag-music festival in New York City. In 1985 a gaggle of drag queens threw a party in Tompkins Square Park in New York's East Village. Over the next 10 years the crowd of drag queens and their fans grew from a couple hundred to 10,000. The show moved to increasingly bigger venues until the mid '90s, when it took over an entire west side pier. No one would say that all of a sudden everyone was "into drag," but for the day, at least, they were.

And look at the Folsom Street Fair in San Francisco, which is older than Wigstock by two years. When the fair began it was a bunch of leather daddies and mommies drinking beer and showing off on Folsom Street. Now it's the grand finale of a week of leather-oriented parties. Did the entire San Francisco gay community suddenly turn into a group of leather aficionados? No. But guys who used to run from the sight of a harness realized the leather aesthetic was all good fun—it could be Halloween every day—and they started throwing on an armband or two and strutting their pecs down Folsom Street for all to see.

While some may lament the death (read: mainstreaming) of traditional subcultures like drag and leather, is it really so bad? Seeing clothes as just clothes—understanding that everything is drag—is a revolutionary outlook. You don't need to look too closely at history or that far around the world today to see fashion used as a method of political control. On Wall Street, CEOs demand that their minions wear only white or blue shirts with their suits every day. In Muslim nations women are forced to hide beneath sweltering black chadors.

In private Catholic schools across America children have to wear uniforms that enforce rigid gender identities and traditional values.

Oh, but if only gay men had truly thrown off the chains of fashion, fads, trends, and styles once and for all. Intellectually, gay men may know—even believe—that clothes are just clothes, and yet they run through trends like nobody else. In fact, gay men have spawned more trends than any subculture should. It's amazing we even have an identity at all. (On second thought, maybe this is why we really don't have an identity anymore.)

Remember blond construction boots and chambray shirts with sleeves that looked ripped off? How about (*really* tight) workout clothes at the gym—and on the street? Mustaches "straight" out the policeman's handbook; anything with Lycra or rayon—together? Sure, now we can laugh about these fashion catastrophes, but at the time each trend was peaking, that look was the most coveted style in the pantheon. Gay men didn't think twice about what the clothes would look like in the future, nor did they think too much about what they meant when they were wearing them. In a beautifully innocent way, "now" was all that mattered.

Top 15 Gay Fashions We Regret Ever Having Worn

1. Overalls with a wife beater or no shirt, one strap unlatched, and optional underwear
2. Espadrilles
3. Thick socks with yellow Timberland boots
4. Tucked-in sleeveless flannels (bears and leathermen excluded)
5. Capri pants
6. Deck shoes
7. Rainbow anything
8. Mock turtlenecks
9. Pirate shirts
10. Leather, fishnets, and grommets all at once
11. Spandex
12. Safety pins as a decoration
13. Anything shiny and textured and tight
14. Anything from the International Male catalog
15. Anything worn by Monroe on *Too Close for Comfort*

Nutsack, Banana Sling, Skivvy, Slinky, and Sultry as Sandra in St. Tropez! Introducing...the Speedo

When I first landed on the gay beaches of America and beyond, a Speedo was *de rigueur*. Even though I'd grown up in straight America, where only poofsters wore Speedos, I learned that old European men also wore Speedos. And the swim team seemed like heaven because they had to wear Speedos. So when I was 18 and on my way to my first gay beach, I went right out and bought a Speedo. I couldn't have imagined wearing anything else.

What was I thinking? Honestly, I have no idea. Maybe I fantasized about joining the imaginary swim team of gay men I saw on the beach. I wanted to be part of the club. I hope I don't sound like I believe I shouldn't have worn a Speedo, or that I wouldn't again someday. What I want to explain is just how deeply ingrained the trend was in my mind. My choice to partake in it was subconscious and, subsequently, my decision (along with millions of other gay men) to segue from Speedos to square-cut suits was equally subliminal.

Square-cut bathing suits—not boxer trunks—arrived in the mid '90s. It would be easy to say that gay men just got bored with their Speedos, but too many other ideas were flying through the gay ether. *Out* magazine and its competitor, *Genre,* featured swimwear fashion stories every few months—acceptable soft-core imagery for aspiring homosexuals. Openly gay designers like John Bartlett and Dolce & Gabbana were unashamed to make their swimwear homoerotic. (I vividly remember a John Bartlett suit I once owned that was cut like a V down toward my pubic hair. Why didn't I just wear a sign that said LOOK AT MY CROTCH, PLEASE?)

Gianni Versace, another gay designer, was selling gold-belted suits with neo-Roman looks. Bruce Webber was photographing Calvin Klein underwear advertisements in which the crotch was king. Webber shot Versace's men too. And Herb Ritts was finding early success with his muscled men on sandy beaches. Skin, sand, and surf were everywhere. The beach was gay Eden.

The Great Gay Swimwear Story also reveals the wayward twistedness of gay fashion and the intricacies of cause and effect that determine what we consider cool. By the late '90s, square cuts were out and loose—but still snug—boxer trunks were briefly (pun intended) in style. Then came...well, remember Birdwell Beach Britches? Not the first time around, but the second, in 1998 or 1999? That's when gays snagged them from straight surfers and made them their own. They were a bridge between tight suits and the looser styles that are popular today.

Birdwell Beach Britches didn't last too long, mostly because gays didn't know what to do with them. They either wore them too tight or too loose. By 2000, gay men went all the way and began sporting knee-length surf shorts, also known as jams. And suddenly, as if over night, gay men looked like all the straight guys on the beach. Everyone from San Diego to Southhampton was wearing loose trunks down to their knees. What was once Speedo Heaven was now Quicksilver Planet.

I don't know if surfers noticed we co-opted their style. I doubt it. If they were paying attention, they might have noticed that the movement of styles from gay to straight men and vice versa is perpetual. We took their surf shorts; they now wear polo shirts in pastel colors. What was the biggest relaunch of 2003? Izod Lacoste. We took their garage wear—work boots and jeans—and now they wear jeans "built" to accentuate their asses produced by Diesel or 2(x)ist—a company that began by hawking underwear to gays.

The latest looks gay men have taken from breeder boys veer toward "street" styles, like skater boy chic. How many gay guys over the last couple of years have worn a vintage T-shirt—or a new T-shirt that simply looked vintage—from an unknown high-school softball team or a made-up physical education department? Or baggy pants or superloose khakis with bulky sneakers like Skechers, K-Swiss, or Vans? All of these were once exclusively the domain of kids on skateboards. Gay men have taken them on as a way of looking younger, tougher, and more "genuine."

Larry Clark's *Kids* (1995) is a decade old, but it just now seems to be catching up with us. The film is easy to write off as a nihilistic exposé of lost youth, but look at the baby doll T's on the girls and the skater boy shorts and tanks on the boys: It's exactly what gay men and stylish young women are wearing now. It's like we want to look as scruffy and "tough" as possible, even if it's painfully artificial. Abercrombie & Fitch, anyone?

The same goes for hip-hop and its sundry styles. While much of hip-hop music and culture is certifiably gay-unfriendly—sexist, homophobic, and misogynistic, actually—the ghetto-fabulous plumage is appropriated by gay men who admire the rebelliousness and aggression of hip-hop stars.

The night I walked into Remington's, the famous gay strip joint in Toronto, the whole bar was rocking to Eminem. This was during the height of the Gay and Lesbian Alliance Against Defamation's effort to get the rapper blacklisted. (Boy, did that effort fail.) No one in Remington's cared; to make things worse (at least for me), the strippers gave their most enthusiastic performance of the night to his music. One guy I was watching was lip-synching—he knew every word.

Of course, there's a level of generic rebellion going on with the embrace of hip-hop music and style by younger gays. They don't want to be told what to do or who to listen to any more than anyone else does. But it's not that simple. There's something macho about the recent adoption of "street" styles that isn't quite as ironic as the leather and Levi's look of yesteryear. While gays of an earlier generation tried on new drag for fun and sex appeal, gay men today cultivate their new fashion through the music they download, the artists they support, the movies they see, and the lingo they use.

Thank somebody—God, goddess, or whomever you choose—that trends are changing faster than ever. If we're lucky, the obnoxious "street" style will be over before this book hits the shelves.

I was recently reminded about how unpredictable gay men's fashion sense is. In 2003 a new bar called Therapy opened in Manhattan (don't get me started on the possible meanings of the name). During the first few weeks a friend of mine went. He's a regular of downtown's somewhat grungier venues, and this place is in midtown, not exactly his usual 'hood. One of the first things out of his mouth after he took in the scene was, "Oh, thank God, not a T-shirt in sight. Gays are dressing up again."

"America's Next Top Model" Fashion Lists

Nolé Marin's Five Best Looks

1. The preppy look from the '80s—clean, fresh, colorful, and all about having fun! An era of colorful clones.

2. Mugler boy from the late '80s—well-dressed (power suit), sexy, and strong. A well-oiled, over the top fantasy guy like Tom of Finland. Similar to Mr. Mugler himself.

3. Versace's Miami look from the early '90s—very masculine and colorful, supermacho, and sexy. Italian fantasy with leather, silver and gold chains, and colorful prints made Versace a leader in his time.

Wardrobe stylist Nolé Marin (and Minnie)

4. The launch of Tom Ford's spring cruise collec-tion for Gucci 1996—a sleek, tailored suit, woven slim-cut pants, leather belts, sarongs, and flesh colored thongs made this one of the killer collections of the season.

5. The Abercrombie & Fitch clone of 2004—affordable, cute, and campy is the young gay uniform of today.

Nolé's Five Worst Looks

1. Combat boots, cutoff jeans, and flannels from the early '90s—Grunge took the runway the wrong way down a one-way street.

2. The "Let's Get Physical" look from the '80s—Spandex is only supposed to be worn by sculpted men, yet all the flabby and undefined men decided to wear them. *A big no-no!*

3. The *Miami Vice* pastel look from the '80s—a cotton candy-colored nightmare, with high-waters and pushed-up jacket sleeves. They definitely should have left it in Miami.

4. Military shoulder pads in the '80s—The mid-career Michael Jackson look "beat it" for a reason.

5. Bangie boy (baggy jeans) of the '90s—Jean jackets and baggy jeans were the staples for the late '80s early '90s. It's now the 21st century. Bangy boys, please take note.

Jay Manuel's Five Worst Male Fashion Trends

1. During the '80s men wore a lot of makeup and placed large shoulder pads in all their clothes! Trying to be Joan Crawford (in my view) was a bad mistake.

2. In the '70s the suit took a wrong turn! We went from slim, well-tailored suits (turn of the century to 1960s) to large double-breasted "roomy" tents! With cheap fabrics and an "insurance salesman" aesthetic, men lost that sharp, tailored presence.

3. During the '70s once again the clog surfaced. *No* man (no matter how good-looking) looks good wearing a clog shoe.

4. Pleated pants are another horrible invention of the '70s that have stuck around till today. The pleats are supposed to allow for more room and added comfort. What ends up happening? Men eat to fill them out! Pants that have no pleats don't necessarily have to be ultraslim; they can allow for room and comfort without looking "bunchy."

America's Next Top Model fashion photo director Jay Manuel with Tyra Banks and Yoanna House.

5. For the last 15 years or so men who need to prove their wealth have started covering their teeth with gold and diamonds! I don't know who started this— Madonna or the hip-hop stars. Whatever the case, someone needs to stop it! Save the *bling* for the body and show those pearly whites! A great smile never goes out of fashion!

Jay's Five Best Male Fashion Trends

1. During the late 1800s men wore corsets just like women. The corset has come in and out of men's fashion, but secretly I think a few "big guys" have kept them around under their clothes. I say, "Why not?" In today's market men are competing against other men as well as women for attention!

2. Today, men's jeans and fashion-forward pants are revisiting a less extreme version of the bell-bottom pant. This brings a little more shape to the man's straight silhouette. Great with boots, and it can conceal both knock-kneed and bowlegged shapes.

3. Military-style clothing has been a hot trend for the last few decades. Not only is it comfortable, it's sexy at the same time. I think men secretly fantasize about being the big hero when they put on their fatigues!

4. Men no longer have to carry the standard briefcase. In the late '80s men started to carry "work bags" that resemble messenger pouches and even oversized handbags! Now most luxury brand companies cater to men with bags in many different styles and a variety of colors (to match that growing shoe wardrobe)! My own father (a conservative doctor) carries a "metrosexual pouch" to work every day!

5. During the first half of the 20th century men stuck to traditional accessories (ties, cuff links, etc.). The '60s changed that forever! Today men wear everything from armbands and wrist cuffs to fashion sunglasses and over-the-top necklaces! It's all about options!

My Affair With an International Male
By Richard Andreoli

"Who would wear that?" a fag with perfectly plucked eyebrows asks his two pals while he holds up a pair of fishnet briefs at the Palm Springs GayMart. They explode into machine-gun rattles of laughter.

The answer, I shamefully admit as I run my hand through a rack of metallic-colored swimsuits, would be me. I want to rub them on my body, my cheeks, inhale their odor and imagine a man's musky scent invading the chemically created fibers. Suddenly, I'm hard.

Yes, that's right: Dirty underwear turns me on.

"Need a dressing room?" An old salesman interrupts my sweet stroking of some lovely Jocko square-cut swim trunks. He's one of a dying breed of homosexuals—the old queen—who came from a time when a queen wasn't a euphemism for a cunt, but rather a lady, a grand dame, someone you'd love to get drunk with over many gin martinis while discussing the heyday of Palm Springs. I glance at the three gay boys, giggling in their own little world like schoolgirls outside of the boy's locker room, then quickly snatch the cute black shorts with 1950s beach girls printed on them and slip into the dressing room unseen.

This pseudo fetish began in junior high when I voraciously studied International Male catalogues. I admired the supersexy models brazenly wearing Speedos, G-strings, and strange foreign wraps that snugly embraced their privates in ways I could only dream about. These men filled my fantasies, and I became an advertiser's wet dream, completely believing that these risqué swimsuits and underpants were exactly what men wore when they were away from the judgmental eye of society. I soon recognized that my short stocky body was ugly, and I knew that International Males would never embrace a tubby-tubby two-by-four like me. I had to do something, but I couldn't handle vomiting for the sake of weight loss, so what choices were left to me?

I'd purchase silk briefs, a polka dot thong, and onionskin workout shorts, of course! Then I'd look just like those models!

Thus hours of fiddling fun ensued as I donned my fancy threads, admired myself in the mirror, and leafed through more catalogues, lost in the magic.

Now, as I slip off my plain 2(x)ist briefs and hear those cackling queers mocking something skimpy and sexy, I realize there were two reasons why I stopped feeding this fantasy. (1) It cost a lot of money, and starting college meant more important purchases... like beer. (2) Gay men might take cocks up the ass, but they think kinky panties are silly, too feminine. Strippers wear them, not someone with a literature degree from UCLA. Even during leather sex, where I could return to the jockstrap with some dignity, dressing in my naughties was only a fond memory, never a fun reality.

"You look hot," says the salesman who conveniently arrives as I step out of the dressing room to admire myself in the mirror. Such a dirty old man, but since he's encouraging me and he's from a generation that will soon be lost to our people, I simply appreciate his enthusiasm without judgment.

And you know what? I do look good! Granted, once I started working out I delightfully discovered that my stocky-flabby body could transform into ghetto booty, but even still, this swimsuit makes my butt look rock hard and my dick look 10 inches long! *Flaccid*! And for only $32!

Okay, that's a lot of cash. That's groceries for the week. That's 10 days of Starbucks. That's two cocktails in West Hollywood! No matter how hot I may feel, it's stupid to spend $32 on something you'll only wear at home, because you're scared of being teased by other fags.

"Tell me," the salesman whispers, "are you for hire? Because with a cock and ass like that you could make a mint!"

I blush, and then see the three bitches—hardly models of masculinity—eagerly peering in as well. Only instead of laughing, they're checking out my bum like a fine piece of meat.

"Am I for hire?" I say, my ever-growing package now aimed at all four. "Let's talk employee discounts, shall we?"

Chapter 7: Queer Media

All That Fags Are Fit to Print: The Mainstreaming of Queer Media in the United States

By Christopher Lisotta

Just around the corner from my apartment is a small gift shop that serves as the local queer emporium. Besides the racks of candles, frames, gag gifts, and lewd birthday cards, there's a sizeable magazine stand. The collection of publications on display is a common sight in pretty much every gay ghetto. There was a time when "gay publication" invariably meant porn. Sure, I can find plenty of nudie mags promoting pouty, shaved male tarts, but scan a few rows down and suddenly I'm browsing through different kinds of gay rags. National magazines like *The Advocate, Out, Genre,* and *Instinct* boast glossy covers touting Hollywood A-listers, both gay and straight. My newsstand even features imports from places like London and Sydney, so if I want to know what the foreign gays are up to, I'm good to go. Nearby are the local gay newsmagazines, which not only fill me in on local news and keep me up to date on cultural events, but also influence national politics, health, arts, and even sports. Their reportage (which is often surprisingly aggressive) keeps me informed about things the national mags just don't have the time to cover.

If you're like me, your first interaction with the gay community at large was through a magazine. Sure, everyone remembers his virgin encounter with *Blue Boy*, but I also recall being at a friend's house in San Diego, just barely out of the closet, and picking up a magazine that had nothing overtly to do with sex. Instead it featured interviews with out writers about the state of gay literature. The idea of reading an article written by a gay man for a gay audience without any shame or recrimination was a revelation.

Nowadays, in a world where even gay magazines have niches—politics, high-end, club culture, arts, and queer rags focused on people of color—we take our media prowess and sophistication for granted. Of course the hetero Academy Award-winning actress wants to be the feature interview for the gay pride issue, since that's bound to boost her ticket sales among those demographically desirable gay men with all that disposable income. Plus, it's hip—that actress knows she's going to get asked fun questions no other publication would bring up, and she gets to give answers she wouldn't dare to offer in places like *People* or *Entertainment Weekly.*

Even more significant is the number of politicians who now include gay publications as a regular stop on the progressive magazine and newspaper interview circuit. Sure, most right-wingers would rather trade in their NRA memberships for an ACLU card than get quoted in *The Advocate*. Nevertheless, an increasing number of Republican elected officials take interviews with respected gay magazines and newspapers because they know queer journalistic standards are on par with the rest of the print world, and they have a track record for getting their facts straight (as it were).

> **"Every straight guy should have a man's tongue in his mouth at least once."**
> **—Madonna, May 21, 1991**

Besides the good content, gay readers also notice the big corporate advertising that surrounds the news copy. Once the sole territory of a few liquor and tobacco companies—which pissed off plenty of community activists who felt the "merchants of death" were profiting from our delayed cirrhosis and lung cancer—major queer magazines now count everyone from car companies, cell phone-service providers, and national retailers as loyal ad clients.

I take for granted that gay news and culture magazines will arrive in my mailbox every few weeks, unopened and ready for my perusal. Of course, if I need to know about some fast-breaking gay story I can surf my way through local, national, and international queer news just by logging on to the Internet. But like so many things in our fabulous little community, just a few decades ago sending out even nonpornographic publications that talked about filthy things like homosexuality could get you in a lick of trouble with some very powerful, far-reaching people.

To learn more about our early gay publishing history I went for a visit to the ONE Institute and Archives, which sits right across the street from the University of Southern California-Los Angeles. Located inside the former Delta Tau Delta fraternity house, ONE Institute is a two-story, red brick building that houses more than 19,000 books related to

LGBT history. In addition to an extensive art and audio collection, the ONE Institute has almost 8,000 periodical titles on file that can be reviewed by graduate students, visiting USC scholars, and even the general public.

Walking in the building is something of a revelation in itself. The library stacks on the first floor open to a second-floor atrium with a walkway ringing the building. Along the second-floor walkway are LGBT-themed paintings and photography that lead to offices, galleries, and ONE Institute's very own museum, which includes banners, buttons, and even a hot pink leather daddy number from the 1970's. Running along one wall is a series of magazines that are about the size of a really skimpy *TV Guide*. Simply entitled *ONE,* the magazine covers are only one or two colors, appear quickly copied, and give off a very loving yet almost homemade feel.

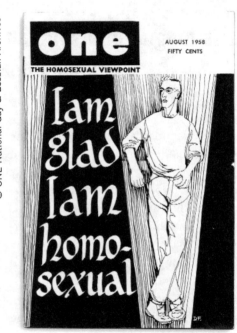

ONE was an outgrowth of the Mattachine Society—a group formed in 1950 in Los Angeles by Communist and labor leader Harry Hay (read more about him in the "Gay Gatherings" chapter)—which followed in the tradition of the "homophile" clubs of the 1920s. Mattachine, which gets its name from masked Medieval performers who traveled across France making social and political commentary through music and dance, saw itself as a serious club where men could come together and discuss homosexuality. Out of the club came the Mattachine Foundation, a legal advocacy group, while in January 1953 the club began a monthly magazine, *ONE.*

According to ONE Institute and Archives executive director Stuart Timmons, the name "ONE" came from Victorian poet Thomas Carlyle, whose quote "A mystic bond of brotherhood makes all men one" resonated with the Mattachine members. For Timmons, the quote sets up a "concept of culture, even a spiritual identity for gay men," and actually spelled out "that gay people are a people, and not just a sex act."

Although *ONE* was one of the first gay publications in the United States, there was a vibrant gay publishing history in Europe between the two world wars. *Der Einige* (The Unique) was a German magazine that followed the gay cabaret culture and chaotic German art world from the 1910s until the Nazis started rounding up gays as degenerates in the

1930s. A similar magazine, the subscriber-based *Der Kreis* (The Circle), appeared in Switzerland just as the Nazis came to power in Germany. It was published until 1967 and featured stories in German, French and English.

Still, *ONE* was a seminal publication, not least of all because it soon appeared on newsstands in this country, something considered an impossible feat for a periodical that called itself "A Homosexual Magazine" right on the cover. "It's peculiarly gay," Timmons says of the earliest *ONE* issues. "The graphics were so good. You don't pick up something that's not attractive, whether it's a guy or a magazine. So they made all those colors and the interior art design very attractive. And actually a lesbian made the design work."

In addition, *ONE* went further than the fledgling newsletters that came out of more socially focused homophile clubs in places like Chicago and New York, where early publications were quickly crushed by zealous government officials looking to stamp out what they considered lewd and antisocial behavior. "The breakthrough transition was from an inactive subculture that was just concerned with getting laid to a more political consciousness to organizing something like *ONE* magazine," Timmons says.

Timmons thinks good old American capitalism overshadowed any sort of moral distaste squeamish newsstand operators might have felt toward *ONE*. "The success of the magazine was partly due to the simple facts of commerce," he explains. "They created a product for an underserved market, and the male physique magazines were already selling." Physique magazines, which had been around for more than 20 years, were outwardly designed for men looking to shake off their 98-pound weakling status and build up rippling muscles, ostensibly to get more babes on the beach. The oiled-up men flexing in little more than fig leafs also appealed to men who were looking for something other than beach babes.

"Those were not marketed overtly to gay men, but the sales were going up *because* of closeted gay men," Timmons says, noting that newsstand owners knew this and figured the same clients would be interested in *ONE*. "It was partially self-interest and partially bravery," he adds.

The rise of Mattachine and *ONE* came just as the Communist and subversive witch-hunts were at their most virulent, and gays were targeted for dismissal in the government and at major universities.

> **"Most of my male friends are gay, and that seems perfectly natural to me. I mean, who wouldn't like cock?"
> —Valerie Perrine, quoted in Leigh Rutledge's *The New Gay Book of Lists***

Before long the government was knocking on *ONE*'s door, and it wasn't for a social visit. According to Lee Walzer's book *Gay Rights on Trial,* the magazine got in trouble in 1954 after Wisconsin Republican senator Alexander Wiley wrote a letter to the post office blasting the magazine, saying it was perverse and wasn't fit to be distributed along with the rest of America's mail. The *ONE* editors knew this was bound to happen, and specifically chose stories and images that could not be construed as overtly sexual or perverse. "There was a conscious strategy to really show gay culture, news, and literature," Timmons says. "They talked about the details of daily life. They were careful to avoid more earthy sexuality issues." But as *ONE* soon found out, mentioning anything that remotely had to do with homosexuality was grounds for government censure.

The October 1954 issue appears to be the queer straw that broke the straight camel's back, even though the magazine had often taken on provocative (but nonpornographic) subjects. The August 1953 issue ran with a cover story that simply asked the question "Gay Marriage?" and the November '53 issue wanted to know "Are 'normals' abnormally interested in sex?" By this point thousands of subscribers were onboard, and plenty more were being sold next to the physique mags. But the October

"Although there are some gay men who prefer small penises, the boastful phrase 'My new lover has an adorable cock like a tiny pink shrimp!' isn't usually going to make the competition jealous."
—Pat Califia in *The Advocate Adviser*

1954 issue had a story written by a lesbian called "Sappho Remembered," a nonsexual item about a woman who leaves her boyfriend for another woman. The story featured nothing more shocking than a kiss on the cheek between the two gals. But this was too much for the censors at the LA post office, who had been monitoring *ONE* issues in the past and who were watching more closely at Wiley's request.

According to Joyce Murdoch's and Deb Price's terrific book *Courting Justice: Gay Men and Lesbians v. the Supreme Court,* *ONE*'s lawyer, a straight man, represented *ONE* for free after even the ACLU shied away from the case. The argument against the magazine's publication and distribution was stark yet simple: If homosexuality was illegal in every state, and *ONE* was a magazine about homosexuality, then *ONE* was a magazine for criminals and therefore clearly illegal.

In 1955 *ONE* filed suit against the LA postmaster in federal court, hoping to overturn the obscenity charges against the magazine. A lower court rejected *ONE*'s claims, and the magazine appealed to the ninth circuit court of appeals, which was equally dismissive of the case. Murdoch and Price quote at length from the three-judge panel's decision, which warned that "social standards are fixed by and for the great majority and not by or for a hard-ened or weakened minority." The panel also went off on "Sappho Remembered," noting, "The article is nothing more than cheap pornography calculated to promote lesbianism. It falls far short of dealing with homosexuality from the scientific, historical, and critical point of view."

Almost immediately *ONE* appealed to the Supreme Court, which up until that time had never discussed a case that specifically concerned homosexuality. Few people thought the court would take the case, since the lower courts had been in agreement against *ONE* and their decisions had been so harsh. But a funny thing happened: The court agreed to review the case. Murdoch and Price argue that the Supreme Court justice's clerks, bright post-law school stars decades younger than their bosses, read copies of *ONE* and found them not obscene but very tame compared to what got written in more traditional men's and women's magazines. For the first time the legal status of homosexuality in the United States was not judged in and of itself as perverse.

Although the justices didn't hear oral arguments in the case, they voted to reverse the decision, which also dealt with appeals brought by two straight nudist magazines. The straight mags took essentially the same position as the folks at *ONE* (and their victories overshadowed *ONE*'s in the mainstream press). Thanks to the 5-4 vote and the one-sen-tence statement striking down the lower courts' interpretations, *ONE* captured the first gay Supreme Court victory in history.

For Timmons, the case's importance can't be overstated. "I think it set a pattern [for a] national publication for gay life that dealt with news, culture, and the expression of a gay point of view," he argues. "This pattern of allowing gay people to express themselves and claim a place in culture is hugely important and has lasted in every LGBT publication today. It started a national dialogue and put it in cold type."

Timmons also notes that *ONE* had some influential subscribers beyond closet cases and the early gay activists looking for something, anything, in print that talked about subjects that had been taboo for so long. "The editors at *Playboy* magazine subscribed to *ONE*," Timmons says. "It's very telling that the

"Do [gay men] love Martha as much as I do? God, I need to be gay!" —Jennifer Garner during an interview for her film *13 Going on 30*

magazine of heterosexuality wanted to understand what was going on in the homosexual world as part of the sexual liberation movement."

The magazine flourished for many years, until internal divisions within *ONE* and

Mattachine weakened the magazine. In 1965 Don Slater, one of the founders of Mattachine and *ONE,* broke from the group and formed his own organization and publication, *Tangents.* The last issue of *ONE* hit newsstands in the early 1970s, just a few years after *The Advocate* was launched in 1967. The world was changing too, as the tumultuous social revolutions of the 1960s and ultimately Stonewall created a new generation of gay activists (perhaps the first generation to truly claim that title) who had little time for assimilation or for tame stories designed to get around rapidly changing obscenity laws. Timmons argues that the generation gap between the now middle-aged *ONE* editors and the longhaired, out and proud hippies who had experience in the civil rights movement couldn't be starker.

"*ONE* and the Mattachine Society became very conservative," he explains. "The homophile movement wanted a buy-in from psychology and religions. The civil rights movement and then the counterculture movement began making demands. That was a big shock, this very impatient new generation, and they got results."

> "God forbid a straight person should acknowledge that there are pleasures associated with his anus."
> —Phil Hartman quoted in *Los Angeles* magazine

The exchange of ideas that the first *ONE* editors hoped to inspire has come to fruition, regardless of whether the 17-year-old gay high schooler trying to communicate with other kids like him in a chat room realizes it. A student of history, Timmons sees both honor and irony in the story of *ONE.*

"I never want to suggest that any individual or institution should get undue credit, because I know there were struggles going on, and there were many heroes who got eclipsed by history, but at the same time it's very important to honor what you've got."

Today *ONE* is almost forgotten, but its legacy survives in every gay magazine on your coffee table, even if they cover issues as unremarkable as the kind of swim suit you'll be wearing this summer. Indeed, if it weren't for the brave souls at *ONE* and their supposedly unwinnable court case, you wouldn't be reading this book right now.

Ted Casablanca's Top 8 Queer-Related News Events

1. Liza and David and their infamous kiss!

There's no brilliant gay writer—Bruce Vilanch, Jim J. Bullock—who could've written it any better. It is so obscenely grotesque, and you can't get any gayer than Liza Minnelli and David Gest. To me, the best gay moments transcend the pigeon-holing, "Is this gay? Is this homo? Who owns it?" I hate that shit.

2. The Ellen DeGeneres and Anne Heche saga

Ellen and Ann had such a journey—and not just to Fresno, but to a really warped place. It became more than just two women coming out—it became a spectacle, and it became about tearing them down. It's like Michael Jackson in that we build up these celebrities and their lives, just to tear them down and enjoy watching it happen.

3. The Career of Harvey Fierstein

You can't have a list like this without mentioning Harvey because he's just done so much. Onstage and off, on-screen and offscreen. Getting awards for playing gay, for writing about being gay, and for thanking his lover onstage when he won the Tony for *Torch Song Trilogy.* Such a trailblazer.

4. Cher retiring. And retiring. And retiring... Britney Spears, losing her virginity. And losing her virginity. And losing her virginity... And is Madonna the mother of Cher, or is Cher the mother of Madonna?

Cher and Madonna have both reinvented themselves a hundred times, but it's very important that the chameleonic aspect be attributed to Cher. But

Madonna had better music, and then Cher stole Madonna's music, and then they got the same friggin' publicist, and you really couldn't tell them apart. And Britney's the bastard child of both of those women. She isn't even old enough to have a camp following, but she's like a young drag queen, because she's not real pretty but she's got a sexy look. She's imminently doable, but not real attractive. Isn't that why we love Barbra, and Liza, and Cher and Madonna—because we can sort of look like them without too much work? So in a way they're all the same person.

5. The straight consumption of queer TV

Will & Grace and *Queer Eye for the Straight Guy* are fine, but they're not great. I know people complain about *Queer as Folk* and say it isn't real, but I think they're a little more real than Will or Jack. *Queer as Folk* didn't cross over to a mainstream audience, but think that's because straight audiences were uncomfortable watching it. I like both *Will & Grace* and *Queer Eye,* but they're safe gay shows. They've been seized by straight audiences in the same way that *The Birdcage* was, and even though straight audiences will say they're laughing with us when they watch these shows, trust me: They're really laughing at us.

6. The Hollywood standard in gay cinema

When women get to play lesbians they get that right-on kiss, and when men play gay guys, they can't. Antonio Banderas and Tom Hanks in *Philadelphia,* it's a little peck. But Charlize Theron and Christina Ricci in *Monster* are tonguing each other. In my mind, *Philadelphia* is a disservice to the gay community because I don't think it showed gay people and what they're really struggling with other than having AIDS in the workplace and enduring that prejudice. But in the movie the Antonio Banderas and Tom Hanks characters didn't have a life, they didn't have sex. Even *Making Love* was better than *Philadelphia,* and that's how many years older? Basically the good stuff is happening with more independent films, like *Monster,* and the bad representation is still happening with the studios.

7. The gay Mafia

The gay Mafia exists only within the gay community. It's like backstage at awards shows when I see actresses being bitchy to each other. It's that same sort of infighting, that same sort of power trip. Money is what really has power. That's it. Regardless of your race, your sexual orientation, or your gender. In this town it's all about money. I only hear about the gay Mafia from gay people.

8. George Michael

I really do think it's appalling that cops were spending their time—and my money—trailing someone like George Michael, who might have been after sex at a public restroom. Big fucking deal! Why don't they go keep somebody from being gay bashed? Why didn't they protect those kids from getting baseball bats to their brains? Where were they then? You know, I spoke to George Michael about it and I told him how impressed I was that he owned it after he did it. Unlike, say, someone who's caught with a cross-dresser and says he was just giving this gal a ride in the middle of the night as a Good Samaritan.

And the 9th item, which isn't an item because it doesn't deserve to be considered an actual "event": The endless debate about Tom Cruise's sexuality

Quite frankly, I think he's more interested in an Oscar than he is in sex. That said, I suppose you have to put Cruise on here because "Is he, or isn't he?" is bound to come up again. But I think it's such a self-hating thing to do, ultimately. Because what you're doing is sending out the message that it's not okay if he was gay. You're sending the message that he's to be burned if he is gay. This is why I don't agree with outing. I think it's ultimately a self-defeating tactic and I think you're screwing yourself in the end.

Ted Casablanca, who is a correspondent for *E! News Live*, writes "The Awful Truth" for E! Online.

"Even if I discover a cure for cancer, the first line of my obituary is bound to mention that I once made a film where Divine eats dog shit. Which would be okay by me."

— John Waters, gay filmmaker

"I'm an openly gay trailer-trash Mexican. How could they not love me?"

—Ice-skating national champion Rudy Galindo

"I don't mind straight people as long as they act gay in public."

—T-shirt worn by Chicago Bulls transvestite Dennis Rodman during a network-TV interview.

"Gay people...were the first to find me, and they get everything, they're so sharp. I'll look out in the audience and I see three or four gay guys right in the front row, or a couple of lesbians, I know it's gonna be a good show."

—Joan Rivers in Denver's *Out Front*

"What do you get when you lock six gay Jewish men in a room together? A Broadway musical."

—Harvey Fierstein after collecting one of *Hairspray*'s eight Tony awards, as quoted in *The Hollywood Reporter*, June 9, 2003

"For everyone out there who thinks the theater is full of nothing but Jews and gays, all I have to say is, '*Oy gevalt,* my lover and I just won a Grammy!'"

> —Hairspray composer-lyricist Marc Shaiman, as quoted in the February 24, 2003, issue of *Daily Variety*

"I can't believe the shit you guys get away with over here [in the United Kingdom]... You're, like, totally gay, and nobody even is fazed by it."

> —Sandra Bernhard, speaking with host Graham Norton on his BBC talk show *So Graham Norton*

"It's these propaganda queens who are really hurting us. These people who put out this lie that we're exactly the same [as hetero-sexuals] and that we're just straight people who fuck our own; that is just not true!"

> —Scott Thompson of *Kids in the Hall* to the *San Francisco Bay Times*

"I believe marriage is between a man and a woman, and I think we ought to codify that one way or another."

> —President George W. Bush

"Should a bullet enter my brain, let that bullet destroy every closet door."

> —Harvey Milk

Chapter 8: Gay Ghettos

How Some Neglected Neighborhoods Became the Major Homo Haunts We've Come to Know and Love

By Christopher Lisotta

When I was a young 20-something gay man coming out in San Diego, discovering the gay neighborhood Hillcrest was like Dorothy coming upon Oz (a bit of an obvious reference, but work with me). For a grad student at UC-San Diego, Hillcrest's mix of great restaurants, alternative bookshops, art house cinemas, and plentiful gay bars provided a welcome break from my much dryer academic existence. But walking down University Avenue was important to me not just for the cultural and commercial delights. For the first time in my life I saw gay men living, working, and loving in a community that was so much richer exactly because all that gayness was concentrated in one place—*our* place.

You know you are there the moment you first step on the street. In theory the neighborhood is no different from the few blocks behind or the few blocks ahead, but you can just *feel* it. Chances are the neighborhood has older buildings that are in their refurbished, reconstituted second prime. The old warehouse is now an interior design firm, the tired beauty parlor is a terrific little independent bookseller, and the hardware store that closed years ago now features the trendiest slacks and shirts in display windows that, for decades, offered passersby nothing more glamorous than Phillips head screwdrivers and table saws. There's less litter—or at least the candy wrappers and disposable coffee cups strewn on the ground next to the neighborhood improvement planters seem to be a bit more upscale.

There are suddenly fewer women, and the men seem skinnier and more clean-cut. And then there is the color—the grays and browns of most urban buildings have pops of bright reds, sky blues, velvety purples, and of course pleasing pinks.

It's the queer part of town—the gay ghetto, baby. Chances are if you are in a mid-sized city or larger there is at least one block that constitutes a gay ghetto. Some gay ghettos have become worldwide tourist destinations—the Castro in San Francisco comes to mind immediately, thanks to the work of slain political leader Harvey Milk, and the area's place in the history of AIDS activism. But what makes the Castro work is the fact that it is so instantly recognizable as the ultimate gay place, not only to the people who have lived there for decades, but also to newcomers just off the bus from Idaho who are desperately looking for a home. Despite all the hindrances in our way, gay men have risked life and limb to be together.

But how did it all get here? How did hundreds if not thousands of LGBT people find each other and decide, Plymouth Rock-style, that they were going to pitch their rainbow flag in the street and claim the neighborhood for all of queerdom? Although the idea of buff pilgrims in pink is a fabulous image, it's not very realistic. The details may differ from city to city, but you can find some common themes that tie together how gay ghettos are born, live, and ultimately die.

The concept of a neighborhood or an area within a city that is associated with gay life is hardly something new. Not very long after cities first developed in America, sailors and explorers looking for a quick gay trick sussed out the streets, parks, and piers where such delights could be found. But the evidence shows that these kinds of cruising and meeting areas were hardly unique to the New World, since guys looking for a colonial freak down got plenty back in the old country, where unofficial but implicitly acknowledged areas of gay activity had existed for decades.

Long before there was even the idea of modern gay identity, men looking to have sex with other men needed places that were easy to access, anonymous, and free of disapproving crowds. At first it was whispered-about sections of parks and certain dark alleys, but over time bars and stores that sold pornography became not only venues to buy booze and get off, but also places where gay men could meet, connect, and communicate.

Even today, of course, cruising areas exist apart from the gay ghettos, particularly for closeted men looking to hook up who have no desire to head to the queer part of town, but still want to get their married rocks off. Although many gay ghettos developed out of that cruising tradition, the reasons they became what they are today are as varied and unique as the larger cities around them. The story of how gay ghettos came to be is not just the subject of snappy disco tunes, but also the focus of a number of serious scholarly studies by academics. The reality is, unlike many other groups that have come to inhabit different urban neighborhoods, we gays have been incredibly successful at making our ghettos work, mainly because they had to.

Out of the Artists Colony

Some of the earliest defined gay neighborhoods, like sections of New York City's Greenwich Village, owe their existence to the tolerant and avant-garde atmosphere created by a burgeoning artist community. According to the Greenwich Village Society for Historic Preservation, the area was known as a bohemian enclave by the 1910s. The throngs of modern painters, theater types, experimental writers, and alternative publishers who flocked to the Village undoubtedly included plenty of queer folk. These cultural pioneers helped create a diversity of thought and political opinion that enabled gay thinkers to publicly express what they had been thinking privately for hundreds of years.

The pointy-headed queers in the Village who were looking to cultivate their extremely unpopular ideas about gay identity found they were in good company; there were lots of people in the neighborhood who wanted to discuss concepts that shocked the polite society of the early 20th century. The New School of Social Research was born in the 1920s, while progressive artists opened institutions to challenge the traditional art beliefs of the day. The 1950s beat movement further defined the neighborhood and provided another welcome outlet for young gay artists who were becoming more unafraid to explore their sexuality in their work.

This all led to a growing gay community that began to congregate in earnest around Christopher Street in the 1960s. Even if you weren't all that artistic, you were quick to realize that you could meet a cute artist or another loving guy in a community where literally anything goes. For all those queer outsiders who couldn't find their place in the world, the Village became a place that accepted you, a powerful draw for men who may have heard of such a place whispered from friend to friend, but couldn't believe what they saw until they got there. Although plenty happened earlier in New York and in other sections of the country, the Village became defined with the modern political gay movement because of the events that took place in 1969 in a ratty little bar, now known the world over as the Stonewall riots. Suddenly the neighborhood carried iconic associations; the Village would be linked to the gay community for decades to come.

Out of the Nation's Capital

Although young gay men have always had informal but highly vibrant social networks to help them meet one another, one 20th century event more than any other developed those narrow strands into beautifully complex webs—World War II. The massive mobilization drew farm boys and grocers' kids from the sticks to the huge human transit stations on each coast, leading many to action (military or otherwise) in the Pacific and in Europe. Old societal customs were shattered, friendships were formed, and young men who thought they were all alone in their same-sex attraction soon realized the guy in the next pup tent had the same manly urges.

When they came back from the battlefields these newly liberated queers had no desire

to return to the fields of the rural Midwest or their hometown Main Street market. Instead, they stayed in the cities together, whether it was in San Francisco on the West Coast or a city like Washington, D.C., on the East.

Brett Beemyn, in his book *Creating A Place for Ourselves,* noted that there were five gay bars in Washington before the war and eleven by 1950. Although the numerous public parks in D.C. were breeding grounds for gay interaction, Dupont Circle drew more of the postwar gays for a variety of reasons. Nearby Lafayette Square was watched closely by the local police, but the park in the circle and the shopping area on Connecticut Avenue provided useful covers for gays looking for each other.

As gay vets started coming together another demographic change was taking place that helped speed the creation of Washington's gay ghetto. Straight couples and their rapidly expanding baby boomer families were dumping their city digs for new homes in the suburbs, abandoning not only the working-class and predominantly white inner cities but also formerly fashionable neighborhoods like Dupont Circle. Many areas suffered from the rapid changes; street crime and neglect made the neighborhoods the nexus of social blight.

Almost as quickly as the middle class moved out, the "bachelors" moved in, happy to buy an elegant but rundown house in a neighborhood that had increasingly failing schools. The first business to cater to this new community was Mr. P's, a bar that acted as a tent pole for other gay-friendly establishments. With the influx of new queer places came a critical mass of safety, where gay men realized they could go from place to place without worrying about a good bashing the way they did before.

In 1971, Earth Works opened, becoming the first nonbar business in Dupont Circle, providing the community a thriving book and magazine shop. With the new neighbors and the businesses, it was only a matter of time before social organizations and community groups started to form, providing services to people in Dupont Circle, but also creating awareness for the rest of the city that the neighborhood was here to stay.

Out of Changing Demographics

Researcher Michael E. Dillinger, a San Diego State University researcher, studied the development of San Diego's gay ghetto, Hillcrest, for the relatively unhip but weighty *Journal of San Diego History* in 2000. He found some interesting things in the neighborhood's renaissance that made it such a special place for me.

In the early 1900s a developer bought tracts of land between 1st and 6th avenues, and founded the Hillcrest Corporation, which subdivided the tracts into small, affordable lots tar-

geting the growing number of singles and small families moving to the rapidly growing city. The young couples stayed in their tidy little homes, growing old as the city grew up around them. Most importantly, newfangled shopping centers got built in nearby Mission Valley in the '60s, forcing small-shop owners in surrounding areas out of business. Hillcrest's commercial streets quickly became the modern equivalent of a coastal California ghost town. The old folks who first moved in during the '20s and '30s were on fixed incomes and could do little about their deteriorating neighborhood.

Dillinger argues that one of the biggest draws to Hillcrest is surprising but makes sense—safety. Since so many of their fellow residents were elderly, young gays and lesbians had little to fear from their neighbors in terms of physical violence. The quiet nature of the neighborhood also meant it was off the radar of the city's vice squad, which patrolled other areas in search of lewd conduct arrests, with a vengeance.

Another close by San Diego landmark also served as an attraction, the city's premier public space, the sprawling Balboa Park jutted up against Hillcrest and served as a regular meeting spot for gay men. Gay men could walk from trysts in Balboa to the new bars lured by cheap rents that began popping up in the 1970s. As Hillcrest's oldest residents began dying off, gay men and lesbians (particularly those who ended up in San Diego after time in the military) were looking for small and cheap places to live. Soon, an open active community that was the envy of the rest of San Diego was born.

Out of Political Need

The City of West Hollywood, the center of gay life in Los Angeles, has the distinction of being its own city. Unlike Dupont Circle, Hillcrest, and Greenwich Village, West Hollywood isn't part of the larger political entity of the megalopolis around it, but an independent municipality with its own government. A relatively young city, West Hollywood was founded in 1984 from an unincorporated area of Los Angeles County with the help of rent-control advocates, elder rights groups, and the LGBT community, which had called West Hollywood home for years.

Although areas of Los Angeles like Mid Wilshire and Silver Lake have had vibrant gay communities over the years, West Hollywood became a gay Mecca for a very practical reason: the LAPD. The Los Angeles Police Department always had an active and overly enthusiastic vice squad that went after gay people and gay bars with a vengeance. Unlike the city of LA, unincorporated areas of the county were patrolled by the county sheriff's deputies, who had vast tracts of land to cover and little time to bust a bunch of queens in bars. Seeing an opportunity, gay bar owners and gay people looking to escape persecution and prosecution moved in, realizing they were in an island free from the stormy antigay seas around them. But there was a price to pay—being a small tract of land—less than two square miles—in one of the biggest counties in the United States meant West Hollywood was never a top priority. Residents took responsibility into their own hands and led the fight for cityhood, with naysayers warning that such a puny little city could never survive on its own. But survive it did, and thrive it did, becoming a draw not only for gays and lesbians but other progressives and immigrants looking for a new life. Since its inception the West Hollywood city government has boasted an active gay component that helped guide the creation of the city and served as a model for other out political hopefuls helping to start a career in their own cities.

Victim of Their Own Successes?

Like any good thing, the creation of the gay ghetto leads to unintended consequences. As the Seattle alternative paper *The Stranger* pointed out a few years back, it was time to figure out where the new gay neighborhood is, since the venerable gay ghetto of Capitol Hill was maxed out. Why? Think about it—what made the burgeoning gay ghetto so attractive was the cost. Young gays from the boonies looking for a cheap place to live had plenty of run-down choices. They also had the opportunity to take entry-level jobs at bars and gay retail spots in the neighborhood, and they were able to meet tons of other new gays also looking for young and frequent love. But as the neighborhood got all spiffed-up, fancier stores came in to cater to the sophisticated new population. Prices started rising. Then hip straight folks, particularly single women, realized that the gay ghetto was a safe, fun place to live. Even couples from the 'burbs started coming into the ghetto, seeking out that new Mongolian restaurant or looking to see an indie film at the restored art deco movie theater just a few blocks away. The straights liked it so much, they started buying homes from the gay pioneers, who were delighted to sell their once run-down homes for huge profits.

Hillcrest is certainly an example of this. Although California—particularly San Diego—is an expensive place to live relative to salaries, the price of real estate in the heart of the ghetto is prohibitively expensive not only for newcomers but also ghetto renters who were hoping that someday they could afford to buy. Gays slowly moved to nearby neighborhoods, like North Park and University Heights, which have experienced mini-gay ghetto booms of their own. But even those areas are out of reach for the young baby gays hoping to find a place in the gayborhood.

Of course some young gays are rejecting the idea of the gay ghetto altogether. For young men who once flocked to the ghetto to find their identity, they look no further than their school's gay-straight alliance or turn on the TV. For many a generation going to the gay ghetto was a necessity, since being out meant they couldn't live at home or in more traditional neighborhoods. How quickly things have changed—gays are no longer perverts not to be trusted, but active participants in rising property values. In San Diego residents of one neighborhood, Azalea Park, recognized all the wonderful qualities gays bring to a community and started marching in Hillcrest's gay pride parade to encourage people to move to their much more affordable enclave. More than a few took them up on the offer.

As gays have more children, the issue of schools starts to come into play as well. The cutting-edge urban neighborhood with the great nightlife was the place to be when you were 25 and out until four in the morning every night. But with the rise of gay 30-something carpool circles and weekend soccer matches, where you live is now dictated by the needs of the little ones.

For some gay activists this is a good thing—we're more accepted now, and good neighbors are admired and respected by everyone in a world dominated by Home Depot improvement and *Martha Stewart Living* rooms. Rainbow flags hang from porches and windowsills in virtually every neighborhood in America. Isn't it a sign of our success that straight couples want to move into the gay neighborhoods, since they too relish the idea of gourmet markets, hip boutiques and well-appointed community spaces? Ironically, it comes back to why gays helped make the ghettos into their image—they wanted a safe, vibrant place where they could be themselves, live in peace, and get on famously with their neighbors. What couple or young adult just starting in life doesn't want that?

Rules for Displaying Gay Pride in the Gay Ghetto

Making the rainbow a gay symbol was cute back in the day, but in truth rainbows don't match any tasteful wardrobe choice and, frankly, they look obnoxious. In any case, the gay community was never a collection of "united colors," no matter how much we'd like to think otherwise. Obviously we can't get rid of rainbows—they're insidious, and fags keep spreading them around, kind of like STDs if you think about it—but we *can* regulate their usage.

Flags and Banners: You are only allowed to hang rainbow flags during events like Gay Pride weekend. Cities are allowed to display the flags, but only if they show extremely good taste. Queer businesses may display them if they choose, but subtle stickers in windows are much more pleasant to look at (or easier to ignore, depending on your preference).

Flag Stickers: When people see flag stickers (Rainbow, Leather, Bear, etc.), they immediately think of how you screw. Triangles are slightly more politically oriented, but not much. You are allowed *one* small, discreet flag *or* triangle symbol (not both) on the back of your car. You may display a red ribbon *or* Human Rights Campaign sticker in addition to a flag or triangle, but that's it. People who use those long, thin GAAAYYYYY or LEATHHHER strips are not allowed anything else on their car or person. Ever!

Bumper Stickers: Political stickers such as HATE IS NOT A FAMILY VALUE are acceptable choices, but as soon as they're outdated, take them off. No fading allowed! Stickers like *It's not pretty being easy* are perfectly fine if you want other people to make fun of you.

Vanity Plates: There's nothing hotter than taking a guy home to meet mom and seeing her catch sight of his license plate that reads SIR4BOY. "Hey mom, guess who I am in the relationship!" Yes, you may very well be a BTM-BOI or LAYNPIPE or a HNGTP, but there's no need to advertise. Plus, friends won't let friends date you.

Affiliation Stickers Demonstrating Double Pride: Rainbow cowboy silhouettes, rainbow Mickey Mouse ears, rainbow States, and the like essentially say,

"I'm a cowboy / Disney / California fag!" These can be confusing. For example, does a rainbow paw print mean you like bears, that you *are* a bear, or that you like screwing large woodland mammals? If a sticker requires too much thought, you must drop it. On the flip side, if it's easy to decipher, then realize that you're showing double Pride in one sticker and that you are therefore not allowed to mix it with any other Pride symbol. Ever!

Adornments: Rainbow antenna balls or license plate frames are fine, but no other Pride object is allowed, and we still reserve the right to mock you behind your back. Mardi Gras beads or any other queer jewelry should be hidden or thrown out once you sober up.

You are allotted one exterior Pride item (a bumper sticker, for example) in addition to one interior adornment such as a disco ball or beanie baby... but you will be teased.

Freedom rings are not allowed! Ever! They were ugly when they came out and they're ugly *and* outdated now. You may, however, keep the set that you bought at 18 for the sake of nostalgia.

Shirts: 2QT2BSTR8! I'M NOT GAY BUT MY BOYFRIEND IS! NOBODY KNOWS I'M A FAG / DYKE / HOMO! These were fun in the '90s, but a vintage Marie Osmond says the same thing *and* it fits your pecs really well. Bottom line: Don't buy gay shirts, and certainly don't wear them, unless they're clever and really say something distinctive about you.

Housewares: Rainbow plates, bathrobes, towels, and the like: Nothing ruins a romantic evening quicker than rainbow sheets. There'll be no ass play for you!

Exceptions to the Above Rules: If you live in a small town, you're allowed to break a couple rules for the sake of progress. But use your Pride power wisely, because there's simply nothing tackier than a gay man who sports too many Pride symbols. When you move to a larger city—say, to New York from Lowell, Mass.— where being gay is as common as getting laid in a park, then it's time to clear out those rainbows. Otherwise, you'll not only be mocked, but you could potentially miss out on some good gay butt-love.

Top 13 Things to Bring When Moving to a Gay Ghetto

1. A rainbow flag, a healthy disdain for the ghetto you're moving into, and the parking permit you stole from your ex who lives in a neighborhood that's closer to the bars
2. Steroids or a gym membership (or both)
3. Teeth bleaching tray and supplies
4. Mystic Tan membership so that you can look unseasonably dark during those long winter months

Chelsea

5. Starbucks card for morning cruising
6. A small dog to walk—preferably a Shitzu—for afternoon/evening/weekend/dog park cruising. Or a high-speed Internet connection. Whichever is cheaper, less work, or cuter by your side
7. A full bar at home for when the cruising pays off
8. Low-voltage halogen lighting so you look even better when you bring your trick inside your place
9. *A Year in Provence* by Peter Mayle, to be placed on the coffee table so that you look intelligent while you're pouring him that drink
10. Subscription to *Us* weekly so that a savvy trick knows what you can really talk about once you're finished in the bedroom
11. Party-size pump bottle of Wet Lube for that same bedroom session
12. Illume candles for the bathroom...and bedroom, and living room. It lets him know you've got some ker-ching ker-ching, creates a mood, and covers odors.
13. A case of Fleet Enemas

Top 11 Things Not to Do Prior to an Internet Date in the Gay Ghetto

1. Eat asparagus
2. Confide your real age
3. Bring roses
4. Bring friends (unless that's been arranged ahead of time)
5. Give your last name
6. Enter his unlocked apartment without permission in case you got the apartment number wrong
7. Get attached to his pet
8. Borrow anything (which will give him an excuse to call you again)
9. Leave out your valuables if he comes to your place
10. Feel obligated to screw him simply because he drove across town
11. Forget to leave his number and e-mail in two distinctly different places in your apartment so that if you disappear the police know where to start looking

You Know It's Time to Leave Your Gay Ghetto When...

1. The rainbow flag becomes an architectural design choice by the local city planners.
2. You unknowingly buy back the gaudy crap you donated last year to the local gay thrift store because it's kind of cute and will go perfect with the new IKEA shelves you're installing.
3. Ordering egg whites, a turkey patty, and steamed spinach for breakfast no longer seems odd.
4. Everyone in your apartment has starred in at least one porn video.
5. You wake up to walk your dog at 3 A.M.
6. You can't walk your dog down certain streets because you've pissed off too many tricks.
7. You start making fun of the new neighbor because he's got a full bar, low halogen lighting, Illumé candles, *A Year in Provence* on the coffee table, a subscription to *Us* weekly, and a small dog.
8. You have sex with that same neighbor later that same evening and dis-

cover the lube next to the bed and an enema case shoved under some school books in the corner.

9. You wish your past Internet hook ups would stop IMing you all the time.

10. You wake up one night to the glow of your own overly tanned body.

11. You begin complaining about all these young body-conscious queens and their superiority complexes...and you mean it.

12. You begin complaining about the shortage of decent leather stores within walking distance of your apartment.

13. You have sex with Jim J. Bullock.

West Hollywood

Chapter 9: Fitness

Building the Perfect Beast
By David Ciminelli

In the fabulously gay ghetto of West Hollywood, if you don't look young and sexy enough to star in a Bel Ami video, you pretty much don't even show up on the city's gaydar. And with another birthday approaching, it's starting to become painfully clear to me that turning 30 in WeHo is vastly different from anywhere else, because it's difficult to age with grace in an urban jungle where body fascism is the norm. Believe me, given the opportunity, the young pretty boys here would happily catapult your 30-year-old ass into the air on your birthday and zap you into oblivion like in *Logan's Run*. There'd be less competition for attention, and they wouldn't have constant reminders that age happens.

Unlike Logan, however, I have no Sanctuary to escape to. I'm still about 10 years too young to connect with my inner Daddy and move to the grittier, "older" side of gay LA known as Silver Lake. And I'm at least 15 years away from even thinking about heading to the gay retirement capital of the world—Palm Springs.

As frustrating as it is, I'm used to not being noticed by guys whose attention I'd be willing to kill for. In fact, I've almost learned to tolerate it. But I have to wonder if I'd be going through mid-life crisis at 30 if I were living in a less glamorous environment. Probably not. But I choose to live in West Hollywood because in a gay ghetto we homos are everywhere, and everything from the neighborhood church to the car wash serves double duty as a meat market. Thus, conforming to the typical West Hollywood lifestyle seems more sensible than moving to a farm in Iowa just to quell my self-esteem issues. The only way to really counter time—and gravity—and feel even remotely visible in Boys Town is to develop a thicker skin, harder pecs, and tighter abs.

The rational side of me, however, cringes at the vacuousness of it all and offers another suggestion: Instead of fixating on the exterior, I could dig deep into my soul, reflect on my enviable inner qualities, and find contentment within the twisted vortex of sex and muscle that permeates West Hollywood. Though that's an appealing idea, good character and solid morals apparently aren't as highly esteemed in these parts as a nice hard ass and baseball-sized biceps.

Before Father Time can wrap his nubby fingers any tighter around my throat, I decide that now is as good a time as ever to try to join the pack and spend every waking hour at the gym, aspiring to be Chi Chi LaRue's next discovery. So I pull out a credit card and join Gold's Gym Hollywood with the hope that in a few months I'll have a body that'll look absolutely fabulous in *anything* from International Male.

The beautiful, tanned god manning the Gold's counter tries to talk me into shelling out another $200 for an add-on membership for the on-site tanning salon.

"But isn't that kinda dangerous and unhealthy, baking in a human microwave?" I ask, slightly baffled. He nods over in the direction of the workout room.

"Look at them," he says, and draws my attention to two lusciously tanned hunks pumping up a few yards away. "You think they look 'unhealthy'?"

For a minute I feel like I'm back in high school and being pressured to buy into everything I know is wrong just to be a part of the popular crowd. It works. I plunk down the extra cash and kick-start my quest to join the popular, buff, and baked crowd.

The general population of the gym is composed of circuit queens, straight guys you'd give your right nut to get it on with, recognizable porn stars, and a few legit celebrities. There's more muscle in this room than on a full season of prime-time wrestling, and everyone is strikingly beautiful. And they all know it.

A bit intimidated by the competition, I wear oversized sweatshirts and sweatpants for the first few weeks of pumping iron. Though they're uncomfortable, the baggy clothes help to hide my waify-by-gay standards 170-pound frame, and the extra padding gives the illusion of bulk. Without the sweats I look like the "before" picture on the posters that advertise the many body-shaping programs the gym offers to transform average Joes like me into envied muscle Marys. I find motivation by reminding myself that with a good workout regimen, in a few months I'll have morphed into the "after" picture.

Hitting the gym regularly starts to pay off within two months. The gay guys at work have started playfully teasing me about my "big guns" the way horny straight boys harass secretaries with big boobs. I'm not complaining.

The flattering feedback inspires me to work out harder, because I crave the ego strokes. And after I get a solid workout routine in full swing—Mondays, Wednesdays, Fridays: chest, arms, and cardio; Tuesdays and Thursdays: back, shoulders, and legs—my self-esteem starts buzzing like the endorphins racing through my body. But that pink cloud dissolves rather quickly when I notice that the guys I see working out during the same 90 minutes I'm at the gym are gaining mass in record time, while I seem to be simply maintaining the few pounds of muscle I've acquired. I begin to suspect that they know something I don't—the number for a good steroid connection perhaps.

With steroids, a simple needle shot in the ass can turn any zero into a superhero in no time. Nowhere is that more evident than at this gym, where it's not uncommon to see an average Joe with a medium build mysteriously bulk up to twice his weight in a few weeks time. I figure if I can just get a good steroid connection, I can easily beef up to West Hollywood standards. However, at this stage of the game I'm not quite up to the fitness level required to infiltrate the gorgeous circuit boy clique and learn their secrets, so I set my sites on this short guy who has an absolutely porn-worthy body and a face to match. It takes a week or so of flirting, small talk, and dropping hints before I finally get him to open up about his workout "supplements." By the end of the week he gives me two phone numbers: his, and the number of his 'roid dealer. I immediately call the latter and toss the former.

The steroid dealer turns out to be a guy I'd seen in various muscle magazines. We meet at my place, where he shows up with a gym bag filled with various drugs and paraphernalia, including needles. Just seeing the needles makes me queasy, and I start to second-guess the situation. But one look at his physique and I'm sold on the idea that he is the all-knowing muscle guru who will take me to the next level in this twisted game of vanity and insecurity.

He suggests coupling two of the most popular steroids on the black market—the injectable Decca and Anadrol tablets. He collects $450 and then offers to give me my first injection so he can show me the proper procedure. A bit insecure about exposing my flat ass to this flawless muscle god, I opt for verbal instructions instead.

Later, once the Hulk has left, I anxiously pull out the goods and stare at the needles for what seems like hours before I actually get up the nerve to inject myself. My head swims in chaos as reason struggles with vanity. One side of my brain warns that it's not worth the risk and that injecting a needle into my body, for whatever reason, officially makes me a druggie. The vanity in me speaks louder than logic and reminds me that I'll forever remain that average Joe no one seems to take much notice of unless I'm willing to take some risks. Hell, what good is a healthy liver anyway if it's wrapped in a bland package?

"You have arrived," I mutter to myself as I take a deep breath and slowly push the long, thin needle into my fleshy butt check.

An hour later the Hulk rings me on my cell. "Oh, yeah, there are a few things I forgot to mention," he says. "You have to increase your eating pattern to every two to three hours a day; force yourself to eat twice what you're used to, because your muscles will be growing quicker and you'll need to keep up with the growth of mass. You'll retain water too. But don't let it freak you out; it'll eventually balance out. Also, because of the heavy increase of testosterone in your body, you'll be horny all the time, and you may experience angry mood swings. So you'll want to a have few joints on hand to help you chill out. And lastly, if you start to notice a breakout of acne on your ass and back, don't worry; it's a normal reaction to the drugs. Later."

Wow, side effects! Who would've thunk it? I assumed the fantasy boys from the gym merely shot a needle into their ass and faster than Superman can rip off his nerdy Clark

Kent disguise, they became superhuman muscle gods. But, no. This is going to take much more effort and is riskier than I thought. The whole point was to sculpt a body that's sexy enough to score my pick of hot men. But who's going to want to get with a horny pot head who has bloated up to Porky Pig proportions and has an ass that looks like it's in need of dermabrasion?!

I convince myself that a hot, ripped body will override everything else, and ass zits and all, it'll be worth it in the end. After all, from an outsider's perspective, the popular steroid queens at the gym seem to be handling the side effects just fine. So I continue with my cycle, injecting myself on schedule.

Within two weeks I start to notice a change—but not of the vascular kind. I conclude it's the overload of testosterone that caused me to create a scene at the supermarket when I was nearly nudged by a car pulling out of the parking lot. Enraged, I threatened someone who looked like the old woman from *Titanic*

HOTTEST SPORTS THAT WILL GET YOU LAID

BASKETBALL—But only if you're wearing 1970s tube socks and those short shorts.
BOXING—Hit me, Daddy! Hit me! *Hit me!*
RUGBY—Few sports make you look so butch (or so sexy in those silky shorts).
SOCCER—Again, we love those shorts (and David Beckham).
WATER POLO—Men fighting with one another in warm water while wearing Speedos...Yum!
WRESTLING—Tell us the singlet doesn't make you hard!
APRÈS SKI—Why not?
And anything requiring a jockstrap

that I'd kick her ass. I decide that whether I like it or not, I have to drop the steroids from my regimen and invest in some popular over-the-counter help instead.

Nine months, a dozen gallons of Creatine, 100 PowerBars, and 20,000 reps later I pick up a 250-pound dumbbell at the gym. His name is Doug. He's not the brightest bulb in the box, but he's certainly the hottest. I recognize him as the model I'd once seen on a flyer for some generic circuit party. He looks a little different without his arm above his head and licking his biceps, but I'm sure it's him. For months I had obsessed over him from afar—usually hiding behind a weight machine while I watched him bulk up between 3 and 4 every afternoon. He is one of them—a flawless, Beemer-driving, A-list queen with a body that deserves its own webcam site.

We're not yet five minutes into our first date—takeout protein shakes at his place—when

I notice that Mr. Perfect has a slight speech impediment. At first his beautiful blue eyes help me see past the tiny imperfection. But then I realize that his subtle stuttering isn't a result of some freaky fate but rather because he's apparently drunk or half-crocked on "tina" (also known by its less cutesy name, crystal methamphetamine).

My suspicions are reinforced when he asks me if I would like something to go with my protein drink as he opens a kitchen cupboard behind him. "I've got pot, coke, GHB, ecstasy, tina..." he announces proudly while waving his arm in front of his supply as if he's Vanna White on crack. His cupboard is better stocked than the prop cabinet on the set of *Valley of the Dolls*.

Not wanting to end up like the guys in *Trainspotting,* I make a crack about watching my figure and politely decline. I just shake my head and look at him while I wonder how he manages to keep himself looking so damn good if he's always smacked out. He must have deciphered the look on my face, because he answers my question without me having asked it.

"You know, this stuff is actually good for you—the GHB is a human growth hormone that gives you the strength to bulk up, while the tina helps you really focus on your workout and suppresses your appetite. Both help you get that 'cut up' look, turning you into lean, mean machine." I stifle a laugh as he flashes a stupid smile that shows the nicotine stains on his teeth. "And," he continues, "I'm always fully stocked should you need anything."

His pitch makes me wonder if this is a date or a staged infomercial for crackheads and body Nazis.

"This stuff will help you sculpt a bod that'll get you laid 24-7," he adds, hoping to seal the deal by using the sex angle. To prove his point, he hits the button on his answering machine. I stand by shell-shocked (and secretly a bit envious) as he listens to his phone messages.

Beep. "Hi Doug, it's Mike from last night. Fuck, man, that was hot. Let's do it again. Call me." Beep. "Hi Doug, it's Jeff. We met last night in the M4M4Sex chat room. Damn, you're a sexy mofo. Really liked topping you. Give me a call. I'm free again tonight." Beep. "Hey Doug-o, it's Kurt, the guy from the supermarket. Really had a good time last night. You wanna hook up again? Give me a ring." Beep... By the time he gets to his final message, I'm convinced the man is a walking petri dish of STDs.

I make a loud slurping noise with my straw, letting him know that I'm done with my protein drink and I'm through with the evening. He takes my hand and leads me toward the other room. "C'mere," he says softly before stopping me at the door to his bedroom, where he drops his shorts and underwear, then turns and flops on the bed, looking at me with a big smile on his face and playfully demanding that I come to him. As I stare at him naked and spread-eagled on the bed, that scene from *Animal House* plays in my

126

head, where the devil pops up on my right shoulder and demands, "Fuck him! Fuck him!" Then an angel appears on my left shoulder to offer reason: "He's a lost soul. Take pity instead of taking advantage of this pathetic situation."

I'm no saint, but I decline Doug's invitation. Looking at him lying there dazed and confused, with a dumb horny look on his face, I realize he would probably fuck a monkey right now if it happened to crawl into the room. I'm not flattered. In fact, it's a big blow, so to speak, to my self-esteem and not worth the risk of going home with a whole slew of STDs. So I leave him lying there naked and let myself out.

Torn between relief and regret, I cruise back home pondering the potentially steamy sex romp I could have had with the muddled mess of muscle I just left behind. There were times—before I actually met Doug—when I fantasized about how fabulous a life he must have: always being adored and envied because he's so hot and sexy and popular. I used to fantasize about the nasty vibe I'd revel in if he ever bothered to look my way. But that was months ago when I was still a mere mortal trying to fit in with the WeHo "in crowd" that ruled the playground in the gay ghetto. I put in a helluva lot of hard work at the gym, even risked ass acne and the destruction of my liver just for the hope that one day a fabulous guy like Doug would pay me some attention, and we'd drive off into the sunset in his fabulous SUV. Instead, I learn he's really just a great-looking jerk whose life revolves around drugs. I think I can do better than settle for a quick, hot lay with someone who probably wouldn't even remember my name the next morning.

It's at this point that I'm starting to understand from where the lofty "West Hollywood attitude" derives. It takes a lot of sweat, time, and determination to look fabulous, and somewhere along that route of transformation from average Joe to muscle god, your self-esteem can morph into outright vanity. Before you know it, you find yourself out of your league and begin overlooking some of the so-so guys that once caught your eye in the days when all the popular boys were ignoring you.

Since then I've become acclimated to my environment. I've worked hard to get my body past the point of the "average build," which is how I used to describe myself on my online profile. Now I'm "muscular and masculine." Guys notice me more now that I can fill out a tank top and look like I can bench press the old me, so why should I settle for "average" now that I can get the attention of the guys who once ignored me?

Now, walking down Santa Monica Boulevard, I stop in front of a coffeehouse to check out the posters in the window that advertise everything from circuit parties to gay underwear plays. Every ad has one element in common—the image of a tanned, near-naked Adonis with a toothy grin. More than a few of the models in the ads look familiar, maybe from the neighborhood or the gym. As I'm reading one of the circuit party posters, in my peripheral vision I notice someone is standing behind me, hoping I'll turn around and notice him. I can't check out the face because a poster interferes with his reflection. But I'm not in cruise mode at the moment any way, and frankly, my dating standards have changed. From what I can tell, the guy is not nearly as built as I like 'em, and he's a bit short for my tastes. But he won't go away—he's intent on waiting for me to turn around and at least say "hello" to him. It perturbs me a bit that this Joe Blow doesn't seem to be able to read body language and get the message that I'm not interested. When I turn to throw some shade and let him know I'd like to be left alone, I realize that there's no one there. I've just dissed my own reflection.

For a moment I stand there reconsidering that move to Iowa. Instead, I take another glance at my reflection and pull out my cell and arrange a follow-up "date" with Doug.

Getting the Bends

By Richard Andreoli

Yoga makes me hate everything.

I first realize this when Poser Girl arrives at my 7 P.M. stress release yoga class 10 minutes late. While everyone else focuses on strong *ujjai* breathing in downward facing dog pose, she enters with a dancer's elegance, air under her feet, and glides to the back of the room and the lone space beside me. She then whips off the brightly colored gypsy-woven fabric holding her sea-foam yoga mat in a tight role and *snaps* out her mat, *slaps* it down onto the hardwood floor, and *s-i-i-i-ghs* into her own off-tempo *ujjai* breath. She gracefully folds her torso until her breasts meet her knees, keenly aware of what her temple really requires, which isn't the ever-so-mundane positions everyone else came to class to practice.

None of this seems to bother our Earth Mother yoga teacher, who tells us to switch to warrior one position, and even though Poser Girl now joins in I'm so annoyed that I almost fall.

You're here to release stress, my "higher consciousness" reminds me. This is the same voice that warns me to stop drinking tequila shots before sickness ensues; I don't always listen to it, but at least it's there. *Forget her perfectly manicured nails,* it says, *her tights and athletic bra that match the gypsy-woven yoga mat tie. Ignore that after class she'll expose her sea-foam tie-die colored thong while climbing into a Range Rover that I'm sure she never paid for. Block out her Jimmy Choo sandals and her ugly feet, all crooked and caving down on one another like a series of collapsed buildings following an earthquake...*

Earth Mother delivers me from my higher consciousness rant with instructions for everyone to proceed through our warrior positions and into plough. I try staying in the moment but fail as soon as the 60-year-old woman in front of me lies on her back and effortlessly flips her legs over her head so that her toes land on my mat. Startled, I immediately look up, past her toenails (which could slice bread) and the dirty soles of her feet, right to her black unitard-covered butt, which is pointed at my face.

This reminds me that I really hate how "everyone is beautiful" in yoga. I mean, I love it in theory, and I really want to buy into it with all of my heart and soul, but I have this huge personal space issue, so yoga essentially destroys all of my beautiful intentions. I try using my third eye to see everyone as brilliant, glowing, spiritual creatures, but when you're in a packed class with barely enough space for you and your mat, and then you're faced with 60-

year-old butt, it's really difficult to (1) consider this "beautiful" and (2) not wonder what your mom has been up to lately.

But rather than continue to stare at this woman's backside (and feel strangely threatened yet simultaneously homesick), I throw my legs over my head and allow my own pelvis to block 60-year-old-mother-butt from sight. Unfortunately, my focus never returns as I now suddenly realize something very significant. You know that joke, "Why do dogs lick their balls?" And the answer is the uproarious, "Because they can"? Well, the humor, of course,

Top 10 Carbohydrates Gay Men Miss Most

1. Aerosol cheese—but Varla Jean Merman is trying to give it a comeback
2. Chicken and matzo ball soup—wait, nevermind. We don't miss that. *L'chaim!*
3. Fluffernutters—besides sounding like a job on a porn set, it's the ultimate decadent delight of peanut butter and marshmallow cream on white bread.
4. Hamburger Helper—and not just because their mascot is a little white examination glove
5. Hostess snacks—because we all love getting a little cream filling from our dessert
6. Krispy Kreme doughnuts—and not just because "cream" is in the name
7. Monte Cristo sandwich—ham, turkey, Swiss cheese, and mayonnaise on two thick slices of white bread, dipped in egg batter, deep fried until golden brown, and then sprinkled with powdered sugar and served with jam on the side…Excusemelneedtopukenow
8. Pizza—which is the only pie a gay man seriously enjoys diving into
9. Rice-A-Roni—because everyone likes a little San Francisco treat now and then
10. Rooty Tooty Fresh and Fruity—because aren't we all, just a little bit?

has to do with the fact that guys generally can't lick their own testicles. Oh, but we can! Because there they are, staring me in the face, a short tongue-flick away. And just then, while wondering if I'm free this coming Saturday night, Poser Girl farts as sharply, swiftly, and smartly as her entrance into the class.

Everyone holds their breath—not because of any odor, but because we're all afraid we'll spill into juvenile fits of laughter—when I am suddenly overcome by an irrational fear: What if everyone thinks it was me? I try looking around to give a knowing glance at anyone watching me, as if so say, "Can you believe her?" But the only things staring at me right now are my own nuts. Unable to do anything, I bubble in my own personal frustration stew.

Undaunted, Earth Mother moves us out of plough, I suppose so that there are no more bums angled into firing position, and tells us to lie on our backs and raise our hips up to form bridge. I consider chuckling so as to convince everyone that I'm an immature guy who laughs at normal bodily functions—and thus by extension proving that I am not the Gas Master—when suddenly a pocket of air becomes trapped between my back and the floor and I make a body fart that's louder than Poser Girl's bootie bomb!

Fan-fucking-tastic! There might have been a question as to who offered the first release, but everyone was listening for future eruptions, and one has undeniably escaped from me! Suddenly I'm "that guy," the person everyone laughs about over herbal tea following class. And even though my boxing teacher once explained that guys with well-defined, muscular backs often make these unintentional body farts, that ego stroke does nothing to assuage my current embarrassment.

I quickly try to recreate the noise, as if to say, "See! It was just air trapped between my mat and muscular back!" But as luck would have it, creating body farts intentionally is nigh impossible; instead, I just look like a fish floundering on the shore. Earth Mother switches positions again, this time to a shoulder stand, where one balances on his shoulders and neck with his legs straight up in the air and toes elegantly pointed skyward.

I try to raise my thighs, but between their weight and my shame I can't create any semblance of balance. I place my hands under my hips and try to prop up my lower body, but my breathing is off, I'm sweating, everything hurts, and I just know I look as pathetic as I feel. Then Earth Mother walks over, takes my legs in her small arms and with amazing power slides me into position with one fluid movement. She kneels in my personal space, commands me to "Breathe," and lets my heels rest lightly on her shoulders.

Before I can worry about whether or not my feet smell, I see it: Through her cream-colored tights her womanhood hovers above my cheek! This is the closest I've been to a vagina since I was born, and it's just sitting there looking at me like my nuts before. I wonder if I should introduce myself. Maybe invite her to dinner. Ask her if she'd like a drink, or if she smokes Camels.

All of my emotions, from fear and embarrassment to frustration and uncomfortableness suddenly cascade through my entire being! I blame Poser Farting Girl for this state of mind and imagine tripping her on the yoga studio steps so that she'll break a leg or arm or both and she won't be able to drive her gas-guzzling, environment-killing Range Rover. And as these twisted ideas flood my normally balanced mind I recognize that there is something inherently wrong about being in a place that should help one attain peace and tranquility, but instead makes anger and humiliation boil throughout all of my chakras.

"I didn't fart!" I want to yell. "It was her! It was Poser Farting Girl!" But before thoughts become words Earth Mother and her womanhood adjust me one more time, forcing my legs even higher. This makes no sense to me. How can she put my bare feet next to her face, allow my big sweaty thighs to rest against her body, and place herself in the line of fire when she undoubtedly assumes that I am the class Gas Master? Moreover, how can she do it all with such a calm, peaceful attitude while I'm on the verge of exploding? Is this woman even human?

Just then, Poser Farting Girl releases another small squeaky bootie prize.

Earth Mother gives me a look that says, "Can you believe her?" and I suddenly realize that Earth Mother is, indeed, quite human. The difference is that maybe she just understands something about this insane world that I haven't quite figured out yet. I guess that's why she's the Yogi, and I'm the student.

We smile at one another, and without any effort my anxieties melt away. I feel fantastic. She lets go of my legs, everyone assumes *savasana*—the corpse pose—and for the last 10 minutes of class I finally know peace.

Namaste.

Chapter 10: Liquor

You Don't Know Jack
By Parker Ray

I don't trust guys who don't drink. Well, I don't really trust guys in general because, well, I *am* one. But I *really* don't trust guys who don't drink. I also don't trust guys who don't cuss, but that's for another time.

I've dated three men who were in AA. The first relationship lasted six months, but he got upset when I went with him to a meeting to "show my support" and he didn't notice my breath smelled of scotch until we were already there and seated. I needed *something* to calm my nerves after the hellacious day I just had at work. And the thought of hearing a drag queen talk about his/her days of prostituting him/herself for a bottle of gin and painkillers but instead finding Jesus and AA and how every day was a struggle and "Why does my mother still hate me?" was *not* what I needed. But I'm a supportive boyfriend and had promised Jack (not his real name, but by far my favorite brand of whiskey) that I'd attend with him.

It hadn't dawned on me that I had done two shots of one of the more pungent liquors until I was in Jack's car. I hid it well enough, speaking toward the slightly open window instead of at Jack, hoping the Oban aroma would wear off by the time we got to our destination. At the meeting, though, his fellow antialcohol alcoholics noticed right away and acted as if I was mocking them. Okay, well I *was,* but only because at the last meeting Jack made me hold hands and say the Lord's Prayer with the rest of the group—even though he knows I can't stand religion. So I decided to get back at him. Petty? Sure. But I flirt by pissing guys off. Most of them love it, and it always makes for great make-up sex.

But not that night. Jack drove me back to my place in silence, even though we were supposed to go out to dinner. A week later we broke up. I actually did the breaking, partly because I knew he was going to do it sooner or later, and also because I missed sharing a bottle of wine with somebody over dinner. Besides, Jack just had a sketchy personality.

In fact, a lot of people in gay AA did. They either replaced one addiction (alcoholism) with three or four others that were somehow deemed less threatening (like smoking, or lots of sex, or insane amounts of coffee, or sugar products). The hypocrisy present at these meetings made me smile because, well, I'm a writer, and we writers like perverse situations that expose human behavior for what it is most of the time: an attempt to convince ourselves that we are in the right and that whatever issues we have can usually be traced back to *someone else*.

The second relationship lasted two months. Clay was sexy and rugged. He drove a truck. He was from Texas and had a hot Southern accent. He loved to get fucked and eat ass. He owned his own condo. Not a bad list of attributes, especially for LA. However, I was attracted to him for purely superficial and sexual reasons, and I didn't realize how much it bothered him that I drank on occasion (and by "on occasion," I mean almost daily). That is, until the day he flipped out because he could taste the Jack (Daniel's, not the ex-boyfriend from above) on my breath when he kissed me. I replied by saying I could taste the meat on his breath (I'm a vegetarian), but that I was dealing with it. He told me it wasn't the same thing. I suggested, in a diplomatic way, that we then go brush our teeth. He said that wasn't the point. I told him I had to go home, disappointed that I didn't get to fuck him one last time. (Damn, and he had a perfect ass. Damn, damn, damn!)

The third relationship lasted just three weeks. (See a pattern here?) I don't think I should even call it a relationship because, from our first conversation, Andy asked me if I thought I drank too much. "For being a writer, I don't drink enough," I joked. He didn't think it was funny. He kept trying to convince me I had a drinking problem. I went three weeks without drinking just to prove to him he had been brainwashed by AA to think that everybody who drank more than one drink a week was an alki.

After three weeks of no red wine or Jack and Cokes and lots of so-so sex and conversations about his gym routine and how he couldn't wait to go snowboarding in Aspen, I started reading *On The Road* (one of my favorite novels) for the umpteenth time, and another Jack (Kerouac) convinced me that my allegiance lay with finely distilled spirits rather than Andy's finely sculpted body. I agreed.

So now I only date guys who drink. I won't even consider a fella who doesn't drink because of the carbs. After Andy I had a fling with Ryan, who liked to take his drinks with him into the shower. The funny thing is, since I stopped dating "recovering" alcoholics, I drink a lot less myself.

My friend Jay and I joke about getting trashed a lot. He thinks 12 drinks in one night is par for the course. I have an almost-empty bottle of Smirnoff on my nightstand for minor shock value, because people always seem to comment on it even though it's seriously been at the same level for two years. Drinking has this almost romantic quality for me, not because I'm obsessed, but because it seems to piss so many people off when I dismiss this glorification as an ongoing joke on my part. Not that I don't care about the alcoholics—I have a handful of good friends who are in AA or who have stopped drinking of their own accord. But I *do* have a serious aversion toward people who've been completely zapped of humor about their situation, about their problems, about just being human.

Some random Friday night: Out at one of the local gay bars with Jay, enjoying my second round of Jack and Cokes. Jay is celebrating his graduation from his DUI class with a nice, big vodka martini. This time, however, he has learned his lesson and knows to crash on my couch instead of being stubborn and insisting on driving home to sleep in his own bed. Jay notices one of the guys from the AA class he was forced to attend standing 20 feet away. "That guy was always hitting on me," Jay says. "He had these really depressing stories to tell every single time, and then he thought I'd want to go out with him. I like my guys with some damage," Jay adds, "but I try to avoid the train wrecks."

"Funny, by gay AA standards, *we're* the train wrecks," I joked with Jay, who had to endure gay AA (doesn't it have a nice ring to it?) as part of his drinking-and-driving punishment.

Jay, who is a writer-romantic too when it comes to anything 40-proof, just looked at me, no expression, and replied, "AA is just another place for homos who have problems to meet other homos who have problems and compare to see who has it worse. Oh, and then to sleep with each other afterward because none of them seem capable of having a lasting relationship with people like us who just drink for fun."

Harsh. But could that be true? Do gay men, whether they are alcoholics, or meth queens, or sexaholics, really play up being a victim in an already victimized community just to get attention? Do they feel that by having it "worse" than somebody else that they can feel better about themselves? It's an interesting contradiction, but you just have to walk around a gay pride event to realize that our "brothers" and "sisters" are full of contradictions.

Okay, now I've got to fess up: I actually don't drink that much—no more than the average gay guy. In fact, if I get into working out for a period of time my body starts to reject excessive amounts alcohol, and I end up having only two or three drinks over the course of a night (when I go out). Why am I then trying to paint a picture of myself as Dorothy Parker incarnate? Perhaps because tragic behavior makes for a good read? No. Okay, maybe a *little*. But what I discovered between my boozy behavior when hanging with my friends and dating guys who were in AA is that many homos have a proclivity to make their issues more important than your issues. Maybe Jay was right.

Take coming-out stories. They permeate queer literature, and sooner or later, when you meet a new gay guy, tales of his "realization" in Podunk, Ark., while living with his military father and deeply religious mother always seem to be just *that* much more dramatic than the experience you just relayed to him. (That's the reason I always let people go first during those conversations. They tell me some huge sob story, and I go the opposite direction and tell them I had no major problems telling everybody I was a cocksucker. It's anticlimactic— and a great way to deflate their self-importance.) There's this hyper-one-upmanship among gay men. One, because we're men. Two, because we're gay. You go to the gym four times a week? I go five. You got 12 numbers at the club last night? That's great, although I snagged 14. Your boyfriend is a doctor? That's funny, mine's a CEO. There's all this competition swimming around us to have the biggest muscles, the coolest car, the best-designed house, the cutest adopted Vietnamese orphan, the perfect tan line—the list goes on. This competition is even more disturbing when it comes to who has the most miserable life story to tell.

Andy, gay AA boyfriend number 3, used to tell me how, when he drank, he would have sex (with *really* hot guys, obviously) in back alleys or other questionable environments. He was almost bragging about it, like the one time he got his ass eaten out behind a dumpster in West Hollywood. *Great,* I'm thinking, *and he imagines I'll want to have sex with him after he's told me that because...?*

Clay, GAAB 2, informed me after a week that he had been sexually abused (albeit by a *really* hot guy) when he was ten. It was like Alcoholics Anonymous had taught him that the only way to remain on the wagon was not to be anonymous at all. You've got to constantly remind yourself of everything bad in your life, because *that's* the reason for your drinking.

Wear your fucked-up encounters like a badge, because only through constant reminders that you're an addict and that you're barely scraping by in life will you be a better person.

Right. No wonder I drank before I went to AA meetings with GAAB 1.

The truth is that when I was growing up in San Francisco I started drinking at 13. At first it was a beer or four over the course of a weekend, but by freshman year in high school, I was a bona fide drunk. Nobody really caught on because I got straight A's (maybe a sign of things to come? AA?) and that was the time that grunge and the whole "let's wear only black clothes" era was ushered in, so my depressive behavior was interpreted as me trying to be cool and "alternative."

During that time I became friends with some on-the-fringe people, and one of my best friends (and, now, looking back on it, probably the first guy I was in love with) was a teenage prostitute with a taste for heroin. Sweet thing was, he would never let me touch the stuff. He just kept me drunk every time we hung out, and never shot up around me. For a guy who got kicked out of his house at 14 and who sold his body to Castro queens who, later, voted against a gay youth shelter in their neighborhood because they thought it would bring property values down, Patrick was usually in good spirits. (Only later would I find out that he was also HIV-positive, something else he dealt with rather calmly.)

When Patrick overdosed in front of me when I was 15, I stopped drinking and went into withdrawal. I was able to keep my situation from my parents, but you could tell something had changed when my running times (I was on the cross-country and track teams at my high school) improved so drastically that I was put on the varsity teams. All of the energy I had poured into drinking I started putting into 12-mile Sunday morning runs in the hills.

I finished high school at the top of my class. I didn't even look at a Jack bottle again until the end of my first year at college, when I started drinking moderately again.

When I stopped drinking at 15, I went to some AA meetings. I was already depressed enough with Patrick slipping away so suddenly—not to mention the thoughts of never again being able to avoid my problems with some vodka shots—and the AA meetings totally turned me off. The ones I went to weren't specifically gay, and since this was also something I was dealing with at the time, I really couldn't relate to many of the stories I heard. Plus, I think I was the youngest person in the room by almost seven years. You know, maybe that was the problem. Maybe I was too young at the time to really see the benefits of AA. It has saved lots of lives, but at those initial meetings I couldn't help but focus on how touchy-feely everybody was. I just wanted to keep to myself and "get better," while everybody else was trying to bond (through their tales of misery) and make friends with people in the same boat. I wasn't in the same boat; I was a sophomore in high school. And when I went to my first specifically queer AA meetings in college, of course I couldn't help but focus on the guys hitting on me. Or, maybe—and this is being optimistic—they just wanted to be friends.

I've been told by a few people in AA that I'm not really an alcoholic—that because I can keep my drinking to one or two nights a week and only sip on the sauce in social situations (er, *most* of the time), I can't be a part of their little group. I have morbid tales to tell, for sure, but I'd rather focus on what's going right in my life. And when I do tell my drinking tales, many of which parallel the drawn-out dramas that I've heard in AA meetings, I can't help but find them humorous.

I know I'm supposed to be "anonymous" and all that, but, really, I'm tired of hiding. Hi, my name is Parker, and I'm an alcoholic. Hi, my name is Parker, and I've never had a good experience in AA. Hi, my name is Parker, and I've had to learn to keep my drinking in check on my own. Hi, my name is Parker, and I'm bored with gay guys (*especially* gay guys) who always want to have cockfights about their issues and problems. Hi, my name is Parker, and I'm tired of writing about my past and I want to focus on how lucky I am not to have let my drinking get the better of me.

Jesus, do you think I'm in denial?

For Guys Who Aren't Boozers...Queer Coffee 101

Want to know how to decipher that cryptic café menu? Looking for a few tips on how to approach that delicious hunk at your favorite coffeehouse? For sober studs or fearless fags who like meeting men outside of the bars, the Goddess Kaffeina has whipped up a quick guide to the types, tastes, and traits of this famous brewed beverage and the men who drink it.

Coffee

This is the brewed stuff. You can make coffee in a variety of ways: old fashioned percolator, conventional drip, French press, or a myriad of interesting methods demonstrated around the world. A no-nonsense, butch drink when taken black. You can learn a lot about a man by watching the kinds of accoutrements he requires for this timeless classic: Is he sweet and creamy or dark and bold? Is he going low-carb and fat free (body fag) or indulging in something a little naughty (free spirit)?

Espresso

The true espresso requires special machinery and finely ground, dark roast beans. The apparatus takes compressed espresso grounds, shoots boiling water across the grounds, which expands them, and presses out only the oils and a small amount of water into the espresso cup. The final product should have a creamy, brown surface and be slightly less than 1/4 cup of liquid. This is the art of coffee reduced to its exquisite essence. The more shots of espresso you take, the butcher you are. Three shots or more and they'll call you Daddy (and possibly an ambulance)!

Cappuccino

This beverage was developed in Italy. It is one shot of espresso with a cap of foam on top and a drizzling of steamed milk in the cup. When more milk is added to a cappuccino in a larger cup, it becomes a latté. The amount of milk involved is directly proportional to the swish in his stride. Milk is the perfect buffer for the higher acidity of poor quality coffees, so this is your best bet if you're abducted by a corporate coffee conglomerate and forced to place an order.

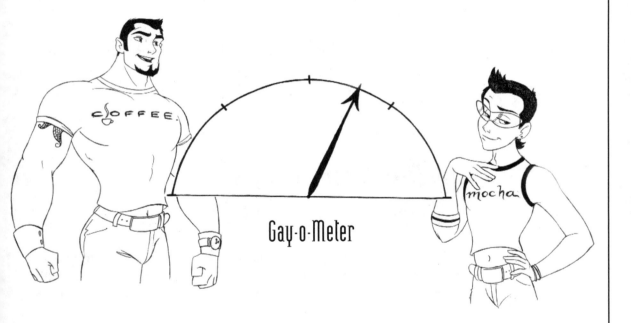

Gay-o-Meter

Café au lait

A French coffee-based drink that contains half coffee and half steamed or hot milk. Could this 50-50 combination be his way of telling you that he goes both ways? Listen carefully for how much emphasis he puts on the *lait* and whether he's looking at you when he says it!

Mocha

The café mocha, the most commonly misunderstood beverage, is simply this: one shot of espresso, steamed or hot chocolate milk, and whipped cream on top if desired. Go directly to nelly, do not pass go! The bigger the whipped cream cone on top, the bigger the tiara. Truly the sassiest drink there is for quenching your inner queen.

That covers the basics. Everything else on a café menu reflects variations in ingredients such as additional shots of espresso, flavored syrups, different types of chocolates, and the final presentation of the beverage. So, while fancy names are fun, know what you like and why. That way you'll be able to order that beverage anywhere in the world.

Remember the stronger the coffee, the more exaggerated your masculine traits. The more additives there are, the higher the reading on the gayometer.

The Goddess Kaffeina is **Laura K. Sutherland**, and she was the first person our editor, Richard Andreoli, came out to. She and her wife, Bonnie Margay Burke, with whom Richard went to high school, made this handy guide for your enjoyment. You can contact them for coffee and love at goddesskaffeina@cox.net.

For Guys Who Do Sample the Sauce... Cocktails 101

The drink a man orders can often tell you a great deal about him, but by the same token what you order will tell everyone else who you are, so know your cocktail! Here's a list of the basic drinks every fag should know when in a bar or hosting a party.

Beer

The type of beer one orders is always open to interpretation. Some think Budweiser is white-trashy, while high-maintenance wannabe artists prefer lagers and microbrews. The bottom line? Go with what you enjoy. First helpful hint: hold the bottle by the neck so your hand doesn't warm up the beverage. Second helpful hint: Nervous drinkers who continually need to sip on something in social situations should order a brown bottled beer so that no one knows if it's empty. This way you can have your action without going broke or getting drunk too quickly.

Martinis

Martinis are so gay and we're all guilty of ordering them, so turn that frown upside down and get plastered! Bars that sell martinis usually offer a menu explaining what's inside that pretty little glass. Go with what sounds yummy, or try one of these classics:

Cosmopolitan—4 parts Citron vodka, 2 parts Cointreau or triple sec, 1 part lime juice, 2 parts cranberry juice. (All I ever hear is, "Cosmo! Cosmo! *Cosmo!*")

Dry vodka (or gin) martini—Vodka (or gin), dash of dry vermouth (if that), olive garnish. (If you ask for it stirred, the bartender has permission to bitch-slap you.)

Apple martini—1 part vodka, 2 parts sour apple schnapps, 1 splash sweet and sour mix. Reverse the amounts of vodka and schnapps if you like it stronger. (My, what a pretty drink you have, my Queen!)

Tang-tini—2 parts vodka, 1 tablespoon Tang, 2 parts water. (Perfect for camping! The new taste sensation that's sweeping the Nation!)

Stupid College Drinks

This is the shit you first drink in life because (1) most don't taste like booze, (2) you remember someone ordering them at a wedding once, and (3) you're stupid and haven't gotten alcohol poisoning yet. Don't order these. Everyone will make fun of you.

Long Island Iced Tea—Gin, rum, tequila, vodka, triple sec, sweet and sour mix and cola. (Lock up the trailer, honey, we're drinkin' fancy tonight!)

Sex on the Beach—Vodka, cranberry juice, pineapple juice and peach schnapps. (Hi, sorority girl on spring break!)

Whisky Sour—Whisky, lemon juice, sugar and a maraschino cherry. (Thanks, Nana...)

Manhattan—Rye/whiskey, sweet vermouth. (Thanks, Grandpa...)

Amaretto Sour—Amaretto, fresh lemon juice, and a maraschino cherry. (Chat, chat, chat—oh, *girl!*)

Fruity Drinks

Cousins to the martini, you order these fun frothy concoctions when in Hawaii, by a pool in Las Vegas, or while being wooed by a Daddy in Palm Springs or Fort Lauderdale. You may only get away with ordering them if your friends join you.

Daquiri—Rum, lime juice, and frozen fruit mixer. (Welcome to Fantasy Island!)

Mai Tai—Light rum, dark rum, and pineapple juice. (Charo and the men who love her)

Margarita—Tequila, sweet and sour mix, or fresh fruit mixer. (On the rocks = *Papi*; blended = *Sí, Papi*.)

Rum Drinks

Mojito—Light rum, crushed fresh mint leaves, lime, and soda. (If he really enjoys it = Brad Pitt; if he's faking it = Ryan Seacrest)
Rum and Coke—The name is the recipe. (Mr. Brady, God bless his soul, on a closeted night out in West Hollywood)

Vodka Drinks
    Rumor has it that the better the vodka, the weaker the hangover; likewise, the better the vodka the classier you appear. Start out the evening asking specifically for Absolut, Ketel One, Grey Goose, or Stolichnaya, and if your money runs low, move on to the house swill.

Cape Cod—Vodka and cranberry juice. No one actually calls it a Cape Cod unless they're uptight or pretentious; vary your options with flavored vodkas like apple, mandarin, or citron. (International gay drink of choice: *Queer as Folk*)
Vodka tonic—With a lime. (Runner up for international gay drink: Will Truman)
Madras—Vodka, cranberry juice, and a splash of orange juice. (Summer in a glass: Jack McFarland)
Vodka and Red Bull—The name is the recipe. (Circuit queens and boys looking for a little kick. Insert any porn star's name here:_____.)
Bloody Mary—Vodka, tomato juice, lemon juice, 7 drops Worcestershire sauce, 3 drops Tabasco sauce, freshly ground lemon pepper, 1 dash celery salt, and fresh dill weed. (It takes so fucking long to make—no wonder you need to be hung over to enjoy it!)
Screwdriver—Vodka and orange juice. (Yawn: Billy Crystal as Jodie Dallas in *Soap*)
Greyhound—Vodka and grapefruit juice. (For gray-haired queens: Uncle Arthur)
Seabreeze—Vodka, cranberry juice, and grapefruit. (1980s closeted Chippendales models)

Chapter II: Club Culture

One-Night Affair
By Smith Galtney

It's sometime in the mid '90s in New York City on a Saturday night. Well, technically, it's Sunday morning, anywhere between 3 and 4 A.M. I've just slipped in the backseat of a taxi cab, and told to the driver, "27th between 10th and 11th," the block where a gay club is located. The name of the club is Sound Factory. It's the best club that ever existed. Period. At least that's what I think.

Traffic is light, but we're still not moving fast enough, because I want to arrive *now*. My stomach is knotting itself into a pretzel, partly because of excitement, but mostly because of the hit of ecstasy I took 10 minutes before leaving my apartment. I have two more hits on me, and a vial of Special K. The vial has one of those screw-on bump dispensers, for easy and discreet use. Both the X and the K are stuffed inside a Zip-Lock bag, which itself has been balled up and stuffed into the nether regions of my underwear. That way, the security guards won't come across them when they search me. Or at least I hope they won't.

In my real pockets are other essentials: lots of cash in case I need to buy more drugs; chewing gum so my chemically aggravated jaw will have something to gnash on; and sunglasses to help my eyes take in that harsh Sunday afternoon sun on the long journey back home. I am freshly cologned and deodorized. The gel in my hair is still glistening, and I'm wearing the same damn thing I wear every weekend: a T-shirt, jeans and sneakers. Because once the DJ spins the last song, and I have danced my last dance, I will be a damp, disgusting mess in need of a hot shower and a rigorous tooth brushing.

The truth is, I have been preparing *all week* for tonight. I've made countless phone calls, finding out which dealers are currently holding what drugs. I've gone to the gym. I've gotten a haircut. I've cleaned my apartment. (Who wants to come down in a pig sty?) I've taken a disco nap. I've spent an exorbitant amount of time cracking open one of those little ketamine bottles. Then I poured its contents out onto a Pyrex dish and waited 24 hours for it to dry, so I could chop and grind the crystallized residue into a fine white powder. After all that—*voila!*—my Special K was ready for bumping and hoarding.

Now it's tucked safely between my legs, and the moment I've been hungering for is getting closer and closer. Like a hopped-up housewife, I want everything about tonight to be nothing less than *perfect*. I want the ecstasy to be fantastic. I want the music to be phenomenal. And I want to get caught up in a one-night love affair, preferably with a man who looks like Ed Harris, only taller. Great drugs and great music would be incredible—two out of three ain't bad, as the old saying goes. But great drugs and great music *and* great sex would add up to the greatest night of my entire life.

I *just* need to *get* to the *fucking* club! That's why my heart feels like it's skipping beats, why my stomach feels like butterflies on a roller coaster. Only it couldn't be on a roller coaster because this cab is moving *too fucking slow!*

Okay, we're turning onto 27th Street. Calm down. Deep breath.

I see an anxious cluster of people outside the entrance to a pale warehouse. But it still feels like an eternity before I'll get inside. For starters, you've got to get past the doorman. Then there's the coat check line, which, given it's the middle of February, is sure to be long as fuck. I step out of the cab—careful not to get too near the hookers lingering in the shadows, who could swipe your wallet without even laying a finger on you—and make my way to the building. Inside its cement walls, music is banging so loudly you'd think the entire structure was ready to collapse.

At the entrance, tall, intimidating figures in jeans and dark blazers stand motionless, unblinking in front of a velvet rope. Inside those ropes are wispier, bon vivant types with arty eyeglasses and short, bleached hair who smile (sometimes) and unhook the rope, admitting 10 wide-eyed, gum-gnashing customers at a time.

I walk past all this and make my way to the end of the line, which is almost at the end of the block. Halfway down, however, I bump into some faces I know—if only I knew their names too—who are gracious enough to pretend as if they're saving me a place in line. Our conversation is completely generic, since everyone waiting in line is basically having it, too:

"I hope tonight's gonna be good."

"I know."

"Were you here last week?"

"No. How was it?"

"Oh, my God, a-*may*-zing. We didn't get outta here until 4 in the fucking afternoon."

"Damn! You're supposed to tell me it sucked."

"It was spiritual. I shit you not."

"Alright, stop it! I don't want to hear anymore."

Top 14 Rules for the Dance Floor

1. Don't compare yourself to anyone else.
2. Just because you want to be groped on the dance floor, or you want to grope that other guy, doesn't mean he (or his boyfriend) wants you up in his business. Don't start dippin' until you know the flavor of the Kool-Aid.
3. Don't start flinging water around even if Pepper MaShay invites you to dive into the pool.
4. You might think this is a magical or spiritual moment, but some of us are just having fun, so don't start talking about Jesus.
5. Stop all the jibber-jabber unless the guy is actually responding to you; otherwise, he wants to be left alone.
6. If you need to smoke, fart, or burp that garlic chicken you had for dinner, go outside.
7. If you do fart on the dance floor, don't start swinging your hips faster; it won't make anything blow away.
8. Wax your back completely. Stubble burns.
9. Wear deodorant, unless you're at a leather event.
10. When creating the "human screen," dance closer to the person holding the party favors, but don't stare at him. Remember: Security's sober and they're watching.
11. Taking pictures on the dance floor is fun for you, but not everyone else who wasn't expecting that flash. Use your cameras in moderation, and be warned: The later it is in the evening, the greater the chance that you'll just look pale, sweaty, and cracked out.
12. Listen to your Mamma! Say "Excuse me" and "Sorry" when you bump into people. Besides being polite, you never know when a cutie might want to stop and talk.
13. Tell a guy what's in your bullet before he uses it.
14. Don't share party favors with the first guy you meet; men are a dime a dozen, but finding K at a party can be a bitch!

"Do you know where I can get any K?"

Fights often erupt outside of this club. From time to time straight guys who can't get in pull guns on the doormen, who, in order to ensure peace on the dance floor, keep a strict policy: If you aren't gay, you have to arrive with someone who is. The doorman knows we're gay because we've been coming to the place for years at this point. Plus, we know the easiest way to get in, which is to draw as little attention to ourselves as possible. Just find a place in line and politely wait your turn until the clipboard-holding bon vivant—who usu-

You Know You've Gone to Too Many Circuit Parties When...

1. You try to keep the beat on any water bottle you pick up.
2. Driving home feels like you're inside a videogame.
3. Security knows your name, you're on everyone's guest list, and promoters celebrate your birthday at their events.
4. You grin whenever you see a commercial for *E! News.*
5. Club friends say, "She's been around forever," when they introduce you to new people.
6. You're dead-set against drinking alcohol because of the carbs and how it makes you feel the next morning, but you've got no problem with snorting a powder that may or may not be a horse tranquilizer.
7. You start believing yourself when you tell others, "Not everyone there is high..." or "It's more like a spiritual experience..."
8. You'll pay $50 for a party you might not even go to, and $50 for something that might be aspirin or Snowy Bleach, but you make a point of refilling your water bottle in the bathroom rather than pay $5 for a new one.
9. You can stand in front of a 12,000-watt speaker for an hour and love every minute.
10. You've partied, driven home, and screwed the same muscle stud four times and you still don't know his first name, much less his last.
11. You have different-colored bullets to match your outfits.
12. You run into Jim J. Bullock.

ally has a name like Derek or Darrell or Hamlet—waves you past the ropes. Like he's doing now, smiling and saying, "Have a good one, fellas."

Once inside, the dim, washed-out lights of the street give way to the moody red, blue and green gels that light the entrance lobby. No longer muffled and caged-in, the music now delivers a trebly, top-heavy jolt. Over clattering high-hats and rib-rattling kick drums, I can make out voices singing things like "Turn it up, turn it up, turn it up! In the mix," and "House is a feeling!" Then there are the noises not coming from the sound system, but from the dance floor itself: high-pitched whistles; screams of ecstasy, passion and pain; and a cacophony of clapping and stomping, as if someone ditched their sneakers for clogs.

In the warmer months I could just rush out and join in the jubilance. But I've got to check my coat—a necessity that seems like it will take an eternity, thanks to the fact that my E is kicking in something fierce now, making the music feel like both an aphrodisiac and itching powder. Everybody is stripping off hats, gloves, scarves, ski coats and polar fleeces—down to a T-shirt, or a tank top, or no top at all. Once again, the sheer beauty of men strikes me: their shoulders, jawbones, lips, smiles, sideburns, biceps, and torsos. And once again, I'm struck by how some of these men—the ones who have bodies like inmates—speak with lisps so thick and piercing you'd think you were standing in a garden full of gay snakes.

Once my coat is checked, I head for the industrial ramp that slowly descends into the club's main space. Halfway down, you have two choices: Keep going straight to get to the dance floor. Or make a left to arrive in the lounge. I choose the lounge because (1) it's not quite time to dance yet, and (2) I need to check in with my friends.

The first ones I see are Jerry and Fred. Jerry looks totally and utterly adorable, like a cross between a white frat boy and a Little Rascal. Fred is taller, with light-brown skin and a spotless smile that makes the club that much brighter. Actually, I want to sleep with them both, but that would be scandalous because Jerry and Fred are something like my gay parents. They took me out to my first gay bar, introduced me to my first gay friends, brought me to this place for the first time, handed me my first hit of ecstasy. Without them, I'd still be doing the same old bong hits in the same old NYU dorm room and hanging with the same old straight friends in the same old dive bars. Befriending them has been like slipping into a parallel universe where the men are eye-poppingly beautiful and call each other "she," and the straight women are rugged—handsome, even—and chase guys the way guys chase girls. Black culture is the end-all and be-all of cool. In Jerry and Fred's world—which is the world inside this nightclub—white boys do their best to undermine their whiteness, either by sleeping with as many black and Latino studs as possible, or just by using the right phrases at the right time.

It's a language I've only recently learned to translate.

"What's up, Miss Thing?" Jerry says. ("Hello, Mr. Smarty Pants.")

"You better work," says Fred. ("Well, look at *you*.")

"How's the music so far?" I ask.

"Oh, it's *fierce*," they respond in near-unison. "She's *completely* turning." ("It's incredible. The DJ is doing a fantastic job.")

We hug each other over and over again, and with each embrace, the ecstasy seems to sink further into my bloodstream—making their arms feel like French ticklers, and their bodies like a second skin. These sensations are like news bulletins, announcing, *"The ecstasy has arrived!"* Trying to fit my white-as-chalk Southern self into this flamboyantly brave new world, I normally feel like a rice cake in a display case full of rainbow-sprinkled jelly donuts. But with the X in full effect, I feel fabulous with a capital *U*. I start working the room, saying hello to Jimmy, who calls himself "Mother Girl," and our friend Peaches, who let me grope her breasts one night, just cause I told her I'd never felt them before (not just her boobs, but *any* boobs, really). I blow kisses to Michael, Brian, Harold, Jeff, Samantha, and Jezebel, our drug dealer, who always shows up wearing a cowboy hat, boots, and a holster with two cap guns.

I also say hello to Angie, Jose, and Luis Xtravaganza. Angie is the mother of the House of Xtravaganza, and Jose and Luis are two of her most famous children, having both been featured as dancers in Madonna's "Vogue" video, as well as on her Blond Ambition tour. Madonna discovered them dancing here at this club, and this is where the entire house holds court every weekend. I knew of this house long before I ever met them in person. I saw them a year before I came out of the closet, vogueing in the popular documentary *Paris Is Burning.* Back then, that movie might as well have been about people on Mars.

But now I'm washing down that second hit of E with a swig from my water bottle. The drugs are great and will only feel better. The music sounds flawless. In fact, Mother Girl just said the DJ, Junior Vasquez, is going to debut his new Madonna remix. He's even going to keep playing until late, late in the afternoon. Yes, it's already looking to be a night to remember, even though it's already morning outside. I pity the poor, clueless souls who, right now, are picking up the Sunday *Times,* or heading to church. I mean, who needs church when we've got this place, where I feel so high, so mighty, and so omnipotent? I hope I never come down.

At this point it's time to hit the dance floor. So it's down to the end of the ramp, where I feel like I'm moving through Emerald City—the main space is a large, dark, square yet somehow cavernous room marked by high ceilings and several rows of support beams. Four monolithic speaker towers rise from each corner of the dance floor. Hanging in the middle of the room is the biggest, brightest disco ball you ever did see, splitting the lights into a million tiny, Technicolor specks that whiz across the walls. Some weekends those walls look black; tonight they look white. But the room never smells of freshly dried paint. Just of dry ice, sweat, and pot smoke: a cross between a gymnasium and a crack den.

Amid all the fog and flashing lights, all I see as I step on the dance floor are disembodied limbs reaching heavenward, smiles without faces, torsos without legs—everything gyrating to the same rhythm, everything in tune to the same melody. The strangers next to me are feeling the exact same thing I am, and therefore they aren't really strangers any more. This sense of communion is turning me on big time, and I actually feel the beginnings of a hard-on in my jeans.

Suddenly, the smoke clears and it's easier to see who I'm dancing with. There's a tall, lanky African-American man who's whipping his dreadlocks this way and that and stomping his feet to the beat. (So *he's* the one wearing clogs.) There's a circle of women working that jeans-and-bra combo. There's an Asian gentleman with a dark, menacing look in his eyes, like his drugs might not be agreeing with him. There's also a...a...wait a minute. There's a guy who looks just like Ed Harris, only taller. He's got his shirt off, and his chest is perfectly hairy, and his dirty blond hair is thinning, and—holy shit! He's looking right at me! Oh, my God, he's moving closer. And closer!

"Hey!" he shouts. Since the music is so loud, we talk right into each other's ears. So close that it already feels like we're making out.

"Hi!" I shout back. "What's your name?"

"Mark. Are you having fun tonight?"

"You bet."

"Are you in it for the long haul?"

"Until the last song, baby."

"Me too."

"Good."

"Good."

Then, with one hand, he gently rubs my stomach with the back of his fingers, his blue eyes staring straight into mine. That's all the courtship either of us needs, really, so we start kissing—soft pecks on the lips for a few seconds, immediately followed by long, deep tongue action. That's when Madonna's voice starts to creep through the mix— "Something's coming over...Mmm-hmmm, something's coming over!"—and the place goes absolutely fucking nuts. Everyone's nudging each other and squealing: "This is the new Madonna single! The new Madonna single!"

We both laugh.

"I guess it's the new Madonna single!" Mark says with a chuckle, before hugging me and burying my face in his hot-ass collarbone. I huff his manly scent—all sweat and Speed Stick—and the music fills my ears. The bass massages my bones, the X makes my eyes feel as if they're rolling back inside my head. And it becomes official: This is the greatest night of my life.

Epilogue

I didn't know that was going to be the last night Sound Factory was open. All I knew was that I left the club, said goodbye to Mark, and went home-only to hear word on Monday that I'd witnessed the club's last hurrah. Thanks to any number of rumors—pressure from community boards or shady tactics from rival venues—the club that I considered the greatest ever was now a thing of the past.

As for Mark, we got together once afterward. In more intimate quarters, it was obvious we didn't have much to talk about. His kisses only felt half as good without the X, and in broad daylight he didn't look much like Ed Harris.

Sure, I kept going out, and I tried to keep the disco flame burning. Junior Vasquez got other jobs spinning at other clubs; I followed him to spaces like the Tunnel, the Palladium, and Twilo. Sound Factory even reopened in a new location, but the nightlife I once knew in the original space began a slow and certain fade to gray. Things either weren't the same in other clubs, or they hadn't changed enough—even the greatest nights of my life started to reek of déjà vu. I'd done all the drugs, seen all the crazy outfits, even heard all the music-most of it was just the same ol' head-pounding house beats tacked on to a new Madonna single.

Next thing you know, I'd turned into one of those wizened disco bunnies—the really surly kind who go off about "the good old days." And I hadn't even turned 30 yet! Newer, younger friends took me out here and there. While they were feeling it on the dance floor, I was standing on the sidelines with my arms folded. "You guys think *this* is fierce? You should have been at Sound Factory!" I'd become just like all the old queens I met at the Factory who waxed nostalgic about the Paradise Garage, the disco that had ruled New York before it. Andrew Holleran, author of the classic gay novel *Dancer from the Dance*, described a disco in the early 70s with one simple sentence: "There was never anything before or since so wonderful."

Exactly.

Today, at the geriatric age of 33, I confess that the only Factory friends I keep in regular contact with are Jerry and Fred-they're still my gay parents and they always will be. As for what other bit players such as Mother Girl, Peaches, and Jezebel are currently up to, your guess is as good as mine. I often spot a familiar face in a restaurant, or on the subway, or passing on the street. *See that guy in the Armani suit? The one toting the briefcase? Every Saturday night, he used to gyrate with a friend on a pedestal, and both of them wore little more than thongs and sneakers.* Sometimes we'll catch each other's eye, as if to say, "Yeah, I remember. I was there." Then we go our separate ways, each of us feeling a little older, a little wiser, and happy to be alive. (Angie Xtravagnza, rest her soul, is but one of the many Factory denizens who have since left this world.)

But no matter how many years pass, or how fuzzy our best memories grow, one thing never fails to take us back: the music. Reminiscing on the early '70s, Holleran wrote, "Any memory of those days is nothing but a string of songs." Likewise, all I have to do is hear "The Pressure" by Sounds of Blackness or CeCe Peniston's "Finally" or "Gypsy Woman" by Crystal Waters, and it's the early 90s all over again: Bill Clinton's running for office, Madonna still has a gold tooth, and I can still count the times I've done X on one hand. Suddenly, my friends and I are dancing, singing, screaming and carrying on. Just like back in the day. Only we don't have to wait in long-ass coat-check lines or stash drugs in our underwear.

Kevin Aviance Tells All!

© David Morgan

Kevin Aviance on Performing

I always fall down because I'm always doing spins and stuff. But I never censor myself, so it's like spin-spin-spin-spin-spin and land wherever I'm gonna land. One time I saw this puddle and I thought, *Jump over it!* But I hit it and flew off the stage! Needless to say, they had to take me to the back, and I was kind of unconscious for a while. Another night I was "having a moment"—How should I say?—an intoxicated moment, and I walked completely off the stage. Walked on and walked completely off. I got back up, though, because I never stop doing what I'm doing.

Kevin Aviance on the Limelight in New York

The Limelight brought you drama. Really obscure stuff. Everyone was in costume, whether it was ugly or pretty or whatever. This was the place to wear a costume. I should say *wardrobe*. We don't wear costumes here in New York.

I think one of the funniest things I've ever seen at the Limelight was a butt-naked old man with a saddle on his back. A crazy night was the Blood Bath party, which was like a massive, murder masquerade party. Scenes of murder and death. Blood grosses me out, and I was at the party, and I couldn't believe these kids. They looked really great, all massacred and stuff. That was really weird for me.

Kevin Aviance on Tokyo clubs

Tokyo is just amazing. They do all the American stuff—the hip-hop and the Afros with the gold earrings and bracelets—but they're Japanese. And the drag queens are hilarious! This one child did "Jingle Bells" like Barbara Streisand while making Christmas cookies onstage. She had a whole thing of eggs and suddenly threw them out into the audience. Of course they were fake, but everyone was screaming!

Kevin Aviance's Language Lesson

There are so many languages in the club culture. I call it Queen's English, and you can totally talk about somebody to their face, and they will never know what you're talking about. But they will think they're in your conversation.

"*Ovah!*" means absolutely amazing. (She's *ovah!* She's just fabulous. She's the top.)
"Rick-Rack" is something handmade, like it was put together and you don't really think about it. It looks good, but you don't get into it.
"Miss Thang" is for everybody; everybody's Miss Thang. Man, woman, cat, dog.
"One of the children." A hot fag.
"Trade" is a hot guy who's straight or straight-acting or you don't know what his deal is.
"Homothug" is a hot black guy who's gay but very masculine.
"Fotch" is your business. (Get out of her fotch!)
"Carter" is face. (Her carter is lo-o-ovely!)
"Gilda" is a wig. (Darling, her carter and her gilda are *tired!*)
"REALLY!" is for someone you wish to dismiss—it's all about how you say it. If someone's talking to you, and you're not paying them any attention, you just say, "REALLY?" Meaning: You're boring the fuck out of me.

If somebody's tired, if you're over them, or you're simply *through,* it's all about the emphasis.
Grit your teeth together and say, "*Tired!*" (She's *tired!*)
Or use the expression, "I'm not having it!"
Or simply, "*Not!*"
Or shake your head and say "Uh-uh" and click your tongue.
Or say, "Ooh, she's a one." Meaning, she's a number 1, as opposed to a number 10.

Kevin Aviance on Drugs

People have to realize something: Not everyone's messed up and high and not everyone's carrying on. But the fact of the matter is clubs, music, all that drama are the ingredients for a good time. A girl has just one night off, she wants to go out and party and have a good time, and so she does whatever it takes to relax her, and you're really not supposed to be up in her fotch.

Kevin Aviance is an artist, performer, and legend. His Web site is www.kevina-viance.net.

Waiting in line at a club can be more painful than genital warts. Okay, that's not true. But it *is* a pain in the ass, so here are Six Sexy Secrets to cutting in line.

1. **Politeness:** Get to know the doormen by name and flirt if appropriate. Never claim to be on a guest list if you aren't and then cause a stink; give them crap and
you'll never get in. When you leave, *always* thank the door staff. They'll remember and do you a favor later.
2. **Generosity:** Buy the doorman a drink. If you don't know him, approach him with a smile, shake hands, and palm him $20. If you act like he knows you and he feels the money, it's easier for him to pretend that you're on a guest list.
3. **Innocence:** On busy nights with lots of traffic, approach from the opposite side of the waiting line and say, "Hey, you just let me and my friends in, but I left my money in the car." The delivery should be casual but firm so that it sounds legit. Mentioning your friends helps because if you look familiar, then he'll assume he saw you moments before.
4. **Pushiness:** Find someone you know at the front of the line and inch your way in. Alternatively, find two solo guys standing together in line and move into the middle or end of them; you'll look like one of the group.
5. **Greediness:** Offer to buy someone a drink if he lets you cut. You'll be amazed at what lushes fags are.
6. **Bitchiness:** Simply cut in line so the doorman doesn't see. If someone complains, say, "Fuck it, I'm not waiting in that line!" No queen will box you. He'll most likely try to save face by saying, "Well get behind me, then!" That's fine because you've still avoided the longer line.

THINGS TO AVOID SAYING TO A DJ

1. Play something we can dance to! (It's not his fault you're in a K-hole and you can't move your feet. Drink some cranberry juice and stop buggin'.)
2. Play something with a beat! (Trust us, unless he's playing Yoko Ono, it's got a beat.)
3. There's this song, and it's got bells and goes like this... (This is not *Name That Tune* and he is not a contestant, and 2 A.M. is definitely not the time to try to figure out your latest crack obsession.)
4. Everybody wants to hear it! (Did they all tell you that while they were taking two-for-ones on your ass?)
5. When are you going to stop playing this shit? (When shitheads like you leave.)
6. My X is peaking! I need to hear ____! (If DJs changed the music every time every queen started peaking they'd never get through a full song.)
7. Will you be playing Madonna tonight? (Um...no.)

Chapter 12: Travel

Looking for San Vicente
By Drew Limsky

For a few years after the millennium turned, Santa Monica Boulevard was an eyesore—torn up, always under construction; tractors and concrete boulders had taken up permanent residence. Or so it seemed. Still, it was magical to me. There I am, cruising around West Hollywood in a silver Mustang convertible, straight from the airport, no shirt, blue skies, looking for San Vicente Boulevard. I'm a sexual adventurer, about to cut a swath through the Golden State.

But let's go back.

Before I started traveling regularly to Los Angeles in 2000, I had only been there twice, the first time when I was 17 to visit my girlfriend Jenny in Beverly Hills. She lived on Rexford Drive in a "McMansion," before the term was coined. There was a tennis court, a pool house, and a strange family, not one of whose members addressed me directly. The mother had become a lawyer late in life, and she had all the defensive confidence that comes with such a belated accomplishment. One night at dinner she went on a tear about the legal inaccuracies in *The Verdict,* the Paul Newman movie that was popular that winter. I was supposed to stay for 10 days, but I was ready to leave after three. Jenny and I had met at an acting camp in New Hampshire (she should have known better) and we tried to date cross-country (i.e., on the phone). For a year, she had begged me to come out, but when I got there something was up her ass. When I called my parents in New Jersey using the Sprint access code they had set me up with, Jenny stood beside me and asked why I was punching in so many digits.

It was a drizzly December, but Jenny took me to the beach in Santa Monica and we sat under a gray sky. We went to Disneyland, which I found aesthetically inferior to Disney World in Florida. We went to Camp Beverly Hills, where I bought a sleeveless, hooded sweatshirt to show off my new muscles (a year of lifting weights in my basement had finally started to show some results). Jenny took me to a Christmas party where she gave her phone number to a guy who was home from college for the holidays. I know this because when Jenny, her family, and I walked into the house after the dinner during which her mother showed off her legal expertise, there was a message on the answering machine from him. We all stood there, unmoving, in the Spanish colonial-style foyer listening to the guy asking my girlfriend to please call him back. It was pretty mortifying.

We went to her father's office so she could type out her college applications. This took some time. When I stepped away to explore, she demanded, "Where are you going?" She dropped her applications in the mailbox without stamping them, but didn't realize it until we were halfway through a live Bette Midler concert at the Universal Amphitheater. I said a few comforting things ("Did you put your return address on them?") that I guess didn't do the trick, because she curled up into fetal position while I discreetly rubbed my leg against the leg of the guy sitting next to me. He was too stoned to realize I wasn't creating a little friction because of the limited legroom. He had on purple wide-whale cords.

On New Year's Eve, Jenny and her friends took bong hits while I just sat there (I didn't do drugs). It was a long night. After she drove me to LAX we didn't speak again for years, not until I was a sophomore at Emory and she was at Vassar and she asked me to come up and see her. I didn't go.

14 years passed before I touched down at LAX again.

In that time I grew up. When I traveled, I went to the water. When I was a kid, I didn't understand adults, why they lay in the sun. What was the allure? I was always hot and bored. That changed when I became a man. Swimming pools are great. Beaches are better. Scratch the surface of a gay man's life and you'll find a story, a host of stories, about water. Our erotic realities can approximate our first fantasies: the swim club lifeguard just sprouting body hair; the camp counselor who showed that he was a man and not a boy in between his tan lines; furtive, lingering communal showers in the college dorm. Sex. This is why we go to the water.

In the '90s I went to South Beach, Fla., for sun and excitement. One New Year's Eve I kissed a dozen guys. I fucked a guy against a sink until the sink fell off the wall. I danced at Warsaw, dyed my hair blond, went for runs on Lincoln Road Mall before its facelift, saw an amazing drag queen bring down the house with Shirley Bassey's "This is My Life." I bought spandex tanks, pumped up at Body Tech, barely ate or slept, came home with a cold.

And then California called me back. A car had hit my close friend Andy while he was cycling in Topanga Canyon, near a hilly suburb called Calabasas. He'd sustained a massive head injury and was in a coma at UCLA Medical Center. The prognosis was not good. I got a ride up to the accident site from the hospital in Westwood and read every sign, noticing everything in LA that I'd failed to notice the first time—the verdant, musical names

California indulged on itself. These were words you tasted, licked as you said them. La Brea. La Cienega. San Vicente. Ventura Highway. Unlikely, spontaneous names, names too dreamy to be applied to permanent things. I didn't believe that Andy could die here—the permanence of death was inappropriate in this place.

I was ashamed that I even registered the handsomeness of Andy's doctor, given the circumstances; I felt my libido kicking in, inappropriately active. I just wanted to rub up against all the California men, unbutton their clothes, and speak to them in California words. *San Vicente.*

I found my way back to my hotel, the prefab Ramada on Santa Monica Boulevard, and then across the street to the gym. Almost immediately upon entering it, I clocked a handsome, sweating boy whose T-shirt was a wet tangle of cotton. He had thick, mesmerizing thighs and a broad, honest forehead. When I noticed him disappear from the gym floor I aborted my fledgling workout and made for the showers.

My friend was dying and there I was, practicing at being a sexual tourist.

I found the boy sitting against the wall on the far side of the sauna. I took a seat on the bench near the door, and we eyeballed each other. I thought there was something so nice, so homey about the boy. Cuddly-sexy. As I looked at the other man—at his unselfconsciously parted thighs and his hair, wetted by perspiration into curlicues—an urge welled up inside me, one which caught and expanded uncomfortably at the top of my chest and rose to the base of my throat, like heartburn.

I looked away from the boy, then back again—I was in California, and so I indulged myself. I imagined myself crossing the room in a soundless sexual fantasy, but actually my longing was for something presexual, or perhaps postsexual. What I had envisioned would have been far more shocking to the object of my fantasy and to those assembled than if I had gruffly pushed my head between the boy's stocky legs. For now, I wanted nothing else in the world so much as to hold the boy's hand in my own as if I knew him, to press our palms together and interlock the fingers. I only wanted to close my eyes beside the stranger, to watch yellow pictures trickle down the dark edges of my brain—to finally know where to go when I needed to rest.

I went back to the hotel alone. I slid off the bed and walked naked onto the balcony, which overlooked a parking lot and a lapping corner of the hotel pool. The floor of the balcony was smooth against my feet, and the wind through the palm trees made my eyes tear. I suddenly had the urge to walk barefoot into the parking lot and down Santa Monica Boulevard, even though no one walked in this city, just to hear the high fronds continue to slice the mild air. These were the pleasures that Andy had spoken of—the wind that was rarely cold; the mountains that broke into bits above the sea; the clean, angular homes clinging onto the hillside as if in a one-armed embrace; the fact that the Pacific Coast Highway was the street where you lived.

On the way back from Andy's memorial service, the friend of Andy's I'd gotten a ride with took the canyon roads too fast, but when we made it down to the Pacific Coast Highway alive I calmed down. The PCH is also called the 1, I guess because if you read the country from left to right it's the first highway that occurs. A highway on the beach. That's something to a New Yorker. I wanted to drive it myself, but my flight was that afternoon. I'd come back. There would be a more appropriate time to savor it, in a convertible, "Ventura Highway" on the radio.

It took me three years to get back to LA.

Because my brother was getting married that September, and there would be the bachelor party in Las Vegas, I knew I would need to do something preemptive, so as sort of an inoculation, I went. I booked a five-day trip to Los Angeles and Laguna Beach, Calif., I perused *Damrons* and the gay *Fodors* and found this place.

The San Vicente Inn shares a name with the street it's on. Easy enough—the whole town's like that. Heading toward the beach on Santa Monica Boulevard, make your first right before Rage and you're there. Across the street from the post office, it's easy to miss, just a couple of pastel-colored bungalows on a steep street pushing upward toward Sunset. It shares a block with a bank and some generic apartment buildings. What you find inside is unexpected: cabin-style buildings set around a sun-splashed pool, thick-cushioned lounge chairs, bougainvillea climbing up white trellises, naked and near-naked men oiled up with suntan lotion. I could hardly wait to find my room and get naked too.

I met some guys at the San Vicente—I didn't deprive myself—but mostly I would meet guys at Will Rogers Beach in Santa Monica and bring them back to West Hollywood. But the inn still represents something important to me: a palpable sense of adult freedom. Go to breakfast in a towel, drop the towel at the side of the pool, lift weights naked in the little open-air gym, and suck in the admiration where the sun always shines and cute houseboys clean up your mess. No one says shit, at least not within earshot.

In time I explored outward from LA, went on guidebook-recommended tours of Russian Hill in San Francisco, ducked into Macondray Lane, the inspiration for Barbary Lane in *Tales of the City*. I had a view of the Golden Gate Bridge from my bathtub at the Mandarin Oriental. I went with a friend to the Russian River, with its one good restaurant—Fife's—and its quiet swimming hole. One winter I drove all night to get to Palm Springs, but I found it a depressing retirement community. I missed the beach.

The south coast always drew me back. There are coves around Santa Barbara—one is in a town called Summerland, no lie—where the men build huts into the crevices of stony bluffs. They collect rocks and long pieces of driftwood and make like Lincoln Logs. It's something to see. And they wait in their handcrafted cabanas, leaning out over driftwood windowsills. Then there's a beach in San Diego called Black's. You have to climb down an entire mountain just to get naked and watch other naked guys. I heard about the drag queen who made it down in heels; I also heard about others who backed away from snakes and pitched right into the canyon.

And Laguna Beach. Laguna is so beautiful you want to cry, just coves and bluffs and views. Rolling green waves. Birds of paradise. They say it looks Mediterranean, the way the town slopes down to the sea, but Europe can't be any better than this. In the '30s, Bette Davis had a weekend retreat on tiny Wood's Cove. A dozen houses sit on the headland above the beach because that's all it can fit, and hers is the one in the middle with its own fortified seawall and a fancy *D* on the chimney.

Perched above another cove, a quarter-mile north of the Davis house, sits a gay hotel and bar. It looks like a ship. White and rickety, it has nautical ledges that architects call eyebrows and a descending arrangement of wide balconies. Give it one good push and it's headed for Catalina. The men spill out of the club and wander alone or in pairs down the steps to the beach, but mostly the men just wait, listening to the sound of the waves crashing. It's louder than the music from the bar. It draws us in.

Andy kept telling me to come out and see him, but I didn't make the trip until his accident in '97. In other words, I didn't make the trip out until he died. But in death he taught me something: that I was part Californian. Now I go to California every month. That's how I learned about the drag queen at Black's and the ship-motel in Laguna. That's how I found Summerland. I met my boyfriend there, on an all-but-deserted beach in Summerland. This is Andy's legacy to me.

Traveling is different now that I write about it for a living, and now that I have Chris. I'm not a sexual adventurer anymore. But you have to give up things to get things. I no longer take calculated walks with my shirt off, the way I did on Santa Monica Boulevard and Ocean Drive. Instead Chris and I calculate other things, like our favorite hotel amenities, because we've gone upscale (no more $60-a-night rooms for me—one of the perks of being a travel writer). So we take note of the rooms with DVD players, rain showers, separate water closets, and feather beds. And the fuck-benches at the foot of the bed.

Some snapshots: taking baths in the 40-inch-wide tub in the French Quarter; getting a couples massage in Chicago; swimming at midnight in Laughlin, Nev., the poor man's Las Vegas; scarfing down scones and lemon curd on the Club Level at the Ritz-Carlton in Key Biscayne, Fla.; nabbing the honeymoon suite in Houston's Lovett House; lighting a fire in our room at the lodge in Zion National Park, Utah; seeing the ocean from the bed in Palm Beach; being naked in our private outdoor Jacuzzi in Big Sur, Calif.; enduring a nine-course French dinner with a PR woman at L'Orangerie in LA (please, no more organ meat); getting lost on Bee Cave Road in Austin and not caring; mountain biking in Moab, Utah; smiling at the woman who leaned over the railing on the riverboat in New Orleans to tell us, "You make me miss my boyfriend!"

With Chris I'm not wanting for adventure. He's been in the Peace Corps and visited some 80 countries and has a high threshold for what he likes to call developing nations but what I refer to as the filthy and the dirty. I gave him a lot of hell for persuading me to go to Guatemala, but once we got there, it was fantastic. We explored the colonial town of Antigua, swam every morning in a lake surrounded by volcanoes, and ate hearty, home-cooked meals for about $15 each a day. I also conquered my fear of overland travel, tiny pud-dle-jumper planes, and large groups of non-Americans. We've also lost a wallet at the Hotel Bel-Air in LA (it was recovered), lost a tire on a dirt road in Belize, and ran out of gas near Needles, Calif.—aside from the moment when I thought I would lose my new cowboy hat while pushing the jeep, it was actually fun.

And our adventures take other forms. We've cut a swath through North and Central America as a gay couple. I've been asked if we needed a king-size bed in English and Spanish. In Belize, the manager of Francis Ford Coppola's Turtle Inn was too shy to ask, which could be the reason why we ended up with an enormous thatched-roof villa with two separate wings. No complaints here. I could finally use the john without shutting the door and running the water to obscure what I was doing in there (Chris's WASPy toilet fear, don't ask), and we were able to have sex at least twice a day on clean sheets.

A world away, in Beverly Hills, Chris and I were getting some sun at the pool at the Beverly Wilshire. I was the one in the Speedo. An attractive blonde in her 30s started chat-ting me up ("Can I look at your *Zagat*?"). After some time—two hours in which our club sandwiches came, were eaten, and plates cleared—her TV reporter husband came over. The talk turned to travel. She asked how often I came to LA. I said as much as I can, and then I gave Chris a meaningful look. It was a look you could have seen from the last row of the Kodak Theatre. Well, they missed the look. They didn't register the Speedo. After the two of them recalled their wedding in Las Vegas, the husband turned to me.

"So Drew," he said, "are you married?"

Beat.

"No," I said. "We're together."

Anyone who says that people only open their mouths in shock in the movies is a liar. Butterflies could have bred children inside those mouths by the time they closed them. I don't know what was worse, their gaping faces or the ensuing our-best-friend-is-gay story (a real gentleman, blah, blah, blah, the Rupert Everett in our lives, blah, blah, blah).

Finally they left us alone. We took another swim and went up to the room, both of us looking very William Holden in our high-collared, white robes. At the Wilshire, there's a DO NOT DISTURB button you can push from the bed. Only time I've ever seen that. We made use of it. The hotel is only a mile or two from my old stomping grounds in West Hollywood. As I reached for Chris I had a fleeting thought: I looked for San Vicente, but in my travels had found something better.

Dennis Hensley's 12 Ways You Can Tell You're On a Gay Cruise

As the Cuba Gooding Jr. film *Boat Trip* reportedly demonstrated—I say reportedly because I didn't see the film and don't plan to—sometimes it's possible to find yourself on a gay cruise and not realize it until it's too late. One minute you're sipping banana daiquiris by the lido deck pool and the next you're getting corn-holed by the ship's swarthy Sardinian coxswain (pronounced "cocks-un") and his buddies in a room without a porthole. Not that there's anything wrong with that. I just think one should know such events might be on the agenda going in.

You see, gay cruises, as fun and free-wheeling as they may be, are not for everyone. Avowed heteros like Kevin Spacey and the boys from N'Sync would probably have a miserable time on a gay cruise. As would self-loathing closet cases and aging dance divas recovering from plastic surgery who just wanted to be left alone and not told how fierce they are every fucking second.

So here then are a few tips on how to tell if the cruise you've just embarked on is actually gay or if it just *seems* gay because of all the froufrou drinks and production numbers. As a former cruise ship chorine (Princess Cruises, class of '91) and an avid aficionado of gay cruises—okay, I've been on exactly one—I feel more than qualified to offer advice on such matters. Believe you me. If Cuba Gooding Jr. had consulted me before *Boat Trip,* I could have saved him adding another turkey to his already spotty resume, thereby freeing him up to focus on his Oscar-bait role as a mentally-challenged football groupie in *Radio.* We all would have been better off. Anyway, you are definitely on a gay cruise if...

1. The Ping-Pong balls keep disappearing.

2. You overhear crewmembers describing the hot tub as "egg drop soup" and the steam room smells like those trees that smell like come.

3. The male dancers in the stage shows are actually *trying*—giving 150 percent to their performances—while their female cohorts don't even bother putting on their false eyelashes. Also, keep an eye out for some jealous "acting out" behavior from one particularly surly girl dancer who is still carrying a torch for her adorably fresh-scrubbed male partner even though he's told her repeatedly that he's "confused" and "just wants to be friends for now."

4. The penises of the passengers who take part in the costume parade on Mardis Gras Night are either tucked into pantyhose or exposed completely. There's no middle ground.

5. The ship's well-regarded bread-maker is given the week off and spends it questioning his very existence, Maytag repairman-style. "Why don't they *need* me?" he can be heard screaming late at night, in Italian, natch. *"Mi no capisce!"*

6. The ship's doctor gets called away from dinner to remove a shuffleboard puck from a guest's ass. When word of the incident gets out, the poor man will explain to his dining mates, "I was just strolling along the deck, minding my own business and enjoying the moonlight, when all of a sudden I fell and was impaled. I mean, what are the chances?"

7. The ship's hairdressers, massage staff, florist, and smoothie maker can't go five minutes without being told how to do their jobs.

8. The drunkest person at the captain's cocktail party is the captain.

9. The Eurotrash crewmembers aren't the only ones in Speedos.

10. The ship DJ, a well-meaning gadget geek from Ireland who thinks Thunderpuss is a professional wrestler and hasn't been sent any new music since last year's dry dock, can be seen crying into his beer and literally pulling out his hair.

11. The Grandma's Bragging Party has been cancelled and replaced by a "Taint Grooming" seminar presided over by the onboard Episcopal priest.

12. The Leonardo DiCaprio-Kate Winslet poses that are playfully recreated on the ship's bow include penetration.

Dennis Hensley, the author of *Misadventures in the (213)* and *Screening Party* and cowriter of the film *Testosterone*, is currently working on a novel about his years on the high seas.

Itinerary for the Jet Set Slut

Sex tourism has always been a hot option for the gays. Tennessee Williams, Paul Bowles, and William S. Borrows traveled to Morocco in the '40s and '50s to explore their wild sides. Similarly, in the 1960s when jokes about the fruitiness of San Francisco started popping up, men from across the globe starting popping wood and popping over to California to taste the treats. And even now when fags vacation a major part of their trip involves exploring the local gay community, but unless you're from small-town America, these bars aren't that unique; however, being in a new ghetto means you're new meat, and that equals upping your choices and chances for boning.

But first, a public service announcement:
Under federal law, if you leave the United States to engage in sexual encounters that are considered illegal within the United States, even if they're legal in the other country, you can be arrested and prosecuted upon your return. These laws were enacted to stop the booming business of child prostitution in countries like Thailand.

That said, here are five places outside of the United States where getting off is as easy as breathing.

1. Hard-Core Cruising

Take 3,000 men (porn stars, couples, high-class hookers, daddies, circuit boys, conservative types, and more) and remove any big-city attitude because everyone's away from home, and trap them on a luxury gay cruise ship. Mix in movies, games, dance parties, and day trips when the ship docks, along with a sprinkling of cocktails (there are even rumors that some homos bring drugs, if you can imagine that!), and the slap and tickle is sure to follow. Ask any guy who's taken a gay cruise and he'll tell you: From orgies to quickies, pieces of ass are everywhere for the taking.

2. Getting Euro-Trashed

Amsterdam is obviously known for its red-light district and pot purchases, but the gay bars—with their back rooms and saunas—offer hot, free fun. The international visitors flocking to Amsterdam also make for some lovely sexual selections. Another mid-size city with a randy reputation is Prague, which boasts a hot underground of bars, back rooms, and the good times that naturally follow. Discos are infested with rent boys who strip and perform simulated sex onstage. Leather is always an option. Both locations love Americans, but check your superior U.S. attitude at the door.

3. Fan of NAMBLA?

The young and mostly Muslim "beach boys" in Kenya are hot tickets. Popular along the Malindi and Watamu beaches, these boys roam the palm-covered sand offering to accompany men back to their hotel rooms. Money being scarce, Kenya has been slow to crack down on the booming sex trade, even though homosexuality is illegal there.

4. Me Love You Long Time!

Those smooth men of Thailand are more than happy to do the job, and in the gay sections there are men on the streets luring you into every bar. The general setup features boys standing on a stage in little white undies with numbers on them so you know whom to request from the manager. They also feature shows that range widely in quality; to get a sense for your options, hit multiple bars and take in all the action. In Bangkok the action happens on Silom Road and Sukhumvit Road. And don't miss the city of Pattaya, where they also have a thriving queer scene.

5. Screw That U.S. Embargo!

In Havana, Cuba, there are several parks where young men hang out and make themselves available to tourists; however, no Cubans are allowed in hotel rooms, and the police are merciless in their harassment of locals. If the police do approach while you're chatting it up—whether it be for sex or cigars— put your arm around the guy and tell the officer he's with you; the police tend to leave tourists alone. Once the deal is made, let him take you to a *casa particular*, which is a private house where you can legally rent a room for private use.

Mama Goose's Stepsister Presents...The Invasion!

By Richard Andreoli

Once upon a time, tribes of Faeries gathered in an enchanted land known as Fire Island. While the communing occurred mostly during the summer months, when the Island was its most bright and beautiful, it was never actually on fire, though the visiting Faeries sometimes were ablaze in spirit.

Anyway, the tribes divided into two factions: those in the bohemian Cherry Grove, and those in the modern Pines. Faeries of Cherry Grove were older, more likely to be artisans, and closer to nature and her various beverages. Many denizens of Cherry Grove delighted in the ways of cosmetics, jewels, and dresses. Meanwhile, Faeries of the Pines were young and muscular and loved to saunter shirtless where others might admire their bare, sculpted chests. They reveled wide-eyed all through the night, enjoying magical delights to lift their spirits.

According to legend, the two factions rarely entwined. Each preferred instead to pass judgment upon their fellow brethren, even though they were all truly Faeries at heart. Only in the magical meadow known as the Meat Rack did these people commingle, but those stories are for another time.

What matters now is the tale of a warm summer evening when a Grove Faerie, resplendent in his finest gossamer gown, journeyed to the Botel, located in the Pines, for a yummy dinner. But once he arrived, this Faerie was denied service because his feminine attire did not suit the tastes of the establishment! He returned to Cherry Grove, sad and malnourished, to speak with the newly crowned Homecoming Queen, Tom Hansen. Disgusted, their new leader decided to stage a protest.

So it was on a hot summer day that the Faerie Queen led her people, all dressed in their feminine finery, onto a shaky water taxi and sailed into the Pines harbor.

The taxi docked! The Faerie Queen stepped forth, leading her followers and prepared for a battle, when they were suddenly greeted with cheers! The Pines Faeries were so shocked and surprised, tickled and thrilled at this "invasion," that they welcomed their fellow Faeries and invited them to libations at a tavern called the Blue Whale. They all suddenly realized they had things they could share with one another, and that made them one big happy Faerie family.

Now every year on the Fourth of July a historical recreation begins at noon in Cherry Grove's downtown. Faeries dressed like their sisters from years past board a ferry and forge to the Pines harbor where they are now greeted by the boldest bacchanalia of badinage in the summer season. The ladies are announced and grand entrances are delivered down the makeshift catwalk, dazzling all in attendance. The event is so well-known that even some of those boring old hetero humans attend the festivities.

And that, children, is how the Invasion of Fire Island was born.

U.S. CITIES EVERY GAY MAN SHOULD HIT BY AGE 35

WEST COAST
West Hollywood, in LA—To meet porn stars and Jim J. Bullock
Palm Springs, Calif.—To meet porn stars and Barry Manilow
The Castro, in S.F.—To meet porn stars and audition for Raging Stallion, Titan, Colt, Falcon, etc.
Las Vegas—in honor of Nomi Malone

EAST COAST
Provincetown, Mass.—To meet porn stars and Jimmy James
Fire Island, N.Y.—To meet porn stars and Sam Champion
The Village-Chelsea, in NYC—To meet porn stars, see Wigstock, and meet the

Queer Eye guys (who will go to the opening of an envelope)
New Orleans—To meet porn stars and enjoy Southern decadence
South Beach, Fla.—To meet porn stars and Donatella Versace
Atlanta—To visit Hotlanta weekend and Backstreet

CITIES EVERY GAY MAN SHOULD HIT BY AGE 55

IN THE U.S.
Russian River, Calif.—For the hustlers
Asheville, N.C.—For the hustlers
Key West, Fla.—For the hustlers
Fort Lauderdale, Fla.—For the hustlers
Dollywood, in Pigeon Forge, Tenn.—Because everything Dolly is dandy!
All of the Hawaiian Islands—For relaxation

OUTSIDE THE U.S.
Paris
Ibiza, Spain
Manchester, England
London
Barcelona, Spain
Sitges, Spain
Mykonos, Greece
Reykjavik, Iceland
Marrakesh, Morocco

Chapter 13: Gay Gatherings

Fast Times at Homo High: Gay Clubs in Our Big Gay World
By Christopher Lisotta

Like lots of gay men, I like spending time with boys doing social, active, and organized things. Sure, I love potlucks and movie nights, but if you were like me as a kid, you were on plenty of school activity boards and organized the decorations for the dance committee, even if you ended up not making out with a girl behind the dumpster in the parking lot. As an adult—especially one who freelances for a living—I've realized those organizing and interpersonal skills first put to good use in junior high school drama club play a big part in my professional and personal life. As a member of the National Lesbian and Gay Journalists Association, I've met other gay writers, gotten lots of great advice, commiserated about the state of media today, learned about my craft, and most importantly, had a great time making interesting new friends from all over the country.

But because public gatherings have been such a dangerous proposition in our queer history, we've had to get together under shrouds of secrecy—or at least without drawing undue attention to ourselves. These days when we think of gay gatherings, we tend to think of hanging out in bars or, on a larger scale, partying it up at circuit events or even skulking about in bathhouses. The growth of nonprofit, AIDS, and political organizations has made gay gatherings more mainstream, but some men wonder if there is more to meeting up than fund-raisers, sex clubs, and dancing until 5:00 A.M.

Just like our straight brethren, we have a myriad of interests that make forming groups a natural development in our social lives. Unlike straight men, however, gay men tend to form groups that have just a bit more flair and excitement about them, or at least take straight events and give them their own special spin. One way to understand all these gay groups is to think of them in terms of a hypothetical high school, but where the halls are filled with gay boys flitting through their days waiting for their extracurriculars to start. Eerily, the gay gatherings highlighted below can be compared to the clubs and experiences we went through back when we had all of our hair and braces were still a cruel metallic reality. So join me on a trip through Homo High's yearbook!

Radical Faeries

Although the idea may seem a bit dated, think about the classic American high school glee club— the people were perky and fun and wanted to create a world that probably doesn't and will never exist. Sounds like a straightlaced version of the ultimate gay consciousness-raising group, the Radical Faeries. Like so many other things in modern gay life, you can trace the beginning of gay gatherings back to a man named Harry Hay.

An actor, protestor, communist, labor organizer, peace activist and father, Hay was a larger-than-life figure in Los Angeles progressive movements before forming the Mattachine Society, the first organized gay group in the United States, in the early 1950s. Gay historians usually credit the eventual founding of every other LGBT organization thanks to Hay's early work, and when he died in 2003, politicians, writers and scholars all mourned his passing.

Long before his death and well after Mattachine was up and running, Hay decided he and his friends needed to address their own spirituality and community. In 1979, Hay, along with his partner, John Burnside, and a small group of friends, founded the Radical Faeries, which biographer Stuart Timmons describes in his book, *The Trouble With Harry Hay,* as a "networking of gentle men devoted to the principles of ecology, spiritual truth, and, in new age terms, 'gay-centeredness.' " Like the word "fag," Hay and his brothers decided to take back "Faerie" and make it celebratory and to create an egalitarian, free-form environment that embraced the best elements of Hay's love affair with socialism.

Using a healthy dollop of Native American spiritual ideals as a foundation, the group came up with the idea of a "Faerie Circle," where groups of men could commune, dance ecstatically, and cast off all the crap they didn't need any more in their lives. The first Radical Faerie events brought together a few dozen gay men for long weekends during which they would take part in pagan rituals, eat communally, and create art. Over time, Radical Faerie communal households formed, and gatherings of all shapes and sizes started taking place all across the globe, but the overall theme remains the same. As Don Kilhefner, one of Hay's friends and a Faerie cofounder said in *The Advocate* in 1987, "The idea was, you came out and the journey ends. The growth stops. To me that didn't make sense. I didn't know what it meant to be gay. Something that was missing from the gay identity was a consciousness, a sense of spirit." For many gay men, the celebratory nature of the Faeries brings them a sense of spirit they never new existed within them.

Family Pride Coalition and Gay Family Weekends

The story of Heather and her two mommies or two daddies now seems decidedly mainstream, but way back in 1979, the idea of queers as parents was a pretty radical one. That year, at the first National March on Washington for Gay and Lesbian rights, a group of demonstrators realized they all had something in common. With kids from previous straight relationships, many a gay man discovered he wasn't the only gay dad out there. In response, the Gay Fathers Coalition was born. After years of growth and well-attended annual conventions, the group became the Gay and Lesbian Parents Coalition International in 1986 and welcomed the mommies. (The organization became the Family Pride Coalition in 1998.)

Besides all the organizing, outreach, medical information, legal services, and social networking the group brought to grateful parents looking for some help and connection, the gay family pride movement realized there were even more needs to meet. The growing number of gay mommies and daddies and their little bundles of joy might do just fine in their day-to-day lives in the gay ghetto or their progressive little neighborhood, but taking the seminal family vacation could be tough in most traditional resorts and kid-friendly destinations. And for families living in smaller communities where life was a fishbowl, going away with other families just like them was an attractive idea.

Long before the first Baby Gap came to your mall, the Family Pride Coalition's Family Week was thriving. In the mid 1990s, Provincetown, the tiny little artist colony on the tip of Cape Cod that has been welcoming gay and lesbian vacationers for decades, was the first destination. Most LGBT visitors up until that time associated P-Town with tea dances, bar nights, and sex among the dunes. During Family Week, instead of ecstasy and harnesses, gay men were bringing with them children's Tylenol and beach pails.

Provincetown made sense for a number of reasons—it was already an LGBT-friendly destination, yet it offered plenty of activities to keep the kids busy and provided parents with enough to do once their children were off to bed. Whale watching, beach trips, hikes, family dances, and activity afternoons suddenly had families from Key West to the Castro making their way to the Bay State for some R&R.

In 1999, the Family Pride Coalition added a second Family Week vacation option in Saugatuck, Mich., a Midwest version of P-Town that also features dunes, art galleries, and vacation fun (with Lake Michigan standing in for the ocean, of course). Family Week has become the yearly highlight for hundreds of gay families, with kids meeting other kids in situations just like theirs and their parents learning about parenting and advocacy for their families as they have a ball in ways they never imagined when they were single and kidless.

Gay Naturists

Okay, we already know what you're thinking—"naturist" means "nudist," and if you throw "gay" into the mix, what that really means is "lots of sex in the woods." Sure, plenty of amorous hikers wearing nothing but their boots have come out of the brambles with more than a suntan after stumbling upon another similarly dressed lover of the outdoors. But for the vast majority of gay naturists, the idea of all-male, all-nude events brings together the best in nonsexual group bonding without the fractiousness that so often divides gay men when they're clothed.

Gay nudist groups exist in most major cities and boast memberships as diverse as the gay community itself. Think about it—if you're at a potluck where everyone's bare-assed, you really can't make fun of anyone's shoes. Plus, snickering over someone's big belly just brings it all back around to your own physical limitations. For naturists, there's nothing more honest than being literally naked to those around you—and that kind of openness will make you more accepting of others. Plus, aren't you tired of putting up all those barriers? For thousands of men, dropping it all and revealing themselves at house parties, beach events, hiking trips, and social gatherings without the specter of drugs and overdrinking proves there's more to gay life than sizing up someone else.

Some naturists have taken their public displays of everything to a new level with a series of annual gatherings. Gay Naturists International, an umbrella organization for local naturist clubs, sponsors a 10-day August gathering in rural Pennsylvania that attracts more than 800 gay naturists a year. Daytime activities include everything from yoga and hula lessons to more esoteric activities like body painting and oil wrestling. It may seem counter-intuitive, but GNI also sponsors costume nights and drag shows. The West Coast version is hosted by the GNI-affiliated California Men Enjoying Naturism (love that acronym!) in September and brings together hundreds of men to the mountains north of downtown Los Angeles for even more *au naturel* bonding.

International Gay Rodeo Association

The cowboy mystique has been a part of gay culture since the first young buck put on a pair of chaps, so it's no wonder the gay rodeo circuit is popular with cowpokes and city slickers alike. Since 1976 gay men who love roping, rustling, and riding have had a way to pursue their hobbies outside the bedroom. Phil Ragsdale, who was emperor of the Imperial Court in Reno, Nev., back in that bicentennial year, decided the court could raise money for the Muscular Dystrophy Association by holding a gay rodeo.

The first event was light on participants and spectators and almost didn't happen because Ragsdale faced resistance from ranchers who were unwilling to loan their livestock. Undeterred, Ragsdale made the Reno gay rodeo an annual event, and soon Gay Rodeo groups were forming in Texas and Colorado, partially driven by the early 1980s *Urban Cowboy* movement. In 1985 gay rodeo groups from California and Arizona joined the pioneers and formed the International Gay Rodeo Association, standardizing competitions, rules and objectives so that participants could easily move from event to event. By 2003 the IGRA had 20 member associations representing 25 states and the District of Columbia, and it achieved true international status with the inclusion of chapters in two Canadian provinces.

A visit to any of the various gay rodeo events that take place across North America during the rodeo season is an introduction to a unique and vibrant culture that goes far beyond line-dancing night at your local country-western club. Thousands of actual gay cowgirls and cowboys spend months preparing for competition, honing the skills many of them learned when they were young pups growing up on their respective ranges. Welcoming of outsiders, the gay rodeos still focus much of their attention on philanthropy and community service, raising tens of thousands of dollars for local charities through special events, dances, and pageants that coincide with the rodeos. The same way some boys travel the country for circuit parties, rodeo aficionados travel to compete in events from Palm Springs to Calgary. Most events have a traditional, gentlemanly, and unpretentious vibe about them, and even the most cynical urbanite can fall under the sway of the gay rodeo's (or at least a gay cowboy's) Technicolor sunset charms.

Gay Games

Gay men have been competing in the Olympics since ancient times, and from the earliest days of the 20th century and the modern sports movement, gay athletes have been a force to be reckoned with. (Consider American tennis player Bill Tilden, who won the men's singles title at Wimbledon in 1920, and competed as part of seven winning Davis Cup teams.)

Still, virtually every gay athlete played in silence, while gay amateurs had no place to practice their sport of choice without their sexuality becoming an issue. That is until former paratrooper and physician Tom Waddell came along. According to Joe Clark, who has written extensively on the Gay Games, Waddell, a U.S. Olympic decathlete who competed in the 1968 Mexico City games, wanted to create an event where gay people could compete without fear of retaliation. He also wanted to avoid the geopolitical tensions that had come to dominate international sporting competitions. By 1982 Waddell and the group San Francisco Arts and Athletics, Inc., started to organize their Gay Olympics, but not before the U.S. Olympic Committee sued them for using the word *Olympic* in their event name. Though thousands of groups and clubs (including the Special Olympics) used the supposedly sacred word without any problems, the USOC went after Waddell. The organization demanded payment for their legal fees and even put a lien on Waddell's home, despite the fact that he was suffering from AIDS.

Thanks to the USOC, the renamed Gay Games were born. At the first competition in San Francisco that year, more than 1,000 athletes competed in 16 events, with no restraints based on nationality, age, sex, or race. As Waddell wrote in the handbook for the second Gay Games, held in 1986, "There are no competing world ideologies in these games." By 1990 the Gay Games went international, with more than 7,500 athletes competing in over 30 sports, while another 1,200 people took place in a cultural festival run alongside the games. In 1994 the Gay Games returned to the United States, and in order to accommodate the growing number of international athletes who wanted to take part, attorney general Janet

Reno waived U.S. policy and allowed HIV-positive people to enter the country without special permits. After a successful run in Amsterdam in 1998, the 2002 Gay Games went to Australia, attracting a growing number of athletes from Asia and other parts of the world and helping to shake the image of the games as merely a North American and European event.

The Gay Games have evolved far beyond an occasion for type-A personalities to pick up medals. The games have helped spur local gay sporting organizations, increase physical fitness in the LGBT community, and foster international understanding while avoiding tensions created by national rivalries. Maybe it's time to try your hand at kickball again...

Men's Erotic Awareness Weekends

It seems hard to believe, but plenty of gay men don't think they understand what gay sex is all about. For most queers, the "learn as you go" method and the occasional sex column gets them far enough, though some long for a better sense of erotic understanding and acceptance. Even more importantly, plenty of gay men feel that society is so hostile toward them that they have to start from scratch to figure out what it actually means to be a man.

Organizations like California's Body Electric have been helping people learn more about their bodies for over two decades. Although you may think you're in for some kind of smelly naked hippie weekend where the only pause in the group sex is for tofu snacking, there's actually a lot more at work here. Instructors like the ones at Body Electric argue that a better understanding of touching, breathing, and thinking makes us not only better lovers but better men.

Several groups offer weekend retreats and even weeklong vacations at rustic locations for men of all ages. Some classes are designed specifically for HIV-positive men, while others focus on the specifics of bondage and submission. Most are based on a foundation of erotic massage, which means sensual touch is encouraged and celebrated, but actual sex between participants or with instructors is discouraged. In addition, the particular kind of eroticism cultivated by these groups usually doesn't involve ejaculation. The idea is that too much of the sex act is focused on coming—and fast ejaculation at that—rather than bringing that orgasmic feeling to all levels of sex.

Be warned, though: Weekends are not geared toward the overly cynical or tragically hip. If you're not ready to put down your guard and let go of your inhibitions, then you probably won't get much out of the experience. Portions of most workshops are conducted in the nude, and participants note that the removal of clothes lowers inhibitions and actually takes the focus off desire and arousal and allows people to connect on an equal, affirming level.

Ultimately, erotic awareness weekends try to help men build relationships with one another based on erotic desire, as opposed to relationships based purely on physical sensations. Don't be surprised if there's a healthy dose of Eastern philosophy and group hugging.

Burning Man

In 1986 San Franciscans Larry Harvey and Jerry James went to Baker Beach and built a crude wooden figure. It was Summer solstice, and Harvey and James burned the figure to commiserate about failed relationships. Both men found the experience thoroughly refreshing and profound, and soon friends were asking them about their experience. The next year the two men (both straight) repeated their ritual, but this time other people showed up to figure out what it meant, exactly, to watch a wooden effigy go up in flames. From these humble beginnings Burning Man has become a yearly weeklong event that attracts more than 25,000 people of all shapes, sizes, backgrounds, and sexual orientations.

Until 1990, Burning Man happened on the beach near San Francisco, but that year the growing festival moved to Black Rock City, Nev., where it took place on a dry lake bed. What goes on? Well, the first rule is there are no rules beyond the Golden Rule. People from all over the world come to the early September ritual in a collection of cars, SUVs, RVs, and even bicycles to create an experimental community based on love, acceptance, art, celebration, and life.

From the very beginning Burning Man has been a place that warmly accepts people of all identities, and gay men have played a vital role in the creation of community. The focus on art (each year there is a theme that helps to build common bonds) and the creation of something beautiful out of the nothingness of the desert has also attracted gay folks. The celebratory, free love, anything-goes attitude taken by many of the straight men also exerts a strong appeal. Burning Man is the kind of place where a loving male-female couple goes for the week to explore the other side of their sexuality, while gay men there with their boyfriends find themselves in multi-ways not just with other guys, but even a few gals.

Burning Man disappears into the desert just as spontaneously as it is created. At the end of the week there should be no sign that 25,000 people lived, loved, and learned on the lakebed. There should also be no trace of the spectacular, ritualistic burning of a giant wooden man. For one week a year participants, drop all their bullshit and party, play, explore, and reflect on what makes them who they are. Not a bad way to spend a vacation.

Uniform Clubs

Training America's future soldiers is no mean feat, and the Junior Reserve Officers' Training Corps has been playing a role in the lives of motivated, clean-cut, and dapper teens who think they want to make the military a career. Whether you were a participant or an admirer, the macho uniforms inevitably held a certain allure. "Hello sailor! Is there a problem officer? Give me 10, soldier!" What is it about this kind of talk that makes gay men quiver in their Kenneth Coles?

There's a bunch of reasons. Deep down we want to be protected by a man who's in control, we realize that a man in a uniform is a cut above the rest, and in general the lines of a uniform—even in a bad polyester—makes a man's body look really, really hot.

For some men this nearly universal attraction to cops, soldiers, and firefighters goes beyond re-renting *An Officer and a Gentleman* on a lonely night or leering at the firehouse during a drive-by. There are several national organizations and about 20 clubs across the country that bring together gay men with a fondness for the uniform.

Some uniform novices might think this is just a spin-off fetish from the leather community, but any uniform-club member worth his spit-shine technique can tell you it goes far beyond just the thrill of power exchange. The number one draw seems to be a respect for authority, while guys into the love of precision and detail also find uniforms a great way to get their groove on.

But if you're looking for a quick game of dress up, move along. Most clubs consider themselves fraternal organizations, where many members collect vintage uniforms and lovingly restore them, which means this gay crowd may have more in common with Civil War re-enactors than leather daddies. And many clubs have stringent membership requirements—like the Regiment of the Black and Tans in the Los Angeles, which require a one-year probation and a unanimous vote in order to bring someone new into the starched and creased fold.

And don't call them costumes! The point is to respect the excellence that the duds signify and impart, and anyone who thinks this is funny won't last long in the uniform subculture. Sure, plenty of guys point out that gays have been victims of homophobes who hide behind their badges and gold bars. But the idea here is to be all you can be, and to do so with a group of like-minded men. It gives "Uncle Sam wants you" an entirely new meaning.

International Mr. Leather

Often there's more to competing in a pageant than just walking around in heels and talking about world peace. Sure, the camp and stage-dazzle factors are both high, but plenty of gay men have an interest in watching individuals transform themselves into winners. Although it's a long, long way from Atlantic City in both spirit and location, the annual International Mr. Leather competition held each year in Chicago captures the thrill of excellence with fewer tiaras and a lot more body mass. For more than 25 years, guys with a love for their chaps and motorcycle jackets have made their way to the Windy City in the hope of walking away with the title that warms the heart of large, grizzly men everywhere: International Mr. Leather.

In 1979, 400 men gathered for the first competition, and the vibe was decidedly "only experts need attend." In recent years, thousands of people (as in men *and* women) have shown up for the event, with newcomers to the leather world as welcome as the experienced old hands. Some folks come just to walk the sponsor hotel's signature leather market, which is basically an industry convention for the S/M set. But most leather boys and girls attend to watch the competition. There's also a lot more going on besides some sweaty guys in leather jocks flexing their pecs (though there's a lot of that too). Potential Mr. Leathers are expected to go through a preliminary interview process with a series of judges, where—as in the Olympics—the highest and lowest scores are dropped from the contestant's total. From there contestants are judged on stage presence and personality as the roster is whittled down to a list of 20 finalists. Judges then look at each finalist in three areas: leather image (0 to 40 points), physical appearance (0 to 20 points), and presentation skills (0 to 40 points), for a combined score that runs from 0 to 100 points. This scoring strategy ensures that looks alone don't get you the coveted title, and that the spirit of leather wins out at the end of the day.

Winners become celebrities for the year, touring the country to visit regional leather events, raising money for charities, and attending benefits. As its popularity has grown, International Mr. Leather has been expanded to include a women's competition as well as something every Mr. Leather needs: a contest for the title of International Mr. Bootblack (that's the adoring and submissive guy who polishes his leather man's boots to loving perfection). Like so many leather events across the country, International Mr. Leather has grown into a spectacle that is popular not only with the diehards but also with the gay guys who love the thrill of their very own pageant. If only Bert Parks knew...

Thankfully, high school is far behind us, but the sense of belonging we all wanted in our gawky adolescent days is still with us, even if we don't necessarily want to admit it to ourselves. Thankfully, none of us is alone, and we can share our interests, desires, and need to have fun with someone else just by coming together.

Bellies of Fun

Bear Runs are organized weekend parties for the bear community that are similar to circuit parties (without all the drugs) and leather festivals (with some leather, but not necessarily *that much* leather). Originally they were envisioned as events where big guys could feel good about themselves in our body-image obsessed community and where they could have fun and hook up with other big guys for a little slap and tickle. The popularity of these events grew, and Bear Runs now happen somewhere almost every weekend. These year-round events culminate with a major bear contest at IBR—the International Bear Rendezvous. The winner of this contest, held annually in San Francisco, becomes Mr. International Bear and represents the community for the year.

Check out what a group of our furry friends (whose names have been changed) had to say about their Bear Run experiences:

"Originally a bear was a big, hairy guy, but then smaller hairy guys started calling themselves cubs. Bears are generally tops and cubs are generally bottoms, but those rules don't always apply. Anyway, once bear events got really popular, you started getting otters (skinny and hairy), wolves (older leather), and muscle bears (steroid queens with hair). It was so much easier when you could say 'I fuck bears' and no one asked for specifics."
—Malcolm, San Diego

"I don't go to any of the organized events at bear parties. I basically contact the guys I've cruised online in bear chat rooms, figure out when we're both free to hook up, and

then make it happen. I rarely even see the sun...unless it's during a pool party or a breakfast buffet."
—Dan, San Francisco

"Being a contestant was tough. You had to be 'on' all weekend, you had to go to every party, and you had to meet-and-greet at official events. The only highlight was the contest itself because I got fucked backstage just before I had to give a speech about my place in the community. I wanted to just pull back the curtain and shout 'This is what it means to be a bear!' But the organizer wouldn't allow it."
—Terry, San Diego

"I look at it this way: I can miss IBR and not have to deal with the IBR flu that everyone leaves the weekend with, or I can go and hang with people I only see at these parties, get fucked silly, and eat really well at the buffet. Flu, schmoo..."
—Randy, Atlanta

"Whenever my friends and I go out to a local restaurant for dinner, women ask if we're football players. Then we start talking, and they figure it out..."
—Marcus, Los Angeles

"One year a contestant's sister came to cheer him on and met the hotel manager's daughter. Next thing you know they're partying with us the whole night, and they didn't seem fazed at all when the

Max Archer (photo by Bo Tate)

bear sex started busting out right in front of them. The next morning they were in the hotel hot tub being eaten out by a bi-bear. Good times!"
—Richard, Chicago

"These bears got pissed because the host hotel in Chicago closed the steam room so that no one could have sex in it. I was like, You tell 'em! We've already been kicked out of every other hotel in the city, what's one more?"
—Benjamin, Chicago

"My favorite memory of Bearquake [in Los Angeles] was going on [Disneyland's] Pirates of the Caribbean with a group of friends and getting stuck because we were too heavy. Other fags would be mortified that they had to turn on the lights and push us, but that's what I love about bears. We just laughed."
—Carey, Los Angeles

Chapter 14: Porn

Porn in the USA
By David Ciminelli

I've had a lust-hate relationship with porn ever since coming (pun intended) across a videotape of godlike porn star Jon Vincent in 1988's *Heavenly,* an unforgettable, snowy sex epic set in a ski lodge where the man-on-man ball-busting was hot enough to melt the slopes. I scored a copy after seeing Vincent's stunningly beautiful body on the box cover, which I spotted in the window of a sleazy downtown combo pawn-porn shop while walking home from high school. I power walked the six blocks home with the videotape tucked under my denim jacket and my heart beating out of my chest, the primal anticipation of seeing hot man-sex for the first time causing beads of sweat to break on my brow. Unfortunately, I had to wait a few days and endure a bout of blue balls as I waited for an opportunity to christen the family VCR with gay porn. I strategically faked a stomachache as Mom was planning a family outing to Burger King so I could stay home alone and manually release some tension with Jon.

For the next few months while my equally horny straight teen colleagues were learning the finer elements of foreplay underneath gym bleachers and in the back of their Dads' Trans Ams, I was secretly learning the ins and outs of gay sex courtesy of hard-bodied top man Jon Vincent and his lucky bottom-boy scene partners.

In one particularly memorable scene in *Heavenly,* Vincent, playing the hunky hero-top man, sits in the ski lodge next to a roaring fireplace with his leg in a cast (a result of a ski injury) while all but one of his pals are enjoying the slopes. Like a king sitting on his throne with Tony Davis as his manservant, Vincent, in his deep, manly, boner-inducing voice, convinces his buddy to service his every desire, which includes unzipping Vincent's pants and taking his uncommonly huge cock down his throat. This was the star's first scene in porn and one that hasn't been...er...topped by anyone else since. It set the precedent for what the ideal top man in porn should aspire to be: big, burly, chiseled, undeniably gorgeous, and muscular, with a gravelly, macho voice that seems created for foreplay talk. Jon Vincent had all of this. And the sexiest aspect of all is the fact that his dirty talk, confidence, and macho demeanor never seemed forced or contrived. He was a genuine sex pig who happened to look like a Hollywood action hero. But not even Stallone or Schwarzenegger ever put in action scenes as unforgettable as this stud's.

After many hours of intense interactive study of *Heavenly*, I decided that while getting stuffed by a hot muscleman like Vincent looked like one helluva hot carnival ride, being the top looked to be a lot more fun. The dominant man gets to control the action and the pace, and he gets to boast about the size of his dick while saying stuff like, "Yeah, baby, take that dick. You like my big cock, don't ya?" What's not to like about that?

As a gay teen just beginning to discover my sexuality, I easily identified with Vincent because he wasn't a walking gay stereotype. I thought of myself in the same way— whether as an unconscious effort to protect myself from any potential homophobia or because my "straightish" personality was merely ingrained, I don't know. But I knew I had little in common with the stereotypical gay characters TV and film were presenting at the time.

Though I wasn't yet out to friends and family, I had already discovered that I didn't relate much to what I knew of the gay community. And because I looked like every other straight rocker dude at my high school, I was able to walk the campus without being pegged as a "fag." I preferred death metal to disco, romance to promiscuity and poppers, and sports to circuit parties. Years later, after I moved to West Hollywood, during a freaky Hollywoodish happenstance I met and got to know John Vincent. I discovered we had much in common along the lines of music, sports, and the way we identify with the gay community.

But before I'd ever met Vincent in the flesh, he taught me quite a few important life lessons, especially in the sexual arena. From his turn in *Heavenly* I learned that tops should grunt a lot, while the bottom squeaks out something that sounds like a cross between a muffled scream and a moan. I found this instructional video course to be infinitely more interesting than my high school's lame sex-ed classes, which concentrated on how not to get a girl pregnant. Education I clearly didn't need.

I was confident that the $25 I paid for the videotape was a solid investment in my burgeoning sex life. After all, porn serves informal instructional and entertainment purposes and is great for strengthening the forearm and grip, but at what cost? This is where the hate part of my lust-hate relationship with porn surfaced, and when I learned firsthand that porn can fuck with your self-image.

Being an impressionable, insecure teen at the time, I noticed that none of the men in gay porn looked anything like me or any other guy I knew. Jon Vincent was the archetypical macho gay porn fantasy: tall, incredibly well built, masculine, and downright sexy, with short dark hair and brown bedroom eyes. And the rest of the *Heavenly* cast was equally flawless and uncommonly good-looking. Like I imagine *Seventeen* magazine was doing to insecure teenage girls at the time, gay porn transformed my typical teen insecurity and body issues into full-blown body dysmorphia. But it was nothing a gym membership and a decent work-out routine couldn't quell years later.

When I moved to West Hollywood in 1991, all it took was a leisurely stroll down Santa Monica Boulevard (also known as "the gay catwalk") to discover that I wasn't the only one affected by porn-influenced body issues. Virtually every guy that passed me had bazooka-sized biceps and powerful chests tucked into baby-sized tank tops. They all looked like porn stars—and more than a few were. And all the local billboards and window posters featured steroid queens and porn stars advertising for the latest gay nudie play and hip circuit party. Even the city street signs warning residents to clean up after their dogs had a silhouette of

a bulging body builder rather than the generic bowling ball-headed silhouettes you're used to seeing on school crossing signs. Without 16-inch biceps you can pretty much expect to remain completely invisible in this town—a life lesson once again provided by adult entertainment.

Gay porn also opened my eyes to other, more interesting aspects of the gay world. Unlike the only other obvious gay men I was familiar with at the time—B-rate celebrities like Rip Taylor, Paul Lynde, and Jim J. Bullock—the *Heavenly* guys were masculine and definitely not swishy, lisping clichés.

I began to imagine that the porn world was a fantasy place somewhere on the West Coast where beautiful, hard-bodied macho California gym boys with insatiable sexual appetites made lots of bank. In return for their hot salaries they were expected to do nothing except screw their equally hot costars and sip champagne while hanging out with Elton John and David

Geffen and arriving at Chi Chi LaRue's parties in the latest model Boxster.

Years later, after I'd moved to LA and scored a job as editor of *Unzipped* magazine—a hip, glossy monthly covering the world of gay porn and sex trends that's best described as a hybrid of *Out* and *Playboy,* but with plenty of cock—I discovered firsthand what lies beyond the fantasy world of porn.

Before accepting the editorship at *Unzipped,* however, I played the same game of mental hopscotch that I imagine any guy who considers working in porn would go through: *What will my friends think? What if Mom somehow finds out? Will my journalism career be forever marred and unsalvageable? Am I going to burn in hell like Jerry Falwell says?* Then I imagined all the parties and hobnobbing with porn stars and started to get excited about the opportunities. Plus, I wanted to find out firsthand if being a "fluffer" was actually a real occupational option in porn, or merely a queer urban legend. And if it was a viable option, I wanted to know where to apply.

In all seriousness, it wasn't really my curiosity about fluffing and hanging out with porn studs that influenced my decision to accept the position at *Unzipped.* I did it because I figured it would be a fun in-between job while I was figuring out exactly what it is I really wanted to do in my journalism career. However, it took all of a month to realize it's an enviable, fun, and sexy gig unlike any other opportunity I have had thus far. Hell, who wouldn't want to step into the role of being queerdom's answer to Hugh Hefner?!

It took some convincing to gain my friends' support, however, as virtually everyone I knew made a strange face the moment I mentioned the words "gay porn." And these were porn-purchasing gay men! Never mind what my straight buds thought. A month into the job every gay guy I knew was calling to ask for a comp subscription to *Unzipped.* Sure, this was homo hypocrisy at its most blatant, but it was also a concrete example of just how seductive is the lure of sex and porn. That notion alone made me feel quite secure in my new editorship.

In fact, my own uptight reservations about working in porn have subsided since joining the staff of *Unzipped.* And after being seduced by the fun of producing a monthly magazine about sex and interesting and important gay issues, what I thought would initially be an in-between job has become an exciting career. When you consider how incredibly racy Hollywood-produced entertainment has become within the last few years (*Temptation Island* is merely TV-sanitized, soft-core porn in prime time) and the way adult entertainment is edging its way more into the mainstream (VH1 scored high ratings with its gay-porn documentary *Totally Gay!* and W Hotels recently added gay porn as a pay-per-view option in its rooms), it seems that *Unzipped* is simply ahead of its time. And in the gay community—where porn is as common a sight as a Madonna T-shirt, and where every local gay rag features a half-naked circuit queen or porn star on its cover—the brazen celebration and exploitation of male beauty hardly raises an eyebrow anymore. It's almost as if we've become desensitized to the once-taboo topic of porn, now that there's a virtual cock in your face every time you turn your head in the gay ghettos across America.

So it's easy to imagine that in a few years' time, an adult magazine like *Unzipped* will be as nonthreatening to gay people as *Maxim* is now in hetero circles. Gay porn will continue to move further away from the dark corners of gay video stores and closer to the shelves showcasing the latest gay-oriented releases. In fact, in some homo havens gay porn has already mainstreamed its way into consumer consciousness. Case in point is the porn studio-owned All World's Resort in Palm Springs, where you can soak up the sun au naturel while watching a porn flick in the making, proving that even on vacation, you can't escape the lure of porn.

Top 15 Things Gay Men Have Learned From Porn

1. "The porn progression"—Grope, stroke, suck, fuck
2. Brothers can do it.
3. Brothas really are bigger.
4. Czech boys—whether or not they're really from the Czech Republic—are hot.
5. Docking
6. Manscaping is important.
7. Subtitles don't really matter, and moans don't have to match the mouth movements.
8. You can shoot things out of your ass.
9. A forearm can fit up an ass.
10. Cauliflower ass is not pretty.
11. "Winking" is not hot.
12. "Yeah...you (really *do*) like that, don't you?"
13. When you're ready to screw, rubbers magically appear and no one ever needs lube.
14. Porn is a universal language.
15. No one really has sex like that.

My adult education in the dynamics of porn continued when, during my first month at *Unzipped*, I got my first glimpse of porn in-the-making after being invited by Raging Stallion Studios to cover the shoot for *Monster Bang #4*. The title alone made it an offer I couldn't refuse.

The studio flew me to San Francisco, and when I arrived onset asking for the director, some of the crew mistook me for a porn newcomer, which was of course flattering. I was even more flattered when the director later extended an invitation to appear in one of his next skin flicks. It was then that my first onset experience became twofold: I initially went there to write about the making of an adult video, and now I was also using the opportunity to feel out a potential career move.

While I was watching the crew set up the first scene, prolific porn performer Matt Sizemore half-jokingly mentioned to me that the adult entertainment biz is what saved him from a hellish life of 9-to-5. But believe it or not, after being on a porn set all day long, making hot sex can become as monotonous and uninspiring as working a day job in a bank. That's the feeling I got after spending most of the weekend on the *Monster Bang* set, where the work hours were long—almost as long as Michael Brandon's dick. Almost. And even standing around watching beautiful men have sex can become too much of a good thing when your stomach is telling you it's time for lunch but the production schedule says otherwise. The half-hour sex scenes on the finished tape are undeniably hot and sexy, but it took most of the weekend, a dozen breaks to adjust lighting and sound, and countless bottles of lube to capture just the right intensity and composition to create the perfect series of scenes.

During that weekend I also learned two more important things: (1) Unfortunately, professional cocksuckers aren't part of the studio budget. Instead, fluffing is just one of the many perks of being a hot young porn star. You're often summoned to help stimulate your fellow workers when the going gets soft. And (2) while some of the clichés of the grandeur of the industry are true, the glamorous world of porn is run just as boringly tight and by the rules, maybe even more so, as any legitimate entertainment business—but with a little hustling on the side. Okay, with *a lot* of hustling on the side. The young, naive beauties are still paid anywhere from a couple hundred to a thousand dollars a movie while the studios churn out big profits. But at least everyone knows beforehand all the legalities, costs, and risks involved because it's part of their legal business contract to perform in an adult video.

On a porn set, before the cameras start rolling, copies of the models' driver's licenses or other legal ID are made, enema sessions take place, and then the sex action begins. Though the work hours are sometimes long and the pay won't make you rich, working in porn is undeniably a good ego stroke that appeals to the vanity in all of us. And so for those who choose to pursue a career path in porn, it can be a good gig if you can get it. Though you may have to turn a few tricks to maintain the fantasy porn-world lifestyle of endless circuit parties and go-go dancing gigs in tiny bars from coast to coast.

The money versus lifestyle issue comes up later in the day. During a break from filming a handsome blue-eyed stud who flew in from Arizona to make his porn debut in the video mentions during our interview that he recently left the mundane business world for the more carefree and lucrative option of hustling and porn. The video work may not pay substantially, but the exposure builds a bigger client base, which help sustain a practitioner of the world's oldest profession.

After spending most of the weekend on the set and getting tips from the pros, I decided that an onscreen career in porn and hustling probably wasn't a good idea for a guy who gets pee shy when he has to use a public restroom. Concentrating on satisfying one man during a hot, steamy sex romp in private takes enough mental and physical energy. I could never focus on catching wood when there's a crew of 10 other guys staring at me and training a spotlight on my dick.

Also, as I stood on the set going over the pros and cons of working in porn, I couldn't help but think of Jon Vincent, who was someone I once saw as a fantasy figure and then came to know as a buddy. In a real-life scenario that not even Hollywood could have scripted, I came across the porn stud on my very first day in West Hollywood, while strolling Santa Monica Boulevard and exploring my new environs. I couldn't believe my eyes when I turned a corner to buy a soda at a supermarket and stumbled upon Vincent in the parking lot. From the looks of the situation he was obviously very fucked up on something and arguing with a drag queen who was trying to pull him into a waiting taxi.

He was struggling to get away, though he was so inebriated he could barely walk let alone stand on his own, and the drag queen was winning the twisted tug of war while the cabbie and I watched in amazement. I stepped in to help because, well, I knew I could take the drag queen with one arm behind my back, and I pretty much knew what my reward would be for helping a porn star in drugged-out distress. The drag queen fled in the cab while I helped Jon hobble the three blocks to my apartment, where it wasn't long before I crossed the line between fantasy and reality and got to know my favorite porn obsession a little better.

That unusual introduction led to a friendship-fuck buddy situation that lasted until Vincent's untimely death from a heroin overdose in 2000. And unfortunately, the inebriated state he was in on the day I met him wasn't an exception but the rule in his life. Though I did see him on a few occasions when he was sober and trying in vain to kick his vices, mostly he was wrapped up in the drug-hazed world of the LA underground.

Offscreen, bisexual stud Jeff Vickers was just as sexy and masculine as his gay porn superstar alter ego Jon Vincent. In fact, it was difficult to tell the two apart. And during sex with him, it was difficult to know whether Jeff Vickers had adopted the porn personality of his profession, or if the porn commodity Jon Vincent was merely the celluloid replica of Jeff Vicker's real-life personality. Jeff had a warm, engaging charm and a genuine personality, but during the throes of hot sex he would from time to time utter the clichéd porn dialogue of Jon Vincent—"Yeah, you like that big cock, don't you, baby?"—and perform with the studied choreography of a prolific porn star.

I recalled these moments vividly during a break in the *Monster Bang* shoot and realized that the side effects of Jeff Vickers life in porn was not something I wanted to experience again, especially from his viewpoint. And even some of the alluring aspects that he spoke of—such as the sugar daddy who bought him a home in upstate New York—didn't outweigh the dark realities that he confessed he had to endure to achieve that material excess.

So I decided on the spot that when it comes to porn I'm content with just being a voyeur. It's the safest sex there is. Like most guys, though, I'm certainly glad there are uninhibited, good-looking men out there who have no issues about getting their groove on for the sake of entertaining the horny masses. Life would be a little lonely and quite dull without them.

John Rutherford's Top 5 Tips for Anyone Aspiring to Become a Porn Star

1. Leave your body hair natural.
2. Keep your hairstyle contemporary but not trendy (wedge cut, *eww*).
3. Do your research on who's who in the business; only work with reputable companies that make quality products.
4. Toss out all preconceived notions of what the porn business is. It will surprise you how many great people are working hard to make high-quality product.
5. Don't overexpose yourself by doing too many movies.

John Rutherford's Funniest Moments on a Porn Set

1. Damien (a star from the early '90s) was going down to suck off his scene partner in a Mustang movie Chi Chi was directing when his hair got caught on his scene partner's coach whistle. Just as Damien put his mouth on the other guy's cock, Damien let out a loud yell. I immediately panned up to reveal Damien desperately trying to get disentangled. We stopped shooting and both of them needed the makeup artist...who was nowhere to be found.

2. Once while assistant directing for a Falcon movie, we were shooting out in the forest alongside an old tree. The cameraman, Todd Montgomery, and the lighting grip were getting the shot and didn't realize that the cables from the camera and light were wrapping around the tree and limiting their ability to move. Without warning, a beehive that nobody saw in the tree came alive with angry bees. They swarmed the models and the crew. Todd, with his diligence to save the camera, started running and got caught in the tightly wrapped wire and flung back like a slingshot, falling onto his ass. By then the models were gone and he was

left alone, so he got up and ran to the horizon, zig-zagging back and forth like in a Bugs Bunny cartoon, yelling, "Will nobody help me?"

3. Another time I was directing in a forest and the photographer, David Lam, thought it would be a good idea to climb the tree for the shot. After getting the shot he realized he couldn't get down and wrapped his arms and legs around the tree limb. Then suddenly he was slipping upside down. He started losing his grip and yelled for help. The models looked up and quickly got out of the way. David then fell from his perch onto the soft air mattress they had been performing on. Thankfully!

4. In Australia the talent and the talent coordinator flew up to Cairns from Sydney, but the crew decided to make the two-day drive in case we saw some pretty shots along the Aussie coast. The weather was perfect, but just as we passed Brisbane and continued along the Gold Coast we encountered some of the worst rain we'd ever experienced in our lives. We couldn't see in front of us, and the road suddenly started looking like a lake. I was lead car in our five-car caravan when we saw a man alongside the road screaming at us. Just as we passed we realized he was warning us in his thick Aussie accent that the road may be washed out and we could be in danger. We put the pedal to the metal and just made it before the road washed away. Not wanting to press our luck, we spent the night in a small-town motel, waking up in the morning with the entire town under water. Thankfully, we'd chosen a motel on top of a hill.

John Rutherford is the president of Colt Studios.

What Made the Writers Hard?
Favorite Pornos and Porn Stars From the Cast of *Mondo Homo.*

Richard Andreoli—I've seen quite a few leather and fetish porns in my time, but the one that originally set my mind and body on fire was the first *Fallen Angel* film from Titan. It was a movie full of the hottest men I'd ever seen, and Kyle Brandon was leader of the pack. He encapsulated every daddy fantasy I'd ever had, in look and especially in attitude, and the fact that he could take it just as easily as he could dish it out made me fall for him even more. I've never really had an obsession with anyone in film, TV, or porn, but if there were someone I'd choose, it would be Kyle. And, honestly, every porn I've seen since then seems to be either trying too hard, or not trying hard enough; I guess your first time really is the best.

David Ciminelli—I've never had a taste for twinkies or chicken and therefore bypassed most of the typical gay porn that was out there when I was coming out in the late '80s. I've always liked men—*real* men, masculine men with mounds of muscles, intimidating Clint Eastwood-like stares, and gruff voices. I found all of that the first time I laid eyes on Tom Brock. A prolific porn star in the '80s, Brock never looked better than he does in famed director John Travis' *They Grow 'Em Big,* Brock's third movie for Catalina. Tall with rippling muscles, wavy brown hair, soft brown bedroom eyes, and the sexiest cleft chin since Kirk Douglas's, Brock looks like he's part Marlboro man and part WWF wrestler—and he's an insatiable sex pig with a huge dick that would make Jeff Stryker feel inferior. Playing a ranch foreman in *They Grow 'Em Big,* Brock looks so incredibly sexy in his tight Wranglers and cowboy gear that he could easily make you climax before he even takes off his clothes. When he catches equally studly Steve Ross beating off to a straight porn mag, he takes him aside and gives him a lesson in man-on-man sex that I haven't forgotten since seeing this flick two decades ago! The only scene that even comes close to topping Brock's and Ross's unforgettable fuck fest is the flick's later four-way with Brock, Dean Chasen, Jay Hawkins, and Eric Radford, four megastuds who get it on in an outdoor orgy scene that has yet to be topped by any other director.

Smith Galtney—Nick Fabrini in *Sunkissed.* Sure, he's often cold and otherwise engaged on-screen. But damn if Fabrini isn't a hot-as-*blazes,* turbo-top in this otherwise shite flick. (The moustache! That dick!! What grindwork!!!) In other movies Nick looks thinner—alarmingly thinner, to be honest—but here, his body's just right: all ripped and chunky and hard, just like a good daddy should be.

Aaron Krach—All I know is that somehow, somewhere I saw this scene at a kitchen table. A brute-of-a-man named Chad Douglas was sitting next to this blond twink (name: irrelevant) at a clear glass kitchen table. They both were wearing these ridiculously short white tennis shorts like they were fresh off the grass at Wimbledon. You could see their bulging baskets through the table, which had no dishes on it. And—*schawing!*—out pops Mr. Chad Douglas's scary, enormous wanker. Fat and round and hanging down his leg from apparently too much blood, sweat, and sex. The thing was beastly. It turned the twink bright red and sent me running to the cupboard to grab some Kleenex. Chad Douglas is too ugly to ever be cast in porn today: another reason why the industry churns out boring videos. They need to bring back the scary, monster men of years gone by. Don't get me wrong. I mean "scary" in the most exciting way.

Christopher Lisotta—I'm so lame. I don't do porn. Allergic to the plastic they make remotes out of. Am I still gay?

Parker Ray—I'm probably the only homo who doesn't own any porn. No magazines, no videos, nothing. I've seen it, sure, but I can't remember any of the guys I've been attracted to in porn. And the faces that go with the names I do know, the ones that are tossed around all the time (Ken Ryker, Jeff Stryker—are they related?)—I couldn't pick them out of a lineup. Maybe I'm one of those lucky guys who has had enough good real sex so I don't need fantasy fodder; I just think about my own past experiences when I'm on my own and it always seems to do the trick. So the only "porn stars" that turn me on are the guys I've had sex with, and I remember their names—well, most of them, anyway.

Dave White—*Spokes.* What's great about *Spokes* is that it's set in a barn and plenty of guys end up with hay stuck to their asses. There's almost nothing erotic about hay stuck to a sweaty ass, but these guys are so into the sex they're having that they didn't even bother to stop and towel themselves dry between takes. It's a testament to the crazy energy of this video that it's populated by guys who aren't even my preferred type—skinny and hairless—and yet I can watch it again and again. I even showed it to a straight male friend once and *he* thought it was cool too. There. An endorsement from the other team.

Crack Addict!

Dave White's Tips on How to Know When You've Officially Watched Too Much Porn

1. Overlooking stubbly, blotchy, shaved asses has become second nature.
2. You find yourself thinking, *You know, this music isn't bad at all.*
3. You keep waiting for Peter Jennings to whip it out on the evening news.
4. Thoughts of actually doing something to get yourself arrested and thrown into one of those all-male sex-jails for a night seem more and more reasonable.
5. You can't come anymore unless there's a remote in your hand.
6. Any fugly guy in a tool belt gets you instantly hard.
7. You daydream about turning your bedroom into a sterile hotel suite complete with wall-mounted phone and 125-watt bulbs in the lamps.
8. You stopped watching *Friends* because they never gave you the money shot.
9. Your local adult video store has given you your own "[Your name here] Recommends..." section.
10. There's no good publicly mentionable answer as to why your hands are so soft.
11. You begin to think of your collection as "erotica" and yourself as an "archivist."
12. Another live naked person in the room throws off your concentration.

Confessions of a Go-Go Boy

By Richard Andreoli

"There are three kinds of male dancers," Marcus informs me. "Showboys who do production numbers at circuit parties and clubs, strippers, and 'dick dancers' or go-go boys." Go-gos, he says, wear as little as possible while gyrating on a raised box, under a spotlight, and have tips shoved down their G-strings.

"Will you be our dick dancer?" asks Parker Ray, my editor at *Instinct* magazine. I look around at the expectant staff who have cornered me in his office.

"Is a pig's pussy pork?" I ask, then quickly purge the Subway sandwich I just ate and prepare for my diet of chicken broth and Tic Tacs. It's time to become *Instinct*'s go-go boy for a night!

With five years experience under his thong, Marcus is my go-go liaison. He explains that most dancers choose a stage name (his is "Lucid"), but I can worry about that after my audition at Mickey's in West Hollywood, where the happy-hour dancers shake their money makers in full view of every passerby.

Auditions generally involve removing your shirt or stripping to your 2(x)ists and boogying on the box to see if you freeze under pressure. Dennis, Mickey's promoter and fairy godfather of go-go boys everywhere, also looks for dancers with personality and a knack for working the crowd.

"But if you're bombing, you'll know right away," Dennis says, "because you won't get any tips."

I earn Dennis's approval and head to Hollywood Boulevard where "Walk Of Fame" stars belonging to Carol Burnett, Cloris Leachman, and Jim Nabors flank the 20-year old store By George. There the staff informs me that dancers usually wear cock rings to appear well-endowed, and they prefer jelly rings or thongs with built-in elastic rings because, unlike metal or leather ones, if daddy gropes you he won't feel the booster.

Then, in a Julia Roberts-esque *Pretty Woman* montage, I march out of the changing room modeling multiple G-strings, jock straps, and bikinis. Suddenly, in black trunks with my ass sticking out like an invitation waiting to be RSVP'd to, my go-go name descends upon me like a fluttering $100 from Truman Capote's ghost. I become "Raven"!

To quote a cliché, here's the breakdown:

Raven's clothes: $60
Raven's spray-on tan: $25
Raven's diet: $10 per week
Being "Raven" for the night: Priceless

I meet Marcus at Mickey's the following Friday, quickly dress in a camouflage thong (to support our men in uniform) under surfer swim trunks, oil up, do double tequila shots, and jump into the red spotlight. The upbeat T-dance music is easy to move to, and I quickly find my groove.

As an older gentleman slips money into my waistband and cops a feel, my boyfriend swoops in like Batman on a mission, pushes me back, and passionately smooches me.

"In the gay community, this is what we call 'marking your territory,'." my friend Alonso dryly observes.

Note: To earn a go-go living, lose the boyfriend or you'll never work again.

Raven's first 20-minute session completed, I observe the following: (1) Staying erect while dancing is not always possible; (2) acting silly is only funny for a minute, then you become bored, and if this were a real job you wouldn't make any money goofing off; (3) having friends tip you is nice, but collecting cash from strangers is awesome!

The bar now packed, customers expect more, so dancers wear less clothing with each set. My second appearance offers Raven's college look in shiny blue UCLA gym shorts, and I pour water over myself, smile at every guy, and ask his name when he's tipping.

By Raven's third set I'm wearing the black swimsuit, feeling no pain, and taking requests. I imitate Olivia Newton-John from *Xanadu* for author Dennis Hensley and do clothed tea-bagging for writer Dave White (who promised $5 and gave me $2—don't think I was *that* drunk!). I make bank as the new boy on the box and realize that scoring bills because someone thinks you're sexy is an incredible rush. I slowly plummet into every negative stereotype about gay narcissism...but then another dollar gets tucked into my shorts and I immediately lift myself back up.

It's tougher work for dancers without friends on hand. Between sets they socialize and flirt with the fans in order to score the almighty green. Happy hour is also easier because the customers are generally older and polite. At night you get drunks looking to grope more and pay less, and the other dancers become more competitive, bitchy, and backstabbing. Think *Showgirls*.

Truthfully, go-go dancing is far more work than I expected. You're "on" the entire time, and I suspect the most successful dancers are exhibitionists as much as money lovers; otherwise it wouldn't be worth the emotional investment. I doubt Raven will ever return.

But I did leave Mickey's with $80 after only an hour's work. And I do have a couple fans now, my student loans are still looming, and a trip to Vegas would be fun.

Hmm. Raven wonders if there are openings for The White Party.

Chapter 15: Sex

What About Those of Us Who Swing Both Ways?
By Parker Ray

After coming out at 17 I couldn't get enough of guys. My senior year in high school was a study in adolescent sluttiness. My freshman year in college was even worse (or better, looking at it from my perspective), since I was far away from home and surrounded by closeted frat boys, sexy science types who never realized they had perfect butts, and other young horny guys my age from all around the country. I don't even remember doing my schoolwork—or even going to many of my classes those first two years.

By the time my third year rolled around I had gotten into the swing of the gay scene at my school. Even worse (or, again, better), I was able to live off campus in a single in the gay neighborhood. Boys at school, men at the grocery store. I was prepared for another year of scholarly seduction.

Then I met Heather. I was first introduced to Heather while at a house party in Westwood Village, the student 'hood that surrounds UCLA. That evening I had some guy hanging on me that I had met two weeks prior. His name isn't important. What was of significance that night was that I spent most of it talking to Heather. My boy toy got trashed and wanted to have sex in a closet or some other stifling setting. I told him I'd get around to it, but he passed out while Heather and I chatted about psychology (which was one of the two degrees each of us was getting).

I realized while sitting there, mayhem happening all around me, drinking my fourth cheap-vodka drink, that I was stealing glances at Heather's breasts. Then her legs, her smile, the way she tucked her hair behind her ear, which, ever since Claire Danes in *My So-Called*

Life, always sucker-punched me when pretty and shy-seeming girls did it. I guess Heather didn't notice me sizing her up—maybe because she knew I was there with another guy. At one point I self-righteously confided to her how I couldn't stand that straight guys objectified women, which is the reason I went out of my way to objectify breeder boys when the chance arose. (Ah, the pompous feminism phase all college-age gay boys go through in order to make up for not giving one shit about females when a cocksucking opportunity arises.)

I didn't return sex-in-a-closet guy's calls, but the next day I called up Heather and asked her out. She thought it meant "hanging out," not knowing that I was sexually pining for her. Once I started having sex with guys I never looked back on the chicks I had fumbled around with. Probably because the sex was just that: fumbling. But now I had experience, and Heather was two years older than me. She was sexy, and I was convinced she knew how to kiss.

After a few weeks of what she thought was just harmless flirting and letting me grope her because, hey, I'm a fag and couldn't *possibly* want more, I laid it on her. "I'm totally smitten with you, and I'm sure now that I'm bisexual," I said. Her expression changed. She stopped smiling and told me I was gay. I told her to give me a chance. She hadn't had a boyfriend in a while, so she did.

If you need to know, we were a great couple. The sex was great, and she helped me appreciate the art of making out again after that string of guys who stopped kissing and went right for your crotch after 40 seconds. But because I defied a neat "gay" or "straight" label, I came up against objections from both sides of the fence.

The gays: My friends couldn't care less that I was dating a girl. It was college so you pretty much had a license to "experiment." One time, though, I was in mixed company with Heather and said the word "fag" out loud. I'd done it hundreds of times before when I was fucking guys. But I guess once you have a girl on your arm, something changes. You're not allowed to say words that gays consider derogatory unless one of their own says it. This gay guy, whom I'd met only once, and who probably thought I was straight because of Heather, yelled "Fuck you!" and went off about "straight" people not having permission to use that word. I was shocked. My friends who were there were shocked. Thankfully, I quickly recovered and mentioned to the guy that I was bisexual and, to prove my point, got up and sat in the lap of one of my friends and started to French kiss him. (Heather thought it was hot.) I guess that proved my point, because the offended queer just sat down in silence.

The straights (or in this case, the straight): Heather and I used to check out guys together. Girls, too, but mostly guys. Because we were in college and "experimenting," she asked if we could have a three-way...with another girl. I said sure, and even let her pick the lady. After that, I asked if we could have a three-way with a guy. I was starting to miss cock, just like I had realized when I met Heather that I missed breasts and girlie bellies. She agreed, but later admitted she thought I liked it too much. She was afraid I would cheat on her with a guy. (She didn't even comprehend me wanting to possibly sleep around with other women.)

Breaking up with Heather was pretty easy. It was her last year, and she was heading off to the East Coast for graduate school. Maybe she didn't take our relationship all that seriously—even though it was my second-longest one. She convinced me that "bi" isn't a term gay guys use when they're in that transition phase between solely messing around with girls to solely messing around with guys.

The last time I saw Heather, before she went to her parents' place and then off to get some advanced degree, I asked her if she appreciated the time we spent together.

"Of course. It was a lot of fun," she replied. "But it never would have worked out in the long run."

Then she said something that I keep in the back of my mind every time I start hitting on a lady: "I don't doubt you liked having sex with me," she said with her beautiful smile, "but you like to suck dick more than me. And *no* girl wants her boyfriend to be better at blow jobs than she is."

How to Host a Home Orgy!

Find a location and make it orgy-proof: Any home or apartment will do, but it's wise to remove the nice furniture and valuables and place them in "off-limits" rooms. Purchase rolls of plastic sheeting from a hardware store and cover the floors for easy clean up. Also cover the beds before placing the cloth sheets on, so that you protect your mattresses. One bathroom should be reserved for taking care of business. Backyards can be used, but make sure neighbors can't accidentally see or hear someone tapping an ass; they'll most likely call the cops. Finally, don't rush out and buy a sling just because you're hosting. A bed works just fine.

Must-haves: Get plenty of condoms and lube, beverages (alcoholic and non), music that suits the sort of guys who are attending, low or dim/indirect lighting, and unscented candles as long as they will last the whole evening and not get in anyone's way (unless we're talking wax torture). Only bring toys if you're willing to share.

Send out invitations: You don't want just anybody showing up, so start with friends or tricks whose tastes you trust implicitly. Perhaps have them each invite one guest as well, but keep your numbers manageable, especially if you're hosting for the first time. More experienced orgy hosts allow unlimited guests to arrive and then either accept or reject them at the door; while this makes things more exciting, it also creates potential drama.

Set the rules: Once everyone's gathered, be clear about what behavior will and won't be tolerated. General rules include safe sex practices, drug or alcohol usage, and how to behave politely in a group sex setting. You can and should kick out anyone who breaks the rules if you feel their attitude diminishes the fun for other people.

Get things going: After the rules it sometimes helps to have a stripper or an exhibitionist couple who is willing to start some action. From there, everyone else will fall in line.

Basic tips:
—Don't try imitating your favorite porn. Dirty talk is great, but too much will distract people and make them laugh when they should be getting off.
—Unless you're the stripper, don't wear sexy underwear, neon jockstraps, or anything that seems inappropriate. Everyone will talk about you years later when someone comes to write a book with a section on orgies.
—Don't claim to be a top unless you really are one, because lying is not only mean, in this case it becomes a huge letdown.
—Bring mints or a small bottle of mouthwash. Brushing your teeth can sometimes be bad if you get bloody gums.
—Be careful with oil-based lubricants like Wet Platinum. They stain walls, sheets, and aren't latex safe.
—Respect the laws of basic hygiene. Clean yourself out before letting everyone bang you on the Lazy Susan.

Stalling for Time? Lie About Your STD!

By Dave White

Men are pretty easy to deceive. A good lie will get you almost anything you want. And if what you want is that hot guy but what you've got is that scorching case of herpes, you'll need to figure out how to buy some time till your outbreak subsides. Here's how not to be a diseased pariah.

You've got: Crabs
He wants: Frottage

The prognosis: He can't have it. And you don't yet know if that Rid shower worked. In the meantime, tell him you're feeling sort of submissive and you need to be fed. A blow job from you won't spread whatever remaining guests you might have crawling around down there, and your willingness to provide unlimited oral orgasms will keep him from asking questions.
Stall time = 1 week

You've got: Syphilis
He wants: Anything more than a mutual jack-off session.

The prognosis: Forget it. You can't touch him. You can't do a damn thing till you take all of those antibiotics and not a moment sooner. If you don't live together, it's easy. Just tell him you're swamped with work and you can't see him till you get your head above water. Phone sex will tide him over. If you do live together then you're probably not having much sex anymore anyway and he won't notice.
Stall time = 2 weeks

You've got: Gonorrhea
He wants: To suck it

The prognosis: You're a heel if you let him. He'll think the resulting sore throat is just a

cold and you'll reserve yourself a seat in hell next to Kevin Spacey. A single 125mg shot of Ceftriaxone is really all that stands in the way of your getting down to love town. Anyone can stall for that long. Start a fight over something stupid. Tell him you need time "to think."
Stall time = A few days

You've got: Herpes
He wants: Near your cock

The prognosis: Herpes is for life, man. You just have to buck up and tell him or you're fucked for, like, ever. No sense driving everyone crazy. And until that particular outbreak goes to sleep, you can give him lots of warm affectionate hugs. Yeah, it's boring.
Stall time = None. Tough shit, Mr. Blistex

You've got: That weird new staph infection that's so hip to get right now but can kill you anyway
He wants: To be anywhere near you

The prognosis: Well, if you get this shit you could wind up in the hospital, which will pretty much give away that you're not up for anal. If, however, you get the milder version of this freaky new skin-to-skin, drug-resistant staph, you'll need to take the Terminator antibiotics and tell him a high school friend died or something, necessitating your leaving town. If you survive, you can eventually do him. Unless he's the one who gave it to you. Then you're screwed.
Stall time = God only knows. Check with your doctor. This stuff can take a long time to pack up and leave.

Code Name: Decepticon!

Dave White Sorts Out What They Say and What They Mean...

"I'm 100 percent top." = "I need therapy to sort out my masculinity issues."
"Nice cock." = "I've seen bigger."
"I like it raw." = "I will give you syphilis."
"No cologne, please" = "I have a B.O. fetish."
"I never do that." = "I have a disturbing secret life."

"Do you party?" = "I'm *this* close to hitting bottom."
"I'm furry" = "You'd better like back hair. A lot."
"I like real men." = "Please be big and stupid."
"I need to get fucked *hard!*" = "I'll tense up when you try to stick it in."
"You're the only guy I let come in my mouth." = "I was the basis for that Rod Stewart rumor."
"Do you want to get together again?" = "I need a boyfriend so bad I can taste it."
"Sorry, this has never happened before." = "Damn it! Not again!"
"I'm just a big bottom." = "I can't keep it up long enough to fuck anyone."
"I'm gonna fuck you all night long." = "I'm kicking you out after I come."
"I don't like to rinse the come off right away." = "You can pee on me if you want."

Why You Should Have Sex With Me Right Now

By Dave White

So there's this weird movie called *Hey, Happy!* that you should totally watch. It's a freaky little Canadian movie I like by a writer-director named Noam Gonick. The plot is convoluted and absurd, but the main story line involves a young DJ named Sabu who decides that, in order to bring on an apocalyptic flood, he needs to have sex with 2000 men. Or maybe he just wants to have sex with 2000 men because he's a slut and decides that the apocalyptic flood is just a nice bonus, like when you get something free with the purchase of an item of equal or greater value. Either way, he has sex with 1,999 men and has his sights set on a UFO-obsessed guy named Happy. After many obstacles are surmounted, they fuck, the flood comes, and DJ Sabu gets pregnant. The end.

Here's why it's a great movie: because they fuck.

Think about it. How many gay-themed movies or TV shows have you seen where the fags get to have tons of sex and don't have to learn a lesson about moderation or true love or some other bullshit like that. In *Hey, Happy!* slutty Sabu is the one doing all the boom-boom and he's the only one that holds the truth. He doesn't have to realize that all that nonstop sex is empty and meaningless or that it's time to grow up and stop having orgasms. All he gets is knocked up, and he's okay with that. We may have more homo-themed entertainment product out there than ever before, but how much of it inspires you to go out and get into a hot threeway? Say what you want about how dopey Showtime's *Queer as Folk* is—and it is—but at least the dudes on that show get it on. Brian Kinney may have a grumpy look on his face when he does it, but the point is he does it.

Not that you have to be some kind of A-list god, TV actor-looking guy to qualify. Everyone should have sex. Look at this chapter's title. You should be having sex right now. Maybe not necessarily with me—although that would be preferable from my perspective—but with someone. Why? Because we're sexy people, and sexy people should sex it up with each other. That's why.

Notice that I didn't say "hot." It's a stupid empty word, one so degraded it means that people like Kimora Lee Simmons or Lorenzo Lamas get to sit behind desks critiquing your symmetry and your flab, pointing at you with a laser thingie and telling you to hang it up. Models are hot. People in shit like *The Fast and the Furious* are hot. Porn stars are hot. Ripped abs and big muscles are hot. But when was the last time you looked at an actor or a porn star or any of the gymrats you could see in your local Bally's gym and felt any actual sexual energy coming from them? Can't remember? That's because actors are about teasing the camera, the majority of porn stars are just punching the clock like everybody else, and most bodybuilders are usually too focused on training for competitions that have, if you can even believe it, absolutely nothing to do with blow jobs.

And blow jobs, gentlemen, are what we should be about. Blow jobs and anal and frottage and group action and one-on-one monogamous vanilla "lovemaking" and slings and dungeons and bondage and role-playing and threegies and fourgies and bisexual flings and mutual masturbation and foot worship and watersports and I forget what else. Oh, yeah, and all the kinky activities those multicolored hankies signify. That stuff too. If you're one of the sexy people, you know that "hot" isn't always what you're looking for. I'm not hot. But you should have sex with me right now anyway.

Notice, also, that I didn't say "sex-positive." Call someone that and you're more or less telling them they're a dullard. The expression meant something once, not so long ago. It used to be a way for the sexy people to suss each other out. Then it became boring. People began using it as a signifier of correct thought, or worse, as something related to your "spirituality." (Not that sex isn't good for your spirit. I just don't want to have to talk to you about it over herbal tea, you know?) And if you didn't measure up to the new definitions then you weren't correct to have sex with. Sex-positivity is for people who put ideology before pleasure, and that's a backward-ass way of fucking. Better to dangerously flirt with stupid hippie-think and call it all "free love" than to get stuck in either of those traps.

I said sexy. A quality that, strangely, in "gay culture," we've lost sight of even as that same culture remains hypersexualized.

It seems silly maybe to encourage fags to have more sex. But I've met a lot of us and we're not the Annabel *"World's Biggest Gang Bang"* Chongs the world thinks we are. Way too many of us are insecure about sex. We suddenly become timid and shy. Or else we get sex, maybe plenty of it, and get the weird-itis afterward. We feel horny, we go out and get some trick, we fuck, we throw away his number, and then two weeks later we see him out somewhere and we pretend we don't know him. (FYI, if he's with his boyfriend or wife that's a good thing, but otherwise you have no excuse.)

If we really want to "be bad" we put on ripped-up jeans and boots and end up in some sex club or bathhouse. Then we go home feeling bad because we don't have a boyfriend or because we didn't hook up with the one perfect guy we wanted or a hundred other stupid reasons. That ain't sexy. That's fucked up.

But back to why you should be having sex with me (or whoever) right now. You should have sex right now because you're free. You're free to do whatever you want to do with whatever consenting partner of consenting age that you choose in whatever country you live in. Even if it's illegal for men to have sex with men where you live. Even then you're free to do it. And the reason you're free to have sex right now is because you freed *yourself*. If that sounds too lame and new agey then step back and rearrange your mind for a second so that it doesn't sound that way. Being free means you have to make it happen. The world out there doesn't want you to feel sexy. But you must.

I'm not advocating better self-esteem or happier dispositions or tantric breathing or special body oils or Marianne Williamson books or even tanning. I'm saying that it's time you looked at your body and saw it for what it is: a sexy machine designed for sex. It's built for having orgasms. You should have lots of them, even if you feel guilty about it. That guilt will subside the more you come. Or "cum," if that's your preferred spelling. Whatever.

But how do you come—or cum—if sex makes you feel all uptight and pinchy? If you *do* feel that old drilled-in guilt? If you need the lights completely off or you need to be out of town on a business trip so you don't run into anyone you know or you can only do it with a total stranger? Is it too late to become the kind of person who wants to whip it out and do the humpty dance at a moment's notice? Do you need a therapist?

You might. But then again, you may just need Susie Bright. Susie is this bisexual chick who writes books about sex. Really fun, smart books about sex. She's as straightforward as her fellow sex-writer Dan Savage, but she's different. She's more like if you had this really awesome older sister telling you about dildos. She talks about sex like it's your patriotic duty. She wears latex dresses. She wrote *Susie Sexpert's Lesbian Sex World* and *Susie Bright's Sexual Reality,* books that all fags should read. Yeah, *Lesbian Sex World,* you read that correctly. Dykes can teach you things. Never forget that. And Susie, by virtue of simply living her life and writing it down, is the awesome sex-ed teacher you never thought you'd have. Her work can help you open the door and face the weirdness of desire.

You might also simply need Lil' Kim. And please don't be that pucker-faced faggot who says he hates hip-hop. You are obligated to love hip-hop. Hip-hop is fuck music. And you need to fuck. Lil' Kim knows this simple true fact of life, and for some reason, faggots seem to respond instinctively to her. Example: Not long ago I was at a strange new West Hollywood biweekly party called "Club Chub." It's for bears and fat boys and guys who think bears and fat boys are sexy (and they are, by the way, just in case you weren't in on that). So the DJ is playing old '80s stuff—which is fine and all because older faggots need shit they can sing along to. But no one is dancing. Then he plays Kylie. A little dancing. Not much. Then he plays Lil' Kim and 50 Cent's "Magic Stick." You'd have thought he'd rung a dinner bell and announced free cheeseburgers on the dance floor. Suddenly, the big boys are shakin' it up and down. Jumping up on the go-go boy's platform. Grinding into each other. The works. It's one of the most inspiring, spontaneously sensual moments I've witnessed outside of an orgy. In fact, it was sexier (and more fun) than some orgies I've seen.

I could sit here and do nothing but recommend stuff—books to read, movies to see—to inspire your "erotic imagination," or whatever. I could enthusiastically exhort you to follow your horniness to the place where it intersects with cultural "texts" so that the two will fuse and you'll be lofted to new heights of sexy. Stuff like the darkly pounding, sensually stimulating indie band Girls Against Boys or the great German fag movie *Taxi zum Klo*, about a guy who's really into public toilets. Or old Prince songs like "Alphabet Street" where the now-disappeared-but-formerly-awesome-Prince-sidechick Cat rapped about "lovesexy" being "the glam of them all"—whatever the fuck *that* meant—and how "life was too good to waste" in a state of non-lovesexiness. Or the TV show *Monster Garage* where these smoking-hot mechanic dudes build cars and you get to watch them get greased up and, well, build cars. Trust me, it's good. But none of those things is gonna mean a damn until you can do some brain surgery on yourself.

First, you must stop swallowing every limp dick the gay media tries to stick down your throat. You know the guys who do this, the guys who won't put on a swimsuit because they're not "ready;" the guys who want their back hair electrocuted off; the guys who can barely even kiss properly because they're so freaked-out about their own desirability. Here is a message for those guys: *Please to unbunch the panties, faggots!*

I say this as a man who writes for a couple of national gay magazines, and I'm telling you that a lot of what gets fed to you about being a sexually competent and active sodomite is hogwash. Almost all of it misses the point. Really, how many articles on developing your abs and lats do you actually need to read? How many pairs of $180 jeans will make you desirable? How much exfoliation is really necessary, and must you drop the cash equivalent of a half-day's wages on the product that will do it to you? How unfat is unfat enough? How pretty and turned out and back-hair-waxed do you need to be to be loved? How much Botox? How many lies about your body are you willing to believe? Because if you're not the sort who can say "piss off" to images of perfection, it can seem like everyone is "hot" but you.

Next, you must stop taking the "hotness" of others so personally. Because I'm not advocating that the porn industry stop employing muscular fantasy men with 9-inch cocks or that magazine art directors change their ways and quit putting cute model boys on the covers. Porn stars and models need work just like everyone else. The media do what they do to reach the biggest number of consumers possible and to make money. But they are not responsible for how you think about your own body or your sexual worth. You are responsible for how you think, regardless of how un-"hot" you may be. And I'm also not saying you shouldn't take care of your body or go to the gym if you feel like it, or that being attractive to others isn't important. If you're not attractive to others then you're not getting laid. Ever.

What I am saying is that—here's where it gets self-helpy—you gotta get it through that concrete skull that you are sexy. Right here and right now. Everything about you at this moment is attractive to someone. In fact, it's attractive to more than just some *one*. Lots of someones. Your inherited tendency toward male-pattern baldness is sexy. Those gray hairs you've been plucking and dying are sexy. Your first and fifth and 20th wrinkle is sexy. Your imperfect teeth, your big nose, jug ears, your unibrow, your belly, your very average cock, your scar, your odd chest hair pattern, your less-than-Herculean arms, all of it. Someone out there sees you and thinks, *Wow he's cute. I wanna hit that.* I'm not lying. I'm right.

And I know I'm right because I am just like you. I am the regular guy that most hot guys don't look twice at. I am the guy who had the misfortune to stumble into a very close friendship with a fag—I'll call him Kevin—who turns heads everywhere we go together. That bummed me out for about five seconds. Then I realized I had been given the superpower of invisibility and I could eavesdrop and spy on everything other people were saying about my friend and me. And here's what they said:

About him: "[various expletives and exclamations over his hotness, blah, blah, blah]"

About me: "..."

Even Kevin's friends treated me like I didn't exist. And I mean that in the most literal sense I can impart to you. I would greet these vacant motherfuckers when they met us on the street and they would never respond to me. It was as if I hadn't spoken to them at all, as if they could see right through me. Afterward, Kevin would apologize for their rudeness. I'd just laugh. I probably should have been offended by them. Instead, I was shocked into thinking it was the funniest thing I'd ever experienced. I was so *not there* to these guys that I even overheard them speaking about me once (proving that, in fact, they *could* see me and simply didn't find me human enough to consider lowering their voices for, but you get what I'm saying). One of them asked, "Why is Kevin hanging out with *that* guy?"

The other one responded with a shoulder shrug and a face that silently said, "Ewww."

"They're not fucking are they?"

"Please."

Becoming Harriet the Spy around these guys meant I could do the same with other hot guys. And what I learned from my eavesdropping is that hot guys infrequently scratch more than surfaces or their own immediate itches. They don't have to. While hot guys get told all the time about their hotness, the rest of us have to learn on our own what makes us sexy. We have to think about it. We have to swim against the tide that tells us "No." And we have to chase the hot guys for a while, find out that it's dumb to do so, learn to ignore the ones who ignore us (a handy mantra: "Fuck all y'all"), stop worshipping as gods the ones who *don't* ignore us, start seeing ourselves the way most others see us, and start living our lives by our own rules.

No, it's not easy. If suddenly seeing yourself as others do were simple, then therapists offices would be empty and Dr. Phil wouldn't have his own show where he gets to yell at people every day. What *is* simple, however, is faking it. That's the next thing you have to do. Anyone can look confident. Any man can walk into a cruisy gay bar and stand up tall and assert himself, shoulders back, head up, chest out, smirk on face, purposeful. You don't have to *feel* like you stand a chance in hell—you can *know* that you're awkward and shy and intimidated by all the strapping alpha males swaggering around the place—but what you can do is front like you've got the biggest dick in the place. It just takes a little practice.

It's not about becoming obnoxious or butch, surly or overly serious (as in that sour Brian Kinney *Queer as Folk* scowl). It's about exuding quiet self-assurance. If you do this, you will get sex. The men you want, the men who want you, will come to you. If they don't, then you just need more practice. It's the best type of vicious circle. Pretend like you know you're the hot one, get sex, feel good, feel like you actually *are* hot, get more sex. You win!

And the goal? To understand that pleasure is good. It's good for your cock, it's good for your complexion, it's good for your heart, it's good for your soul, and it's good for the other guy you're experiencing pleasure with. It has nothing to do with ego or neurosis. It has everything to do with feeling like you just got your electricity switched on. It has everything to do with joy. To deny yourself real physical pleasure, real fun with another person, is stupid. So don't be stupid anymore. Be sexy instead. Got it?

Contributors

Besides collecting really cool but ultimately useless pop culture crap, **Richard Andreoli** works as a freelance writer in Los Angeles. His words have appeared in *The Advocate, Instinct, Cargo, Frontiers, IN Los Angeles,* Playboy TV, and a variety of—how do you say?—"adult" publications. This past year he interviewed both Lynda Carter and Jennifer Garner (and Jennifer complimented his biceps). He can now die a happy man. Talk to him at www.richardandreoli.com.

Contributing writer **David Ciminelli** has served as Editor-in-Chief of various Southern California publications, including *IN Los Angeles,* and has written for *Daily Variety, Instinct,* Gay.com, and Universal Studios' Horror Online. He is the editor of *Unzipped* magazine and is writing a book on "homocore" bands for Alyson Publications. David lives in Silver Lake with his two Rottweilers, Britney and Christina.

Smith Galtney is a freelance writer living in New York City. His work has appeared in *The New York Times, Rolling Stone, GQ, Spin, The Village Voice, Out* and *O: The Oprah Magazine.* A former writer at VH1 and the music video network Fuse, he is currently trying to complete a screenplay/novel/whatever.

Born in Michigan but raised in LA, **Aaron Krach** is a writer and artist who now lives on Manhattan's lower east side. A former editor at various homosexual publications, he is currently a senior editor at *Cargo* magazine. His first novel, *Half-Life,* was published in May 2004, and his life didn't change one bit. He is still hard up and single. He is steadily at work on a new project (he's just not sure what it is yet). Check him out at www.aaronkrach.com.

Drew Limsky is a freelance journalist and *MetroSource* columnist whose travel writing has appeared in *The New York Times, San Francisco Chronicle, BusinessWeek, USA Today, SmartMoney, New York Daily News, Genre* and the *Robb Report.* He has stayed in more Ritz-Carltons than you have, and can be reached at drewlimsky@aol.com.

Christopher Lisotta is a journalist in Los Angeles. He first came to town to work in the television biz, but was so attracted to the idea of writing he felt he had to do it full time (that, and the show he was working on got cancelled). He is a frequent contributor to *Frontiers, IN Los Angeles, LA Weekly,* and *The Advocate.* He also writes for the Gay.com and PlanetOut.com network and can be heard delivering news on Sirius Satellite Radio's OutQ news service. His Web site is www.christopherlisotta.com.

Parker Ray is Editor-in-Chief of *Instinct* magazine, co-author of *Going Down: The Instinct Guide to Oral Sex,* author of the upcoming *How To Get Laid,* and just an all-around righteous babe. He likes to paint, surf, read, and pretend he's a rock star during his free time, which usually amounts to about 13 minutes per week. Parker currently resides in Los Angeles.

Dave White grew up to be a debaser. He writes a lot and gets paid very little by *Instinct* magazine. He has also written for *The Advocate, Glue* and *LA Weekly.* You can find his blog at www.livejournal.com/users/djmrswhite.